Scribe Publications
POST-WAR LIES

Malte Herwig is a reporter, broadcaster, and historian. He is known for his in-depth interviews and investigative features, and his articles have appeared widely in US, British, and German publications, including *The New York Times*, *The Guardian*, *The Observer*, and *Vanity Fair*. Herwig was the only journalist to interview former SS captain and convicted war criminal Erich Priebke.

For my father,
1927–1972

MALTE HERWIG

POST-WAR LIES

translated by
Jamie Lee Searle and Shaun Whiteside

SCRIBE
Melbourne • London

Scribe Publications Pty Ltd
18–20 Edward St, Brunswick, Victoria 3056, Australia
2 John St, Clerkenwell, London, WC1N 2ES, United Kingdom

Originally published in Germany as *Die Flakhelfer* by Anstalt in 2013
First published in English by Scribe in 2014

The translation of this work was supported by a grant
from the Goethe-Institut, which is funded by the German
Ministry of Foreign Affairs.

Typeset in Minion Pro 12/17.25 pt by the publishers
Printed and bound in the UK by CPI Group (UK) Ltd, Croydon CR0 4YY

National Library of Australia
Cataloguing-in-Publication data

Herwig, Malte.

Post-War Lies: Germany and Hitler's long shadow.

9781925106145 (AUS edition)
9781922247650 (UK edition)
9781925113280 (e-book)

1. Nazis–History. 2. National socialism–Germany. 3. Germany–History.
4. Germany–Politics and government.

Other Authors/Contributors: Searle, Jamie Lee, translator;
Whiteside, Shaun, translator.

324.2430238

scribepublications.com.au
scribepublications.co.uk

Contents

'History is the lie commonly agreed upon.'
— *Voltaire*

List of Abbreviations

BDC: Berlin Document Center

BDM: Bund Deutscher Mädel (League of German Girls)

BfV: Bundesamt für Verfassungsschutz (Federal Office for the Protection of the Constitution)

CDU: Christlich Demokratische Union (Christian Democratic Union)

CIC: Counter Intelligence Corps

FDP: Freie Demokratische Partei (Free Democratic Party)

FPÖ: Freiheitliche Partei Österreichs (Freedom Party of Austria)

FRG: Federal Republic of Germany, West Germany

GDR: German Democratic Republic, East Germany

GRH: Gesellschaft zur Rechtlichen und Humanitären Unterstützung (Society for Legal and Humanitarian Support)

HVA: Hauptverwaltung Aufklärung (Main Reconnaissance Administration)

MCC: Ministerial Collection Center

MfS: Ministerium für Staatssicherheit (Ministry for State Security)

NKVD: Narodnyi Komissariat Vnutrennikh Del (People's Commissariat for Internal Affairs)

NSDAP: Nationalsozialistische Deutsche Arbeiterpartei (National Socialist German Workers' Party)

NSDStB: Nationalsozialistischer Deutsche Studentenbund (National Socialist German Students' League)

NSFK: Nationalsozialistisches Fliegerkorps (National Socialist Flyers Corps)

NSKK: Nationalsozialistische Kraftfahrkorps (National Socialist Motor Corps)

NVA: Nationale Volksarmee (National People's Army)

PDS: Partei des Demokratischen Sozialismus (Party of Democratic Socialism)

RIAS: Rundfunk im Amerikanischen Sektor (Radio in the American Sector)

RSHA: Reichssicherheitshauptamt (Reich Main Security Office)

SA: Sturmabteilung (Assault Division, Nazi Brownshirts)

SD: Sicherheitsdienst (Nazi Security Service)

SED: Sozialistische Einheitspartei Deutschlands (Socialist Unity Party of Germany)

SPD: Sozialdemokratische Partei Deutschlands (Social Democratic Party of Germany)

SS: Schutzstaffel (Nazi Protection Squadron)

ZAIG: Zentrale Auswertungs- und Informationsgruppe (Central Evaluation and Information Group)

Prologue

This isn't a family memoir, but it could be — the collective family memoir of every single person who grew up in the old Federal Republic of Germany. There is still time left in which to ask questions. The last members of the *Flakhelfer* generation, the schoolboys conscripted as Luftwaffe (air force) assistants towards the end of World War II, are still alive. They are our fathers and grandfathers, and it is they who shaped the Federal Republic — as artists, academics, politicians, journalists, and lawyers.

So let's begin with a family memoir, after all. The *Flakhelfer* and I are not too far removed. My father, Günter Herwig, born in 1927, was one of them. He's 86 now, the same age as grandees of the old Federal Republic such as Günter Grass, Hans-Dietrich Genscher, and Martin Walser. My grandfather, Walter Herwig, was born in Kassel in 1880, almost a hundred years before me. As they both came late to fatherhood, the Herwigs skipped a generation, and I was born within earshot of the 19th century.

My father came into the world in the Weimar Republic, but his childhood home was rooted in the German Empire. And not just politically, for their grand five-bedroom apartment was located directly on Kaiserplatz in the Hohenzollern quarter of Kassel, the former imperial residence. My grandfather, however, could no longer refer to his shipping company as an 'Imperial Carrier' because, much to his regret, the German Kaiser — who had been fond of holding court in nearby Wilhelmshöhe Castle and the Kassel Staatstheater — was by then long gone. But the family business flourished nonetheless, not least thanks to its overseas links, which in 1929 earned Walter Herwig the title of honorary consul of Peru. Before swastika flags came into fashion, the consul used to adorn his Maybach limousine on the Peruvian national holiday with the standards of both Peru and the Weimar Republic.

It was a peaceful time. As a child, my father would listen from the third-floor window to the sound of the former military band playing 'merry, light-hearted compositions' in the concert pavilion in front of their building.[1] They played on until 1934. Then the new ruling powers changed the tune. The National Socialists tore down the pavilion in order to make room for grandstands; from then on, parades were held there on Reich War Veterans' Day. It was only fitting that, in 1938, the future warlords would rename Kaiserplatz after a battle; it became Skagerrakplatz, after the Battle of Jutland.

And so my father had one foot in the Kaiser era, yet had to march into the Third Reich with the other. A photograph from the 1930s shows little Günter Herwig on the street, smiling dutifully into the camera and raising his right arm in a Hitler salute. Beneath it in the photo album is a note written by my grandmother: 'His first *Heil Hitler.*' Did he know what the gesture meant?

On 1 December 1937, ten-year-old Günter became a member of the German Youth, the subdivision of the Hitler Youth for ten- to 14-year-olds. There, little boys were to be moulded into the future heroes of Hitler's regime. But my father wasn't hero material. He was too lazy and self-sufficient to take any interest in the Third

Reich and its preoccupation with marching and indoctrination. In 1938, the school sent a blue warning letter to my grandmother, informing her that her son was idle and complacent, and that his sense of participatory spirit was profoundly lacking: 'He spends most of the time sitting there on the bench, pink-cheeked and sated, and appears to be utterly content with the world around him. Admonitions have no impact whatsoever.' Signed: 'Heil Hitler! The class teacher.'[2]

Not that the young Günter felt any kind of inner conflict with the ruling ideology. He simply didn't bother himself with it. He didn't take any interest in marching, either, and was hauled up before a Hitler Youth court in 1943 for having gone AWOL after the roll call at the beginning of a march. He liked theatre, but not the theatre of the Brownshirts. According to the penalty ruling of the Kurhessen Hitler Youth, he had broken ranks with the march formation because he had sprained his ankle during an amateur dramatics performance. His unauthorised decampment was punished leniently: a warning 'for the duration of the war'.

The war would have destroyed him, had it lasted any longer. After his Reich labour service and time as a *Flakhelfer*, my father received a letter in 1945 summoning him to an entrance examination for the navy in Vienna. The defeat of the German Reich was just a few months away, the German armies were retreating on all fronts, and Vienna wasn't even on the coast. But even in the spring of 1945 at Marine Commando II, my father told me, the officers were still paying attention to the table manners of the young recruits who were expected to save the Reich.

In the end, when he was handed his marching orders in Vienna and ordered to report to the relevant office, my father did what seemed like the only sensible thing: he crumpled up the piece of paper and absconded.

Indifference is a powerful force that is often underestimated, even by dictatorships. If everyone had been like my father, the *Volksstaat* might soon have collapsed from a lack of interest on the part of those involved. But that wasn't what happened, and the Third Reich needed more heroes than the few students, workers, and officers who lost their lives in the courageous struggle against injustice, and who have since had to act as an alibi for 'the other Germany'. Brecht was right: 'Unhappy the land that needs heroes'.

My father isn't a very good example of the 'practically ridiculous German longing for role models' of which Margarete Mitscherlich once spoke — either before or after 1945. No, my father wasn't a hero and didn't want to be one, either for Hitler or for the resistance. Young Günter Herwig was not swift as a greyhound, tough as leather, or hard as Krupp's steel — as Hitler Youth were expected to be. Instead, he was pink, soft, and complacent. So my father adopted a completely unheroic form of passive resistance in the Third Reich, and there was very little the powers that be could do about it. They met open rebellion with reprisals, concentration camps, and death sentences. But no state could be made with lazy 'national comrades' like him, let alone a 'Thousand-Year Reich'.

My father didn't like to trouble the past, but the past troubled him. Whenever there was something about Hitler or the Holocaust on television he would change channels. He preferred animal documentaries. He never had to experience war at the front. But he did witness the destruction of his hometown of Kassel, which was reduced to rubble by Allied bombs in 1943; the corpses in the street outside the bunker in the Weinberg part of the city; the sirens; the firestorm.

I often asked him about his memories of those times. When he was an adolescent, did he know what was happening to the Jews? 'They lived in a different part of town,' was his answer. But he also told me how surprised he was when his Jewish paediatrician disappeared one day.

Today, it seems to me that I was asking the wrong questions — or else I wasn't asking the right ones. I was sceptical when my father told me that my grandfather had protected a Jewish employee at his haulage company. At school, such stories had been revealed to be self-serving lies all too often. So I sought out the man in question, and he confirmed that my grandfather really had saved him by letting him work for the family firm. The consul had been a really fine man, the employee told me shortly before he died, and he always thought of him with gratitude and respect.

Wrong question, right answer? Because what did I really know about my grandfather? No one in the Herwig household had held a high opinion of the Nazis, according to my father, and he always told me that his parents were bourgeois nationalist conservatives. I was 37 when I first asked whether my grandfather had actually been a member of the Nazi Party. The question had often lurked in the background of our conversations, and my father answered without further ado: Yes, Grandfather had been in the Nazi Party, because he had run the family business with his brother, who was a freemason, and therefore ineligible to join. 'Someone had to join the party.'

Right question, wrong answer? I couldn't ask my grandfather. He had died of a heart attack at home in Kassel in 1944. So I was late in learning that the old stories were far from being over. That everything we had learned at school about repression in the Adenauer period (1949–1963) had affected us, the generation swamped by history, even more directly than we thought.

Four weeks after my grandfather's sudden death in August 1944, the sirens wailed over Kassel again. My grandmother was so inconsolable over the death of her husband that my father and his sister had to drag her into the air-raid shelter. 'She wanted to die, and she would have if we hadn't taken her with us,' my father told me. A bomb fell into his nursery and destroyed the whole flat. Mother, sister, and son crept through a hole in the wall into the next-door cellar and survived.

'Strange as it may sound, it was a stroke of luck for your grandmother that the house was bombed,' my father said: 'All the memories of her life beforehand were destroyed along with the house.' My grandmother searched the rubble for days afterwards.

Then something happened that my father still describes as a miracle. Beneath the rubble and ashes, one piece of paper had survived the destruction. It was the last letter that Walter Herwig had written to his son. 'All the best once again, my dear Günter, for this new year in your life. With love, your father.'

INTRODUCTION

The Recruits

I f memory were a concert, the Last Judgement of the German
past might sound a little like this: 'Tones of terror from
childhood overlap with memories of marching songs and
hymns, popular melodies, vulgarities, boozing. The ringing
photoflashes from Riefenstahl's Nazi Nuremberg offend us, glaring
ignorance slips from the throes of the fanfare, the stupid harmony
of the conformers and followers.'[1]

With his *Requiem*, first performed in 1993, the composer
Hans Werner Henze wanted to make a stand against this 'stupid
harmony of conformers'. In his memoirs, he depicted himself
as an opponent of the Nazi regime, for which he served as a
Wehrmacht soldier at 18 years of age. In 2009, while researching
in the Bundesarchiv (German Federal Archives), I discovered
that the truth wasn't quite so simple: the man who became the
modernising father figure of classical music after 1945 had joined
the National Socialist German Workers' Party (NSDAP) as late
as 1944. The discovery of his membership card caused a scandal,
but Henze played it down. It must be a 'feint' on the part of the
Nazis, he claimed, a fake. He alleged that he had been enrolled in
the party without his knowledge as part of a collective enrolment
arranged as a 'birthday present' to Hitler from the *Gauleitung*,

the leadership of the regional branch of the NSDAP. Much of the German media accepted his self-excusing claim without criticism, ignoring the index card or rejecting his NSDAP membership as an 'unproven allegation'. When the famous composer died in 2012, the obituaries restricted themselves to reproducing his official biography. After all, Henze had long been regarded as 'an artistic authority beyond all criticism'.[2] The idea that he of all people — a man who had always engaged critically with the horrors of the Nazi era — should himself have been a member of Hitler's party just didn't fit the picture.

Henze is not the only member of the so-called *Flakhelfer* generation whose youth in the Third Reich is now appearing in a new light. Ever since the NSDAP membership cards were handed over by the US to the German Federal Archives in 1994, more and more well-known names have surfaced. Politician and artists, academics and journalists, leftist liberals and conservatives. They all have just one thing in common: they grew up in the Third Reich and after the war went on to become prominent intellectuals and leading figures of the young Federal Republic of Germany (FRG). A list of these names conjures up a cultural pantheon of the German post-war era: Martin Walser, Dieter Hildebrandt, Siegfried Lenz, Hans-Dietrich Genscher, Horst Ehmke, Erhard Eppler, Hermann Lübbe, Niklas Luhmann, Tankred Dorst, Erich Loest, Peter Boenisch, Wolfgang Iser — in recent years, despite their impeccable post-war careers, a whole generation of father figures have become suspect for having participated in National Socialism before 1945. However, with the exception of Eppler, none of the individuals in question who are still living have ever admitted to signing a membership form. The NSDAP — a club of accidental members?

As more names emerged, the public became confused, while

the men under the spotlight clammed up, feeling misunderstood. Their attempts to depict their party membership as having been accidental or unwitting became ever more suspect. In the face of the 'predominantly unreliable sources and evidence' available, the newspaper *Frankfurter Allgemeine Zeitung* expressed its hope that, in the case of Hans Werner Henze, the 'evil spirits' would soon sink back into obscurity.[3] Furthermore, another newspaper stated, the composer simply didn't deserve to have his life-long artistic and political engagement degraded to some kind of exercise of penance 'on account of an unproven allegation'.[4]

It is a new curtain-closing debate, one in which a younger generation is expected to brush aside even the slightest of doubts on the biographical integrity of their role models, and to accept a black-and-white past peopled with evil Nazis and the good founders of the Federal Republic who got rid of them. The idea that even fractured biographies have the potential to be instructive and exemplary simply doesn't fit into the dogma of these later-born high priests of *Vergangenheitsbewältigung* — the struggle to come to terms with Germany's past.

The events that played out among the ranks of the Federal Republic's intelligentsia carried over into the homes of normal German families: if you believe the stories, Hitler seized power over the Germans in 1933 as quickly and abruptly as he disappeared again in 1945, without any of their own relatives having had anything to do with it. The Third Reich was Hitler and Himmler, Goebbels and Göring. But Granddad wasn't a Nazi, nor — in light of the events that followed — was there ever any mention of the fact that Grandma had made doe eyes at the Führer along with her friends in the Bund Deutscher Mädel (the NS League of German Girls).

Or have we children and grandchildren of the *Flakhelfer* —

those final eyewitnesses of the Third Reich who, now in their late eighties, grew up in the Nazi dictatorship, were sent to war at 17 and, after the downfall in 1945, helped build the Federal Republic and shape it to the present day — simply not been listening attentively enough? Is it perhaps also down to us if, over 60 years after the war ended, we are still astounded to find out how extensive the entanglements of the Third Reich's totalitarian system of rule really were?

The great public uproar in Germany over studies into the institutional involvement of the Auswärtiges Amt (the Federal Ministry of Foreign Affairs) in the Holocaust, or the Allied interview recordings of German prisoners of war shows just how deep the rift has become between the life experiences of the *Flakhelfer* and the sanctioned historical understanding of today's society. This rift is also the only possible explanation for why the NSDAP memberships of prominent citizens of the Federal Republic, such as writer Martin Walser or politician Hans-Dietrich Genscher, were willingly suppressed not just by the individuals in question but others, too, and why such revelations continue to cause controversy.

Since the Goldhagen debate in the 1990s about the wholesale involvement of 'ordinary Germans' in the mass slaughter of the Holocaust, rarely has a historical topic been discussed as heatedly in the German public sphere as the question of whether someone could become a member of the NSDAP without their own cooperation and knowledge. It jars with that clear-cut relationship between good and evil that shapes our 'enlightened' conception of the history of the Third Reich: white roses and black medals, Stauffenberg and Hitler, resisters and accomplices.

Even today, over six decades after the NSDAP was banned, there are still all kinds of creeping myths about it in Germany that are rooted in the immediate post-war era. In reality, only around 15 per cent of Germans were members of the NSDAP. In this context, it sounds ludicrous to still claim that only force, and never opportunism, played the decisive role in a person's decision to join the party. Indeed, why would a party that from time to time even imposed enrolment freezes be interested in signing people up without their knowledge? The truth of the matter is that the NSDAP was far more popular than people are willing to admit today. On the one hand, after 1945 no German wanted to claim any involvement with the party; on the other, the myth is still perpetuated that the enrolment of entire half-year groups was carried out in secret.

The American occupying forces knew better, however. By pure chance, a huge treasure trove of information fell into their hands in the autumn of 1945: more than 10 million party membership cards, which were supposed to have been swiftly disposed of in the last days of the Third Reich. An SS commando delivered the 50 tons of Nazi files to a paper mill in Munich in April 1945. But the owner refused to destroy the mountain of documents, and handed the material over to the American military authorities, who then set up the Berlin Document Center. As early as 1947, the Americans were able to establish with the help of those papers that no National Socialist (NS) organisation had ever been collectively transferred into the NSDAP, not even the Hitler Youth or the Bund Deutscher Mädel.

Michael Buddrus, the top authority on the history of the Hitler Youth, established in a report in 2003 that there had been no automatic corporative party enrolment of members of certain cohorts or NS organisations. Any allegations to the contrary, he said, were 'myths which originated in the attempt to ease the burden of responsibility in the immediate post-war era and which, through frequent rumour-mongering, developed into a willingly perpetuated "common knowledge" which unfortunately bore no resemblance to historical reality'.[5]

Even the historian Armin Nolzen, an established authority on NSDAP history, was surprised by the debate: 'Do you know any political party in history which carried out collective enrolment?' he asked. The collective-enrolment argument was, he asserted, a post-war attempt to fend off the theory of collective guilt. According to Nolzen's summary of the current state of research, there is no proof of unauthorised enrolment carried out by Hitler Youth leaders. The prerequisite for enrolment in every case was 'the personally signed enrolment form of each 18-year old youth who they deemed "worthy" of joining the party' — and, until the very end, that was still a minority of all Hitler Youth members.[6] The fact that involvement in Hitler's party prompts a collective denial from many Germans even today remains just as astonishing as the naivety of the historians and columnists who want to draw a line under the unpleasant debate.

Over the years, I have undertaken research on numerous occasions among the 10 million index cards of the NSDAP's membership records, and have found a number of eyewitnesses from the time. I have spoken with Hans-Dietrich Genscher about Nazi files, with Günter Grass about the Waffen-SS, and with Martin Walser about the Nazis in Wasserburg. The dramatist Tankred Dorst told me about the morbid character of the young people in the *Jungvolklager* (youth camps), while Iring Fetscher told me how he succumbed to Goebbels' seductive demagogy on the 'People's Radio'. Former chancellor Helmut Schmidt told me he hadn't known that the Americans checked the Nazi past of both himself and his entire cabinet (in which two ministers were former NSDAP members) even as late as 1980.

The leading democrats who are the subject of this book were not all *Flakhelfer sensu stricto* — in other words, they were not all born between 1926 and 1928 and called up as Luftwaffe assistants. The expanded generational term used here includes all Germans born after 1919 whose youth was shaped by the Third Reich. At first glance, the fact that the Nazi past of this group has only been critically explored in recent years is not surprising. Post-1945, all four of the occupying powers decreed youth amnesties for those born after 1919. But then this amnesty was joined by amnesia: the youthful aberrations were forgiven — and forgotten.

This book is not about guilt and accusation, nor about the youthful sins of those who made a significant contribution to the development of a civil post-war society after 1945 and to the success of democracy in the Federal Republic. This book tells the unknown history of the youngest NSDAP members of the Third Reich, from de-Nazification to the present day. It is not about the war criminals, the mass murderers of the Jewish people and ardent National Socialists whose crimes in Germany, although dealt with belatedly, were reviewed from the 1960s onwards with a thoroughness that compensated for lost time. Instead, the focus is on those individuals who — on account of their age — were labelled as 'Hitler's last heroes' and yet at the same time became victims of Nazi propaganda as teenagers. Dictatorship, war, collaboration, perceived or actual opposition to the system, and ultimately its total collapse caused an existential instability among this generation, which many of its members tried to suppress after 1945 through an intensified engagement in the new democracy. They joined Hitler's party at 17 or 18 years of age — too young to be perpetrators, but too old to escape ties of guilt with the Third Reich. Caught hopelessly in between, they were a generation of young people who regarded themselves as both 'without ties and entangled', as the sociologist Heinz Bude writes: 'Ensnared as children, betrayed as young adults, they retreated, disappointed and insecure but functioning, back into the private and concrete, dedicating themselves quietly and efficiently to the rebuilding of Germany.'[7] Without father figures, a common 'language' with which to describe their experiences, or history, these 'deftly adaptable but grimly determined young men' of the *Flakhelfer* generation compensated for their existential uncertainty by becoming, in Bude's view, 'the de facto, even normative pillar generation of West Germany's re-emergence'.[8]

But one decisive aspect must be added to this portrait of a hard-working *Flakhelfer* elite in post-war Germany. The special engagement of this generation amounts to much more than the quiet economic activity portrayed by Bude in his sociological study *Deutsche Karrieren* (*German Careers*), which is based on the success stories of individual managers in the land of the economic miracle. The *Flakhelfer* also include numerous dedicated democrats who sought a way out of their generation's lack of language and history by scrubbing away at the moral stigma of the German past and decisively shaping the social discourse of the Federal Republic to this day. The writers Günter Grass and Martin Walser, born in 1927, are still among the most important and prominent voices of German literature. Their contemporary Hans-Dietrich Genscher, after having been a federal minister for decades and playing a significant role in the negotiations for German reunification, still exerts considerable political influence today. And there were many other career trajectories that, although they may have begun in the Hitler Youth, did not lead into the NSDAP. Former Luftwaffe assistant Joseph Ratzinger, for example, became one of the most powerful Catholic theologians since the Second Vatican Council and served as Pope Benedict XVI from 2005 to 2013.

They are the representatives of the old Federal Republic in which they came of age. The fatherless became *uber*-fathers; those without language and history created a new language and made their own history. These *Flakhelfer* made a dedicated contribution to the Federal Republic's acquisition of a new historical identity, the moral core of which was rooted in the memory of Germany's guilt.

But this new beginning had a price: in order to be able to dedicate themselves to the democratic rebuilding of the Federal Republic, many former *Flakhelfer* denied and suppressed their own involvement in the Third Reich. They not only distanced themselves from National Socialism, but also formally de-Nazified themselves by dismissing — to this day — their NSDAP membership as a 'feint' or a birthday present to Hitler, with the aim of creating the impression they had been involved in the NSDAP without their knowledge.

And so Walser, Genscher, and co. became experts at *Vergangenheitsbewältigung*, at coming to terms with Germany's troubled past. They became the nation's conscience. They knew that they were being self-opinionated in their speeches. And yet even they were suppressing certain significant details of their own pasts in the Third Reich.

It is hard to reproach individuals for having become members of criminal organisations such as the SS (the elite corps of the Nazi Party) or the NSDAP, on a more or less voluntary basis, when they were only 18 years old at the time. Accordingly, this text is not about allocating blame, but about understanding. It is about reconciling the historical witness accounts with the stories in the newspapers. One cannot be understood without the other. Memory is not something to be picked and chosen at will, and that applies to both the survivors and those born afterwards. The fact that the *Flakhelfer* grew up as a fatherless generation — their fathers either dead or compromised by their participation in the Third Reich — doesn't make the matter any easier. Perhaps it is only their grandchildren's generation, with greater chronological and emotional distance, that can draw closer and try to understand them — an impossibility for the children of the *Flakhelfer*, whose relationship with their parents was characterised by a deep rift.

The story of the *Flakhelfer* is also one of great secrecy, one which is embarrassing to many people. It reflects the post-war history of the Federal Republic, with its many trade-offs, half-truths, concessions, and ritual adjurations, but also the genuine wish for repentance.

In fact, the Federal Republic to this day maintains that institutional continuity between it and the Third Reich cannot exist. Even in 2011, the German federal government answered a parliamentary enquiry from the democratic socialist party Die Linke with the assertion that institutions of the Federal Republic cannot have a Nazi past on account of the fact that such institutions have only existed since the Republic came into being in 1949: 'Departments and other institutions of the Federal Republic have no continuity with institutions of the National Socialist dictatorship.'[9] This legally correct response ignores the fact that, in numerous ministries and authorities, there was in all probability a considerable continuity in terms of personnel between the Third Reich and the Federal Republic, as recent studies of the Bundeskriminalamt (Federal Criminal Police Office), the Auswärtiges Amt, and numerous other authorities show.

The state-decreed memorial anniversaries and events that commemorate the resistance to Hitler and the Holocaust serve just as much as a sign of moral responsibility as the restitution payments to concentration-camp internees and victims of forced labour. But, nearly seven decades after the end of the war, these gestures threaten to become a collective symbolic trade of indulgences if they absolve contemporary Germans from asking critical questions.

For it is not just the numerous *Flakhelfer* who conceal their involvement in the Nazi Party — the FRG government, too, employed skilful tactics to delay the return of the NSDAP membership files from American possession for decades. The US had wanted to return the much-analysed archive to their German alliance partners back in the 1960s. But in the capital, Bonn, there was the fear that public pressure would then force them to open this Pandora's box, which contained the names of many of post-war Germany's leading politicians.

Even in the early 1990s, a senior government official listed in the files as an NSDAP member sat at the cabinet table: Free Democratic Party politician Hans-Dietrich Genscher. For almost two decades, Genscher, as foreign minister, led the department responsible for restitution negotiations with the Americans. As a special favour to Bonn, the US sorted the names of senior German politicians out of the main files to save their Cold War allies from embarrassing revelations. In this manner, the NSDAP files of more than 70 prominent German politicians disappeared into the safe of the American director of the Berlin Document Center (BDC) between the 1960s and 1990s — including Genscher's. Admittedly, before the return of the documentation the Americans neatly slotted the files back into the main archive. However, the names of the politicians whose Nazi legacies were once hidden away in the safe were supposed to remain a secret forever: the US State Department demanded that all BDC files relating to information requests on individuals were to be destroyed upon their return to the National Archives in Washington.[10] It is only thanks to chance that the list of the politicians in question could be reconstructed.

By the 1970s, the Document Center had already become a controversial relic of the occupation era, and one which Stasi spies also took an interest in. At the height of the Cold War, neither the FRG government nor its US allies were able to decide what should be done with the archive. Its return to the Federal Republic — which by then had been financing the archive for a long time — was delayed again and again. When the Bonn government's hand was forced by a Bundestag (parliamentary) resolution in 1989, Genscher's emissaries asked the Americans not to take the government's demand for the immediate return of the NSDAP files literally, and instead to reject it citing technical difficulties. The strategy proved to be successful — the NSDAP files were not handed over to the German Federal Archives until 1994. A few weeks later, the public found out about Genscher's party membership. Why did it take so long? Why is the shady archival legacy of the NSDAP still being argued over today?

The story of the *Flakhelfer* — and with it that of the Federal Republic — is inextricably linked to the fascinating history of the NSDAP membership files and the document centre in Berlin, a story which will also be told here.

I spent five years researching the NSDAP membership files in the Federal Archives in Berlin and studying the administrative deeds of the former Berlin Document Center. I was able to rely on the support of the last director of the BDC, a former US government official, whose testimony threw a controversial spotlight on the Nazi files.

At the centre of this book, alongside the (post-) history of the NSDAP index, lie the portraits of the NSDAP's final members, whom I spoke to about their time in the Nazi Party. It is they — not high-ranking former Nazis such as Adolf Eichmann and Hans

Globke —who shaped the Federal Republic after the war, despite the fact that they were indoctrinated by National Socialism early on. But even today, the debate surrounding the guilt and involvement of the German people is still tied to Eichmann and Globke and fetishists of *Vergangenheitsbewältigung*.

In their groundbreaking work *The Inability to Mourn: principles of collective behaviour*, psychoanalysts Alexander and Margarete Mitscherlich stated that the undifferentiated view of one's own actions and others' suffering was at the root of the German inability to mourn victims and perpetrators. Even today, there are barely any nuances between demonisation and the cult of guilt. And yet there can hardly be a more informative example of entanglement and sin than the *Flakhelfer* generation, who spent their whole lives processing the experiences of the first 18 years of their existence, decisively shaping the arts, politics, and academia in the Federal Republic of Germany in the process. From their voices arises a musical score of memories, a German requiem. It is a lesson about corruptibility, and about what we can learn from those who were corrupted.

CHAPTER ONE

The Funeral Pyre

The 'Thousand-Year Reich' was already teetering towards its demise when, in 1944, the 35-year-old Polish Jew Salmen Gradowski buried a few hastily scribbled pages of his diary not far from Crematorium III in the Auschwitz concentration camp.

As a member of the *Sonderkommando* — the prisoners forced to work in the crematoria — Gradowski witnessed at first hand the mass murder in the gas chambers. He didn't survive the camp, but his written account was found after the end of the war. It begins with the words: 'To the person who discovers this note, please search everywhere, scour through every centimetre of earth. Dozens of documents are buried here, mine and those of others, which can shed light on what happened here. Search so that posterity may find the traces of the millions who were murdered.'[1]

By the time World War I drew to an end, Germany and large parts of Europe lay in ruins. But not only were the clues about the murdered buried in the smoking funeral pyres of the Third Reich; those about the perpetrators were, too.

The imminent end to their rule did not halt the National Socialists' desire to destroy; on the contrary, it seemed to spur them on. Until the very end, the downfall was managed with horrifying efficiency: death marches were organised; prisoners, civilians, and deserters were executed; and soldiers were sent to futile deaths.

'If we go under,' Goebbels announced at a press conference in March 1945, as if the end were still a possibility rather than a certainty, 'then the entire German people will go down with us, and in such a glorious way that even in a thousand years, the heroic downfall of the Germans will be at first place in world history.'[2]

In reality, though, the National Socialists' trust in their own posthumous reputation was so scant that they had long since begun to erase the evidence of their crimes. Any incriminating documents that hadn't already been annihilated by Allied bomb attacks were to be destroyed or hidden.

By October 1944, the Reich Minister for Home Affairs had commanded that all important files be destroyed due to the threat of enemy occupation, 'in particular those of a secret and political nature, and those which could be of significance for the enemy in conducting its warfare'.[3]

The order to destroy the Nazi bureaucracy came from the highest level, but the destruction was also carried out in individual initiatives by lower-level officials.[4] The perpetrators were intent on erasing all proof of their own involvement in the National Socialist mass crime.

But in its attempts to destroy its own tracks, the murderous efficiency of the National Socialist administration failed. The Third Reich left reams of papers behind: from the mountain of files to secret orders, from the fastidiously kept archive to the hastily hidden party-membership book, thousands of tons of written records from the Nazi Reich survived.

After 1945, even millions of ordinary Germans — the followers and accomplices or those who realised late what had been taking place — were intent on getting rid of all the compromising evidence from the Nazi era. In the files of the East German Ministry for State Security, which searched high and low in the living rooms of the 'Workers' and Farmers' State' for Hitler picture books and other Nazi kitsch, there are lists of confiscated objects found tucked away in secret drawers of old cupboards, in ventilation pipes, cellar crates, between balconies and roof tiles, or cemented into window frames.[5] The same would have applied in the West: anyone who had been part of it all, particularly party members, never spoke of it, or pleaded mitigating circumstances when questioned.

A hasty decision

By the spring of 1945, the US Army had reached Munich, and anxiety was growing among the upper ranks of the National Socialist Party. While the remaining men in the German population were summoned into battle by rallying calls, the leaders in Munich organised their own escape.

First, though, an embarrassing legacy needed to be disposed of, one which under no circumstances was to fall into the hands of the victors: the central membership index of the National Socialist German Workers' Party, that orderly catalogue of perpetrators and followers which provided information on millions of party comrades. The card index was still in the administration building of the NSDAP Reich Treasury Minister at Königsplatz, lurking like an explosive device.

Stefan Heym was a war reporter in Munich with the American troops when the city was seized, and later worked his experiences into the novella *Eine wahre Geschichte* (*A True Story*). In it, he imagines a scene in which the last conclave of Nazi leaders are looking for a way to quickly dispose of the incriminating material:

'The card index?' said someone. 'Oh yes — the card index ...'

Everyone knew precisely which card index was being referred to. Munich, the so-called 'Capital City of the Movement,' was home to the extensive card index of the National Socialist Party, an index of seven million party members both at home and abroad, complete with all personal details. Each card held information about the individual's professional role, official positions, awards, addresses, connections and other relevant remarks. The cards of members who the Gestapo didn't completely trust were bordered in red. It was a first-class and very useful card index, a true masterpiece of German efficiency. Except, at this moment in time, it was a catastrophe.

'So what shall we do with it?' asked the man who had mentioned it in the first place. All those present could imagine what would happen if the card index fell into the enemy's hands. Because if it was the intention of the Americans, English, French and Russians to rid Germany of all its Nazis, all they would need to do was pay visits to the individuals listed in alphabetical order in the index.

'Burn it!' declared the Gauleiter [regional Nazi Party leader] who was leading the meeting. 'Just throw it in the furnace and be done with it!'

He stood up to leave. He was in a hurry to put some distance between himself and the Capital City of the Movement.

But the man who had posed the question wasn't satisfied. 'We can't burn it,' he said.

'Why not?'

'Have you ever tried to burn cards that are packed so closely together? They may singe a little around the edges, but they won't burn.'

'Then separate them!'

'Seven million cards?' asked the man who had been the first to mention the index. He could feel that the others resented him for this; they just wanted to get away, and he was holding them up. But they couldn't argue with him, because none of them would dare to admit in front of everyone present that they were willing to surrender seven million members of their party to the enemy.

So he persevered: 'You said that we should separate them and burn the cards individually. Do you have an idea of how long that would take? How long do you think we can hold Munich for?'

The participants of the meeting fidgeted on their chairs and waited for someone to come up with a sensible idea. In the end, a small man stood up. So far he had not said a single word in the meeting, because he was actually very clever and had already organised his escape back when the others were still talking about hedgehog defence positions in Witebsk and Minsk. 'Why don't we have them pulped?' he suggested.

'Pulped! Yes, of course!' said the Gauleiter, assuming that the matter was now dealt with.

'But where?' said the man who had brought the problem up in the first place. He was stubborn.

'In a paper mill, you idiot!'

'I know that a paper mill is where you pulp things. But do you happen to know a paper mill that we still have under our control?'

'Bring me a Munich address book!' ordered the Gauleiter. 'At once!'

The book was brought. Never before had so many perspiring faces leant over a single address book. They found the names and addresses of various paper mills in the suburbs of Munich.

But as soon as they checked the addresses against the entries on the tactical map on the wall, they realised that the routes in question had either already been taken by the enemy, or were in the process of being taken.

At long last, they found a small paper mill that was situated in a part of the city that was still relatively secure.[6]

This is likely to be a fairly accurate depiction of the Nazi leaders' embarrassing deliberations about what was to be done with the dangerous burden of evidence. But what happened next would exceed the imagination of even the most daring of writers.

The miller of Freimann

On 18 April 1945, a hastily assembled SS convoy left the centre of Munich with its controversial cargo. The heavily armed SS men were responsible for making sure that another several hundred kilograms of debris were piled onto the still smouldering bonfire of the 'Thousand-Year Reich'. Himmler's people needed 20 trucks disguised as civilian transports and several days in order to fetch the membership cards and letters from the fire-resistant safes of the NSDAP Reich Treasury Minister in Königplatz and deliver them to the Josef Wirth paper mill in the Munich suburb of Freimann. There, the files were to be destroyed before the American troops marched in.

But the SS hadn't reckoned with the paper mill's owner.[7] Hans Huber was no friend of the Nazis. His brother Karl was a neurologist, and had emigrated to the US after 1933 when the new leaders forbade him from practising as a doctor because he had married a Jewish woman. Now Karl lived in New York, and Hans was being ordered to help destroy the secrets of those who had persecuted his brother.[8]

The miller was an astute man, and soon realised what kind of papers he had piled up under his roof. Before rushing off, the men of the SS commando gave the order, accompanied by the threat of all possible punishments, to destroy the papers at once. But Huber was not prepared to accept any more orders, especially not by April 1945. He decided to hide the files under some other old papers until the SS had withdrawn and the Third Reich had come to an end.[9]

At the beginning of May, the war was entering its final week when a young Polish Jew following the US Army found out about the transport. Michel Thomas had taken part in the emancipation of Dachau with the Counter Intelligence Corps of the 45th Division, and immediately set off to see the miller of Freimann. 'At first I thought it might be gold, or other treasures of some kind,' he later told his biographer, 'so I took one of the Jeeps and drove to the paper mill. When I arrived, I saw mountains, absolute *mountains* of papers. The SS had simply unloaded everything, ordered that it be destroyed, then fled again.'[10]

Thomas pulled a drawer from one of the archive cabinets that had been flung on the heap and fished out one of the cards. It didn't take him long to realise that these were the membership cards of the NSDAP, and he spent the next few hours clambering over the mountains of files and putting together a selection of the most interesting documents as proof of his discovery. Alongside the party membership cards, the hoard of documents also contained party correspondence, personnel files, and curious Nazi kitsch. Next to a written order signed personally by Himmler, Thomas found an art print depicting the execution of the Württemberg-born court Jew Joseph Süß Oppenheimer in Stuttgart on 4

February 1738, an SS album with watercolours from the Greek campaign, and files from a trial which Hermann Göring brought against *Der Stürmer* editor Julius Streicher, during which the latter's paedophiliac penchant for young boys was revealed.[11]

Before Thomas returned to the 7th US Army headquarters in Munich with the evidence he had gathered, he made sure that a delegation of military police were summoned to guard the mill night and day.[12]

But if he thought that the Americans would welcome his discovery with open arms, he was mistaken. 'I took the samples to the military administration and told them I had arranged for guards to watch the mill. Now it was their job to pursue the matter further, because it was outside of my jurisdiction. They said that they would take care of it, but they didn't.'[13]

Even when Hans Huber turned up in the office of the American commander of Munich with three sacks full of NSDAP membership cards, they still seemed only vaguely interested in the contents. Whether this was down to the newly established US military administration being overstretched, or to Huber's inadequate command of English, the result was the same, as it often is with bureaucratic matters: at first, nothing was done at all.

The fact that the occupying forces eventually realised the importance of the files was thanks not least to the persistence of Munich woman Anny Olschewsky, who had been interned in the Dachau concentration camp for eight months. Her Polish father, brother-in-law, and brother had been executed by the Nazis as opponents of the regime. After Munich was liberated, 37-year-old Olschewsky approached the military administration and was employed by the security officer of the 3rd US Army as an assistant on the document search.

She soon chanced upon a hoard of Nazi papers in one of the

NSDAP administration buildings. In the summer of 1945, she took two sacks full of Nazi documentation to the office of Major William D. Brown and tried to impress upon her American superiors that this haul couldn't possibly be everything, that there must be more somewhere.[14] When it was established that the sacks came from Hans Huber's paper mill, where the majority of the files still were, the aggravation caused was considerable: 'Any idiot' should have realised the significance of the documents being stored there, complained the archive consultant of the US military government.[15] But it took another two months before Major Brown was able to convince his superiors in Berlin and Frankfurt that they had to act quickly.

If one believes Stefan Heym's *True Story*, the brave miller was even temporarily taken into custody by the Americans after he received death threats from his fellow countrymen, who feared that membership cards bearing their names might be found under his roof.[16]

In October 1945, the Americans eventually sent a team of 16 former concentration-camp internees from Dachau to the mill, accompanied by officers of the Counter Intelligence Corps (CIC). There, they set to, separating waste paper from the treasure trove of files. What they discovered in those paper mountains, piled high up to the rooftop, exceeded all their expectations. The central membership index of the NSDAP contained the names of over 8 million party members, along with their membership cards (of which there were more than 10 million due to duplication), personal data, passport pictures, and other documents. Major Brown and his people had, as *The New York Times* rejoiced, 'hit the jackpot'.[17]

The index cards were the crown jewels among the files plundered from the Third Reich by the Allies. They were seen by many as 'the key for blowing open the NSDAP's underground activities, for exposing members abroad and for swift de-Nazification'.[18] Once the American experts had recognised the importance of their discovery, they quickly turned their attention to evaluating it.

The files were still being stored in Huber's mill when the leader of the US military administration in Bavaria, Lieutenant Colonel Joseph Hensel, shared the first information gleaned from them with *The New York Times* in October 1945. Many Germans claimed that they had become party members only under duress or even without their own knowledge. After the discovery of the central index, Colonel Hensel left no doubt about what he thought of such statements: 'These files contradict all the stories that these people were forced into the Nazi Party. They show that all members made an application and were obliged to pass various tests before they were admitted into the party by the Nazis'.[19]

By the evening of 20 October, the sorting work at the mill was complete. Loaded with 72 postal sacks full of NSDAP membership cards, the last truck left Huber's mill at sundown, transporting the files back to Munich, where the SS had packed them up just six months earlier.

Their discoverer, Michel Thomas, emigrated to Los Angeles soon after the war and became a successful language teacher, counting Hollywood celebrities such as Barbra Streisand, Grace Kelly, and Woody Allen among his students. The documents that he took from the Freimann paper mill in May 1945 remained in his possession. After his death, the American archivist Robert Wolfe, who himself had fought in World War II as an officer and who was responsible for the looted German military files in the National Archives in Washington for over 40 years after the war, paid tribute to Thomas's unique discovery: 'The success that the victorious powers had in punishing war crimes and de-Nazifying Germany was largely attributable to the possession of and access to the Nazi Party's files, discovered, identified and reported by the CIC agent Michel Thomas.'[20]

Decades after the end of the war, the NSDAP index would still reveal new names and end many a career that had been newly begun at the zero hour. It would lead to diplomatic incidents and tough restitution negotiations between the conquerors and the conquered. Even today, many still claim that their names were included in those files without them ever having known they had become card-carrying members of the party.

Operation Goldcup

By spring 1945, the American secret service and reconnaissance officers in the entourage of the US Army had advanced into the conquered German regions. The Allied troops managed to secure some important documents even while still on the advance. 'A genuine race began to reach certain target objects,' writes the historian Astrid M. Eckert, 'and such trophies were jealously guarded at the risk of serious diplomatic complications.'[21]

Since August the previous year, US soldiers had been allowed to collect trophies and souvenirs.[22] The members of Operation Goldcup, however, were less interested in Göring's marshal's baton or Himmler's SS dagger. Under the command of the Supreme Headquarters Allied Expeditionary Force, they were responsible for collecting documents from German government ministries, and had been tasked with seizing the holy grail of any occupying power: in this case, the Nazi bureaucratic memory bank. Whoever possessed the archive also possessed the power of interpretation over history.

For the victors, the looted documents served as a basis for war crimes trials and the de-Nazification process. But they also served the writing of history. Without the sources from the National Socialist administration, it would have been just as impossible to achieve an exact understanding of the perpetrators as it would be to understand the fate of the victims without testimonies like Salmen Gradowski's diary. Key documents, such as the only surviving minutes from the Wannsee Conference, where the genocide of the Jews was planned on 20 January 1942, were later discovered in the archive that the Allies had already stored away.

Even today, documents are still appearing that shed new light on these dark days of German history. The archival legacy of Nazi rule still occupies Germany, as can be seen from the public debate surrounding the official study of the role of the Auswärtiges Amt (Ministry of Foreign Affairs) in the Third Reich, which was commissioned by the former German foreign minister Joschka Fischer in 2005.[23] Many important discoveries from the historical record are due in no small part to the collective efforts of the Allied occupiers, begun in the spring of 1945, to protect the documents from annihilation or bring them out from their hiding places into the light of day.

The document hunters compiled lists of their target objects even while they were still on the advance. As soon as the dust from the battle to seize an official building or authority had settled, the combat units of the US Army reported back to the Goldcup agents at base, saying whether they had found important documents on location. The reconnaissance officers had to ensure the safety of the archived documents in the briefest of time frames. If the German officials working in the building in question hadn't already left by the time the Americans arrived, they were imprisoned and interrogated.

In order to cope with the sheer mass of discovered documents, the occupying forces had no other choice but to put the fox in charge of the henhouse. They had to quickly recruit additional German workers, whose backgrounds were checked with varying degrees of strictness. The Allied directive that Nazis and militarists should be removed from all public authorities as well as positions in culture and the economy also applied to the Ministerial Collection Center, in which the majority of workers were Germans, under the supervision of occupying officers.[24] An active Nazi was considered to be someone who had held a post or other verifiable position in an NS organisation, who had been an active follower of the NS ideology, or who had voluntarily supported the NS movement. Anyone who had been awarded Nazi medals was also considered to be suspicious.

Officially speaking, those who had been nominal members of the party did not have anything to fear. Quite the reverse, in fact: the Americans were aware that the 'removal of certain categories of persons can lead to individual injustices if an investigation reveals that someone who was fired for formal reasons was only a nominal Nazi'.[25] However, those who were considered to be nominal and reformed Nazis were still reported to the headquarters of the US armed forces.[26]

In the summer of 1945, the list of those to be dismissed initially included all NSDAP members or supporters who had joined before 1 May 1937. Even those who had been admitted into the NSDAP at the age of 18 after four years of Hitler Youth membership had to be removed from official roles.[27]

Admittedly, the officers of the American military government responsible for the dismissal or recruitment of compromised Germans had considerable discretionary powers when it came to deciding what would happen with the individuals the Allies considered to be hostile. Among others, these included nominal party comrades who had joined after 1 May 1937, members of the Waffen-SS (the military arm of the SS), SS candidates, SA members (Nazi storm troopers, or Brownshirts) who had joined after 1 April 1933, as well as non-commissioned Hitler Youth officers, and members who had joined before 25 March 1939. In practice, the decision mostly rested on a short interrogation that lasted just 15 minutes.[28]

So, from the beginning, the conquerors were reliant on the collaboration of the conquered. Some NS functionaries and Wehrmacht (armed forces) officers believed that they could buy the lenience of the victors by offering information on hidden archive sources and testimonies about administration practices. As early as April 1945, the Americans had drawn up a detailed catalogue of tasks for officials in higher-ranking roles.[29] Hitler's bureaucrats were to take up their service again, but this time for Uncle Sam.

For this purpose, the selected German bureaucrats were immediately placed under the authority of the Allied High Command and control officers on location, provisionally named as doyens, and entrusted with the temporary management of a ministry, department, or authority. Their first task was to compile a complete list of the personnel under their command. In this, members of the SS, Gestapo, and SD (the Reich security service), as well as the names of all NSDAP members, had to be marked with a star.[30] The German bureaucrats were not allowed to leave their administration building until they had presented personnel lists and further information, and were responsible with their lives for the documents entrusted to them. They were expressly warned by the American control officers that 'the deliberate destruction, removal, tampering with or withholding of files or archive materials' could be punishable with the death penalty.[31]

A central file-collection point — the Ministerial Collection Center (MCC) — was established at Camp Dentine near Kassel, under American and British leadership. According to a secret memorandum dated 12 June 1945, Lieutenant General James L. Williams, in the name of the later military governor Lucius D. Clay, was in command.[32] Files from the Reich ministries and other authorities were to be collected at the MCC in order to facilitate the development and control of the Allied administration of the occupied territory.[33]

A British diplomat described the MCC as the 'skeleton of German government authorities'.[34] This can be taken in a completely literal sense: the Third Reich had finally sunk into the grave of history, and a new Germany was to arise. The arduous process of evaluating the files was the first step towards the construction of a new German administration.

The task that stood before the American military archivists and their German helpers was an overwhelming one. Within six months, around 1.5 million kilos of files were transported from thousands of discovery sites throughout the Reich to the MCC. There, in the centre of Germany, files piled up from more than a dozen Reich ministries and authorities. The 70,000-volume-strong library of the Auswärtiges Amt was among the documentation to arrive in Kassel, as was the formerly German loot of two chests full of files from the Polish weather bureau. In order to gauge the horrific consequences of Hitler's war, all you had to do was glance at the 450-ton mountain of documents from the Wehrmacht information office listing soldiers killed in action.[35]

In the capital, the American military government seized the premises of the Reich postal department in Berlin-Zehlendorf just two days after the war ended. Officially, the building near the Krumme Lanke lake had been declared to be a telephone amplifier location. In reality, it was where employees of the 'research facility' in Hermann Göring's Ministry of Air Travel had been intercepting phone conversations between Berlin and the west of the Reich.[36]

Now, though, there was radio silence at the large subterranean bunker facility on the Wasserkäfersteig. For the next 50 years, the rustle of secret Nazi files would fill the cellar rooms of the Berlin Document Center, which started its work on 10 May 1945 and would continue for almost half a century.

The black market

The defeated Germans soon realised how important looted documents were to the Allies. Shortly after the war ended, therefore, the illegal trade of Nazi papers began to take off. Given that the breakdown of the four-power administration was already looming, the German file-dealers used the competition between the Russians, Americans, British, and French to their advantage, hawking interesting files to the highest bidders from the four sectors.

'Many German documents,' reported a British Royal Air Force officer, 'can be obtained in exchange for money or goods (coffee, etc) from their "owners". Only these "owners" know the location of the documents, some of which are in the Russian sector. Some of the documents are regularly peddled in all four sectors of Berlin and sold to the authority that offers the best price.'[37] For a certain sum of money, the officer conjectured, a huge range of documents could probably be acquired. The British were not averse to joining in with this game of file Monopoly in the divided city.

Offering archives to the Americans, however, was a more dangerous game, regardless of how they had come into one's possession. In 1948, the discoverer of the Kaltenbrunner reports, which contained Gestapo information about the alleged conspirators in the Hitler assassination attempt of 20 July 1944, offered his find to the Institute of Research into the National Socialist Era for 200,000 deutschmarks. Yet he was out of luck: not only was the recently formed research institute devoid of any funds, but the US Army also got wind of the unethical offer, immediately seized the bundle of papers, and shipped them to Washington.[38]

Contrary to American fears, it soon became clear that German file thieves were rarely driven by ideological motives. There was little interest in Nazi-biased literature, but when it came to film and car magazines, some German workers were even prepared to risk their daily hot meal from the US Army soup kitchen.[39]

American soldiers had a tendency to make off with documents as war booty, too. In 1949, an article in the newspaper *Christ und Welt* under the promising heading 'A People with no Yesterday' criticised with barely concealed indignation the 'naive greed for souvenirs of the GIs, Tommys, Poilus and Ivans' who had allegedly impeded the collection and evaluation work of the Allied bureaus. 'The trade of valuable Reich files is said to have blossomed in America long after the end of the war,' the article declared.[40]

Even high-ranking officers were not beyond being overtaken by a sudden desire to acquire Hitler mementoes. General George S. Patton, for example, revealed himself to be particularly cavalier in this regard. After CIC officers found an original copy of the Nuremberg Laws signed by Hitler in the safe of an Eichstätter Bank, they handed it over to Patton, according to their instructions. It seems, however, that the self-confident general didn't feel personally bound by Eisenhower's directive that official Nazi documentation was not to be taken for private use. Viewing the document as his personal property, he generously donated it to an American library.[41]

Individual documents repeatedly vanished from already established collection points, too. This meant that just a few Allied soldiers had the task of searching a large number of German workers. During the examination of files from the German Foreign Office, a researcher from the British Foreign Office established that, among other documents, the last draft of the retreat order given by Otto von Bismarck and Kaiser Wilhelm II's personally signed response to the withdrawal of his pilots were both missing.

Even Nuremberg Chief Prosecutor Robert Kempner almost fell out of favour with the guardians of the files. For obvious reasons, his office was greatly dependent on the evidence that had been collected by the Allies. And yet it happened again and again that originals lent to Nuremberg were never returned, presumably disappearing into the pockets of employees of the tribunal. 'Some of these people,' fumed the British custodian of the German diplomatic files, Lieutenant Colonel Thomson, 'are more interested in acquiring scoops and souvenirs than in collecting evidence for the trials.'[42]

The expert archivists of the American military administration knew that prompt action was needed if the loss of further files was to be prevented and the use of currently available objects safeguarded. Between January and February of 1946, the last document treasures made their way back into the former capital of the Third Reich, now-divided Berlin, in eight freight trains with 25 carriages apiece.[43]

The various pasts of Günther Nollau

Cats, as the saying goes, have nine lives. So, it seems, do some secret-service agents. The young lawyer who sat down at his typewriter in the summer of 1945 and carefully filled out the questionnaire distributed by the mayor of the city of Dresden was no secret agent. But he was to become one of the most powerful in Germany, in fact.

A new life had begun for Saxon-born Günther Nollau that summer, as it had for many of his fellow countrymen, and he intended to help get it off to a good start, beginning with the questionnaire in front of him.

Nothing had changed when it came to his date of birth: 4 June 1911. The birthdays of his parents, wife, and children, and his frequent changes of address due to the turmoil of war, didn't create any problems for him, either, as he filled in the answers. Under religion, he wrote 'dissident'.

Then came the difficult questions, the ones which were probing even on paper, and of these there were a great many: Had he ever been a member of the NSDAP? What official roles or leadership positions had he occupied? Had he ever been a member of the SS, SA, HJ, BDM, NSDStB, NSKK, NSFK, or the SD? In which other organisations connected to or led by the NSDAP had he been a member?

These were not simple questions, and they demanded carefully considered responses. Especially the million-dollar question of the post-war era, concerning NSDAP membership. It was a complicated matter; there were things that needed to be explained, elaborated upon. But the questionnaire only allowed half a line for the answer. Nollau thought for a moment, then began to type his view of things: 'No. However, I was informed in May of 1944 that I had been accepted into the party on the 1.1.42 (transferred from the NSKK). I received neither a membership card nor a party book, and was not duty-bound. Therefore, no membership.'[44]

This clearly exceeded the framework of the question. But as an experienced criminal defence lawyer, Nollau knew that the truth could seldom be captured with a simple *Yes or No*.

Once he started to get things off his chest, his responses sped up: He had been a member of the NSKK, the National Socialist Motor Corps, from 1 May 1939, but had never held a leadership role. He had also joined the Volkswohlfahrt (the NS public welfare organisation) and the Rechtswahrerbund (the NS association of German legal professionals), but without ever occupying an official position.

Finally, he was asked whether he still held in his possession any files, card indexes, receipts, money, or other papers from any of the above-named organisations. If he did, the questionnaire cautioned, every object was to be reported immediately to the authorities.

As complicated as the circumstances of Nollau's party membership were, a simple answer was advisable when it came to incriminating evidence. Relieved, he typed 'No'.[45]

The files, in any case, had vanished. There was no reason to believe that a few incriminating papers would have survived the inferno that had claimed entire towns and cities. All of Nollau's personal documents had been burned on 13 February 1945, the day that Dresden was desolated.

There were more important things for a young family man like him to think about, such as getting hold of food, and the search for shelter or missing family members.

And so the summer of 1945 became a new beginning for the survivors, a zero hour that of course never really existed. War criminals like the concentration-camp doctor Aribert Heim were able to continue practising without any interruption. Ideologues like the SS captain Hans Schwerte were able to declare themselves dead and be resurrected under a new name as democratic citizens of the Federal Republic. And even if these were exceptions, albeit numerous ones, the majority of Germans had still incriminated themselves by turning a blind eye and thereby participating in the Third Reich.

For the followers, too, the seemingly impossible now became possible. Many were not only able to start a new life, but also to retrospectively correct their old one. It is one of the greatest ironies of German post-war history that the de-Nazification process encouraged the misrepresentation and suppression of the past rather than its exploration. The matter-of-fact questionnaires must have seemed like an invitation to rewrite the past and edit events in the hope that there was no proof to the contrary.

In addition, the authorities even made it easy for individuals to rationalise their party membership. On a questionnaire produced by the district court in Saxony, the question relating to NSDAP membership was presented with three possible answers: a) *No*, b) *Yes, with anti-fascist involvement*, and c) *Only nominally.*

Günther Nollau carefully continued to de-Nazify himself as the Third Reich moved further into the past. On a questionnaire for the Police Presidency of Dresden in March 1947, he answered the question relating to party membership with 'No, just party applicant'.[46]

Nollau's ambiguous answers to questions about his NSDAP membership are a prime example of the dichotomous approach to the recent German past. His answers may have extended beyond the intended framework of the questionnaire, but not the framework of what his fellow countrymen reported about their own party membership. Again and again, former party members claimed to have been accepted into the NSDAP without their knowledge — inventing, in some cases, elaborate excuses as to how and why they had joined the party.

In July 1945, Nollau explained his NSDAP membership to

the state justice administration of Saxony by saying that during the Third Reich he had been subjected to intense moral pressure that had caused him to join the party. After years of unsuccessful attempts to gain accreditation as a lawyer he had, therefore, reluctantly joined the NSKK and then the party.

But this contrite admission wasn't enough to secure permission to practise as a lawyer again in the German Democratic Republic (GDR). Nollau's party membership must have seemed like a curse: in the Third Reich he had needed to entangle himself; in the new Germany, he needed to extricate himself.

In fact, NSDAP membership alone would soon be considered to be a venial sin, in both East and West Germany. Basic party members without specific roles were quickly exonerated as followers. And for all those born after 1 January 1919, a youth amnesty eventually came into force in all the occupied zones.

The Soviets placed more value on the significance of personal responsibility than on the existence of a Nazi Party membership book, at least in theory. On 16 August 1947, the highest authority of the Soviet military administration in Germany announced Directive 201, according to which a legal prosecution would only take place if the files revealed proof of 'personal culpability'.[47] For this reason, the ruling powers in Moscow decreed that it was absolutely essential to:

> differentiate on the one hand between former active fascists, militarists and persons who are genuinely guilty of war crimes and crimes of other kinds committed by the Hitlerists, and on the other the nominal, non-active fascists who are capable of breaking with the fascist ideology and, together with the democratic ranks of the German people, taking part in the effort to rebuild a peaceful democratic Germany.[48]

NSDAP members who had solely 'paid membership fees or taken part in meetings where attendance was compulsory, or those who had exercised insignificant or routine obligations as was required of all members' were also classified as followers.

The assessment of personal guilt was often incredibly arbitrary, particularly in the Soviet NKVD special camps that were in existence until 1950. However, mere NSDAP membership — subject to the ethical 'cleansing' of those involved and a swift avowal of allegiance to the Socialist workers' and farmers' state — was not considered an impediment to a career in the SED (the governing Socialist Unity Party) or the Ministry for State Security in the GDR.[49]

In the decades that followed, the Ministry for State Security continually targeted evidence of personal involvement in war crimes, denunciations, and related information, while a mere party membership was at best a catalyst for the attempted compromising of a West German politician.

The fact that comprehensive de-Nazification was soon called to a halt, even in the Soviet-occupied zone, is down to the new ruling powers' sobering realisation that there were simply too many former party members across all strata of German society. It was impossible for all of them to be completely neutralised. In the case of East Germany, Directive 201 can be seen as an effective propaganda tool, a peace offering with which the new state could win its own eternal followers. Accordingly, the directive proclaimed that comprehensive arraignment of 'all former nominal, non-active members of the Nazi Party would only impede the democratic rebuilding of Germany'.[50]

In the years before the ruling powers came to this pragmatic conclusion, however, young Günther Nollau continued his efforts to rebuild his life. In August 1945, Nollau wrote a long letter to the lawyers' chamber in Dresden, in which he once again tried to explain the circumstances of his party membership. The seven-page-long confession is a fascinating document. Not only does it reveal the half-hearted, wavering opportunism that led young Germans like Nollau to join the NSDAP, but also, in the shifts between contrite disclosure and skilful concealment, the future secret agent's true calling: the foggy grey of the intelligence service.

Nollau's testimony shows how a young lawyer in the Third Reich could be moved to join the party for career reasons, without any particular ideological conviction. Despite his summa-cum-laude doctorate, his licence to practise as a lawyer in the Third Reich was denied for many years on account of the fact that he had not proven his willingness to support the National Socialist state. 'What was I supposed to do, restrict myself to some bookkeeping position just in order to avoid joining the NSDAP, when their true character wasn't yet obvious to me back then and my view was based purely on my own stubborn aversion?'[51]

One day he was allegedly told that, as an NSKK member, he would be transferred along with the young men from the Motor Hitler Youth into the NSDAP. Even though he had already received his accreditation as a lawyer by then, Nollau swiftly complied and signed the application form, considering it too risky to refuse.

In the letter to the lawyers' chamber, Nollau admitted to probably having paid membership fees at one point, too, although he claimed that he never wore the party insignia. He went on:

> To me, the most significant point about my case seems to be that I didn't join the Party from the outset in order to make things easier for myself, but rather took a chance to see whether I could achieve a position worthy of my education based solely upon my professional achievements. When this proved itself to be

impossible, and only after I had sacrificed many years, I decided, albeit with a heavy heart, to make concessions.[52]

Nollau wouldn't have been a good defence lawyer if he hadn't followed up with a reference to bureaucratic circumstances. He had done his homework:

> As I ascertained from the NSDAP's organisation manual, issued by the Reich Organisation Leader in 1943, an individual was only accepted into the party and considered duty bound to it once they had received a membership book issued by the Reich leadership or a membership card (according to pages 6c and 6d of the organisation manual). When I filled out that first questionnaire, I classified myself as a member because I wasn't yet aware of the differentiation that had been made up until that point.

But it wasn't over yet. In order to be able to practise as a lawyer in Dresden again, Nollau needed to do more than just de-Nazify himself. He also had to produce proof of his anti-fascist stance in the Third Reich. According to Directive 160 of the Soviet military administration from December 1945, a person could only be exonerated if 'despite their official membership or application for membership or other external feature, they had not only acted passively, but also, to the best of their abilities, actively put up resistance to the National Socialist dictatorship and suffered the consequences as a result'.[53]

In pursuit of his exoneration, Nollau claimed that, as a lawyer in Krakow, he had not only represented hundreds of Polish people, but also protected clients from the Gestapo, and freed prisoners from concentration and labour camps. On account of the fact that all the written evidence of this had been lost, Nollau acquired assurances on oath from some acquaintances. With this, he had de-Nazified himself.

However, even in the new Germany they didn't want to give a former member of the Nazi Party permission to practise as a lawyer that quickly. The justice department had him submit assurances on oath, and fill in questionnaires again and again. On 13 November 1945, Nollau wrote in his new curriculum vitae that he had been transferred from the NSKK to the party, but that he had possessed neither a membership card nor a membership book, and that he had neither been duty bound nor sworn in, and that he was 'therefore, not a member of the NSDAP'.

His mother declared on oath in a statement that her son had only joined the NSDAP in the end because she, as a war widow, had convinced him to do so by appealing to his sense of duty and gratitude towards her.

Nollau eventually got his licence back, but it was revoked again just a year later by the Justice Ministry of Saxony — after all, in 1945 he himself had admitted that his admission into the party had been authorised. Once again, Nollau set to, writing letters and accounts of his past, and sending them to the Soviet military administration and Saxony's minister of justice. He had indeed applied to be admitted to the party, he said, but had never been a party member. Eventually his petition was successful: from February 1947, he was allowed to practise again.

For a while, the bureaucratic walk on eggshells regarding party membership seemed to be a thing of the past for Nollau; but then, on 26 February 1949, he was arrested during a visit to a political prison in Dresden. He had brought cake to a client who was being held on suspicion of fascist involvement. After Nollau was released in March 1949, he fled to the West and was hired the following year by the BfV, the Federal Office for the Protection of the Constitution, in Cologne. There, the versatile lawyer (whose nickname among his colleagues was 'Dr No') soon began his steep ascent as an expert in counterintelligence. At the peak of his career, after the exposure of East German agent Günter Guillaume in 1975, Nollau was accused of spying for the East himself, and had to step down as president of the BfV. The newspaper *Die Welt* wrote of the man who had been a member of the NSDAP, the conservative-liberal, centre-right CDU, and the centre-left SPD: 'His reputation has been stained brown.'[54]

CHAPTER TWO

Members Only

T he first members of the NSDAP were a railway locksmith and a sports journalist. In 1919, Anton Drexler and Karl Harrer founded the German Workers' Party. A short while later, the small right-wing extremist organisation renamed itself the National Socialist German Workers' Party. The party manifesto targeted individuals with the same mishmash of nationalistic philosophies as those who followed other right-wing splinter parties.

'What made the NSDAP increasingly attractive towards these people was the radicalism with which Adolf Hitler presented its slogans,' writes historian Mario Wenzel. The party set out to achieve an extensive pervasion of German society, as Hitler made clear in his 1938 Reichenberg speech:

Then a new German youth will rise up, and we are already training them from a very young age for this new State. What they will learn first and foremost is to think in a German way, to act in a German way. And if these boys and girls join our organisations at ten years of age and, as it so often is the first time, feel and experience the fresh air, then four years later they will go from the *Jungvolk* [the section of the Hitler Youth for boys aged ten to 14] to the Hitler Youth, and there we will keep them for another four years, and after that, instead of handing them back over into the care of our old sires of class and status, we will take them immediately into the party and the workers' front, to the SA or the SS, to the NSKK and so on ... and they will never again be free, not for the rest of their whole lives.[2]

No German boy or German girl was to escape his clutches. The political sect that began in a haze of beer in Munich soon developed into a ramified mass organisation. By the end of the Third Reich, two-thirds of the German population would be part of its branches and associated societies. However, party membership was a different matter, and the percentage of party members in the German population as a whole was significantly smaller. Those who joined tended to have good reasons to do so.

At the beginning of 1933, there were 1 million members. After the NSDAP seized power, the number climbed to 2.5 million in just a short time. The new members were derided by the 'old fighters' (bearers of the Golden Party Badge, with a membership number below 100,000) and the 'old party comrades' (who had joined the NSDAP before 30 January 1933) as 'March violets', because they had only started to follow Hitler after his clear victory in the March elections of 1933. On 1 May 1933, therefore, the party imposed a membership freeze, which was intermittently lifted thereafter. By the end of the war, there were 8.5 million NSDAP party members.[3]

This meant that less than 15 per cent of the German population were party members — the NSDAP was intended to be an elite group. But in fact, it was much more popular than is admitted today. 'With the exception of practising Catholics and the industrial proletariat, the NSDAP found support and members in all strata of society. By the end, their group of supporters represented a more balanced social structure than all the other parties of the Weimar Republic.'[4]

It is often presumed that Hitler Youth leaders carried out unauthorised enrolments. To do so, they would have needed to fake the signatures on the enrolment forms. But so far there is not one known example of a faked signature by a Hitler Youth leader predating 8 May 1945.

The enrolment procedures for the year groups born in 1926 and 1927 were probably managed in a much more oppressive manner than those for the preceding year groups. Indeed, Armin Nolzen, one of the foremost experts on the subject, refers to the assumption that there was a statutory quota for enrolment from the Hitler Youth and BDM as 'pure fiction'. But it is also clear that the internal guidelines in individual Hitler Youth districts were abused considerably. According to Nolzen: 'Certainly the pressure in this area would have continually increased, reaching its peak with the enrolment drive of 1944.'[5]

Regardless, researchers have found that nothing happened without a personally signed enrolment form. Nor, Nolzen concludes, was there automatic enrolment for any of the Hitler Youth or BDM year groups whose members were accepted into the party between 1937 and 1944: 'The individual always had the opportunity to decide whether they would sign or not.'[6]

The fact that members of the Hitler Youth made use of this opportunity is shown in an SD (security service) report from 1943, 'Recruitment of Youth into the Party', the authors of which observed among many youths in the Reich an 'indifference' and 'lack of willingness' to serve the party: 'Some stayed away from the enrolment ceremony even though they had signed the enrolment form, while others weren't even invited to the ceremony by their HY leaders. In addition, it was observed that even HY and BDM members who had served for eight years in the NS youth organisation and who were now being summoned by their group leaders to fill in enrolment forms made "impolite comments" and refused to do so.[7]

So, clearly it was possible to refuse. It is obvious, of course, that courage was needed to do so, and that a lack of courage is human. But it is remarkable that the long-lasting impact of the Nazi Party leads many Germans to forget and suppress their memories even today. Time and time again, otherwise critical historians and columnists seem to feel the inclination to bring a premature end to the necessary debate.

'But I de-Nazified myself'

The debate regarding NSDAP membership began where it was least expected: in the Germanists' ivory tower, usually only of interest to academics themselves. It was in the literary field, specifically, that people started to discuss whether someone could have become a member of the Nazi Party without their own knowledge, as well as how this was to be dealt with after 1945. The catalyst, perhaps unsurprisingly, was supposedly harmless research into the NSDAP card index in the Federal German Archives.

Christoph König, the editor of the three-volume encyclopaedia *Internationales Germanistenlexikon 1800–1950*, which provides information on nearly 1500 Germanist scholars, checked the resumes of those listed for the period of the Third Reich, and where NSDAP membership was cited, mentioned this in the short biographies.[8] Long before commissioned historians investigated the history of German ministries and authorities, and offered unequivocal proof of the continuity in personnel between the

Third Reich and the Federal Republic, König's encyclopaedia listed the Nazi connections in the field of German philology, in which former NSDAP members helped one another get back into high-ranking positions after the war. The Goethe researcher Hans Pyritz (1905–1958), for example, had been a member of the SA and the NSDAP, but was regarded as having been 'exonerated' by a German de-Nazification court verdict after the end of the war. He later hired Heinz Nicolai (1908–2002), a former party comrade whom he had once promoted to the rank of SS Untersturmführer in the Third Reich, as assistant chair at the University of Hamburg.[9]

The most notorious case of a 'new beginning' in German post-war academia is also listed by König: that of the Germanist Hans Ernst Schneider (1909–1999), who as an SS *Hauptsturmführer* was section leader in Heinrich Himmler's personal staff and worked in the SS Ahnenerbe institute, the Nazi's pseudo-scientific Aryan history research foundation. After the defeat of the regime, he covered up his identity with the help of his SD contacts, had himself declared dead, and remarried his wife under the name of Hans Schwerte. In 1958, he earned a post-doctoral qualification in the recent history of German literature — with his thesis *Faust and the Faustian*, rather fittingly — and later, in 1965, became a professor at RWTH Aachen University. At the height of his career, believed by others to be a left-liberal, he was promoted to rector of the university, and, after his retirement, was awarded the Federal Cross of Merit. When Schwerte's double identity was revealed in 1995 it caused a scandal; he lost not only his professor title and pension, but also the Federal Cross.

Schwerte's explanation — 'But I de-Nazified myself' — is not devoid of a certain logic. The political theorist Claus Leggewie, commenting on the cases of Schwerte and Günter Grass (who concealed his membership in the Waffen-SS), observed that the retrospective discovery of the crimes of the Third Reich had also 'silenced those whose personal de-Nazification is believable'.[10] After all, the individuals in question genuinely had contributed to defending the fledgling democracy against reactionary forces: 'They placed their private, political and social existences on new foundations without making their transformations public. They thought they were already doing enough — Grass as a man of letters and public intellectual, Schwerte as the advocate of a "critical" German philology ...'[11]

The publication of the *Internationales Germanistenlexikon* was preceded by a protracted battle between the editor and the surviving scholars whose careers in academia had begun in the 1940s. *Der Spiegel* reported that some of these 'Unroused Nestors' (senior academics) had tried to put pressure on König and prevent the publication of their NSDAP membership.[12]

Compared to the approximately one hundred Germanists in older age brackets whose Nazi pasts König revealed in the encyclopaedia, the cases of the 'aged men who had once let themselves be moved to join the party as callow youths of 18 or 19 years of age' seemed harmless.[13] Or they would have, if it hadn't been for the persistent denials of the numerous individuals in question, who claimed that they had become Hitler's party comrades without their own cooperation or knowledge.

The Berlin medievalist Peter Wapnewski claimed not to be able to remember any agreement on his part, and created an entirely new category in the history of political-party research by classifying himself as an 'unwitting party member'. The Tübingen rhetoric scholar Walter Jens explained that it could be possible that he 'signed some scrap of paper', but claimed that with the best will in the world he couldn't remember having done so, thereby trying to wipe the 'absurd and petty' issue from the table.[14]

'All my friends in my resistance group were in the SA or the NSDAP,' claimed 88-year-old Goethe expert Arthur Henkel.[15] According to his testimony, he only applied for membership in order to be able to emigrate to Sweden for a teaching role. Henkel's claims could be interpreted as a desperate attempt to escape the tricky position he found himself in. In just one sentence, his own NSDAP membership, as well as that of his friends, is made into a condition for conspiratorial resistance. However, even after emigrating to Sweden, Henkel continued to dutifully pay his membership fees.

In order to establish legal certainty, König commissioned historian Michael Buddrus from the Munich Institute for Contemporary History to prepare a report to clarify whether someone could have been accepted into the NSDAP without their own knowledge. Buddrus's verdict was unequivocal: even if enrolment may have taken place under considerable external pressure, it had not been possible to become a member of the NSDAP without one's own knowledge. There had never been automatic collective enrolment; every membership of Hitler's party was individual and 'a result of the enrolment form and attached questionnaire being personally signed by the applicant'.[16]

There were still membership targets, of course. According to Hitler and Hess, no more than 10 per cent of the population were to become members of the elite NSDAP party, and these were ideally to be recruited from the Hitler Youth. Later, the quota for party enrolment from the Hitler Youth was raised to 30 per cent of each year group, and the enrolment age was reduced to 17. Hitler Youth district leaders did admittedly receive mandatory enrolment quotas, writes Buddrus in his report. However, he continues, 'we can rule out the possibility that regional leaders, confronted with these, took it upon their own initiative to pass on names to their superiors in order to fulfil their quotas'.

Even the lists containing many hundreds of names that were sent to the NSDAP's central membership authority from 1942 to 1943 were allegedly checked 'in each individual case; if, for example, there was no handwritten signed enrolment form attached, then enrolment was refused, even in 1944'.[17]

In short, the automatic collective enrolment of members from individual year groups never took place. According to Buddrus, such claims were 'continually perpetuated myths which arose in the exoneration attempts of the immediate post-war era and which, through frequent rumour-mongering, advanced to become willingly collaborative "common knowledge" that bore no resemblance to the historical reality'.[18]

The American occupying forces had already established by 1947 that no organisation had ever been completely absorbed into the NSDAP in this way. This also applied to the youth organisations, whose members were neither collectively nor automatically transferred. In fact, only a minority of individuals from these groups were put forward for membership of the Nazi Party. As we have seen, the historian Armin Nolzen also states that enrolment applications had to be signed personally by each candidate. After years of intensive research into the NSDAP party archives, he is baffled by the discussions about allegedly unwitting NSDAP memberships. The argument of collective intake was an excuse from the post-war era, he claims, intended to fend off the collective-guilt theory. He also asserts that there was no automatic intake for any of the Hitler Youth year groups whose members were accepted into the party between 1937 and 1944. It was, admittedly, ultimately up to the Hitler Youth unit leaders to decide who was allowed to transfer from their organisation into the party. But a prerequisite in every case was the applicant's signature on the enrolment form — and the intake amounted to less than 10 per cent of all the Hitler Youth. According to Nolzen, there is not yet 'any empirical proof whatsoever of HY leaders signing their charges up without their knowledge'.[19]

For legal reasons, König ultimately decided on the technically correct, albeit cumbersome, formulation that there was no 'evidence for the handing over of the membership card constitutive for membership (§3, Paragraph 3, NSDAP regulations)'.[20] The assessment of the enrolment of 17- and 18-year-olds, however, was a different matter. In his report, Buddrus, too, had written that he could not deduce any defamatory elements with regard to the enrolment of 18- or 19-year-olds into the NSDAP: 'But in many cases, the later lives of the young individuals in question clearly demonstrated that the youthful delusions, or rather unreasonable demands, which they had been exposed to in the final phase of the Nazi regime resulted in them taking paths in life which proved these indoctrination attempts to have been futile.'[21]

This is exactly the point: the significance of a corrupted generation's educational self-emancipation can only be recognised if its precarious beginnings are no longer denied. For therein lies their achievement: pulling themselves, on their own steam, out of the ideological quagmire of their youth. This achievement cannot be properly appreciated if the life stories of those in question are smoothed into biographies of seamless integrity, imputing to them a youth of resistance which was immune to all NS factions and taking on all too literally the myths created later.

Just a single signature

Berlin, in the summer of 1943 — seventy-odd years ago, a human lifespan. The news from all over the Reich was unsatisfactory, even alarming. Reports arrived, 'according to which party enrolment would be desirable for a considerable number of youths'. When it came to events they were obliged to attend, allegedly they had not 'been bitten by conviction', and only a small proportion had a 'positive and convincing' perception of the party.[22]

It was also said that many young people deduced from witnessing 'mistakes and shortcomings the right to turn their backs on the party'. It even appeared, apparently, that they had 'deliberately turned down joining the party'. In short, the number of Hitler Youth members who were indifferent to or rejected joining the NSDAP was 'so great that it could not be overlooked', warned the security branch of the SS in a secret report for the party leaders on 12 August 1943.

The defeat of the National Socialists' 'Thousand-Year Reich' was already imminent, and Hitler was running out of heroes. A quota was needed. Hitler's private secretary Martin Bormann decreed that 30 per cent of young boys from each year group were to be transferred into the NSDAP, and on 11 January 1944 he lowered the intake age for party enrolment from 18 to 17 years. At the beginning of 1944, Reich Youth leader Artur Axmann arranged enrolment ceremonies across all regions, in which selected members of the 1926 and 1927 year groups would be transferred into the NSDAP.

Still children in many ways, the *Flakhelfer*, labour-service conscripts, and school pupils were dragged into the disastrous machine that was the Third Reich. When the NSDAP membership cards of known figures such as Martin Walser and Dieter Hildebrandt came to light in 2007, a whole generation was suddenly regarded with blanket suspicion. 'You can have sex without penetration and smoke hash without inhaling — but can you be an unwitting member of the NSDAP?' asked the newspaper

Neue Zürcher Zeitung.[23] *Die Welt* even printed a 'hit list' of the suspects and posed the question: 'What will be revealed next?'[24] The catalyst for the revelations had been Günter Grass's 2006 confession that he had been in the Waffen-SS. If even Germany's most famous living writer had been part of it all, then who else? Who else had forgotten and suppressed the organisations they had enrolled in or been coerced into as a young man?

The names read like a *Who's Who* of academia, the arts, politics, and the media: SPD politician Horst Ehmke, journalist Peter Boenisch, sociologist Niklas Luhmann (all born in 1927), philosopher Hermann Lübbe, literary scholar Wolfgang Iser (both born in 1926), as well as the sculptor Günther Oellers and dramatist Tankred Dorst (both born in 1925).

In none of these cases is there evidence of a signed enrolment form. Ehmke, Lübbe, Oellers, and Dorst all told me that they had no recollection of having applied for membership (Boenisch, Luhmann, and Iser are deceased).

Despite the unambiguous findings of researchers Michael Buddrus and Armin Nolzen, who regard party enrolment without individually signed application forms to be improbable, the issue of the NS index cards is still controversial among some historians. 'It is plausible,' said historian Hans-Ulrich Wehler, that 'certain Gauleiters gave telephone orders that the HY leaders who were still there should be enrolled'. For those born in 1926 and 1927, enrolment without personal knowledge is possible, he alleged.[25]

The historian Norbert Frei is another who regards unwitting memberships as being a possibility. In a 2007 interview with *Die Zeit* he said, 'Ostensibly, both existed: the strict regimental rhetoric of the enrolment procedure and the sloppy reality of enrolment as it actually took place.'[26] Frei went on to give his view of the revelations about the Nazi pasts of Walser and Hildebrandt:

'This is about something which is just as sad as it is banal, that in the second half of the war 50 per cent of individual Hitler Youth year groups were collectively transferred into the party.'[27] When I quoted Frei's assessment that one could have become a Nazi Party member without one's knowledge in an article I wrote for the German magazine *Stern* in 2011, the historian threatened to sue, trying in vain to get a gagging order from the courts. Even today, Frei has not produced any evidence to back up his statement.

Back in 2003, in another article for *Die Zeit*, Frei had argued in support of his former teacher Martin Broszat (1926–1989), a leading historian of NS research in the Federal Republic and long-standing director of the Institute for Contemporary History in Munich, when it came to light that Broszat, too, had been enticed into becoming an NSDAP member. At the time, Frei regarded it as 'unlikely that Martin Broszat had known about his enrolment in the party'.[28] As evidence, the historian cited Broszat's application to the University of Leipzig from 1946: 'In the questionnaire for his admission to study there, he responded to the question "Were you a member of the NSDAP" with *No*; by making a false statement, he would have been taking a great risk under the political circumstances at the time.'[29] But in the face of the numerous falsifications and fibs on record for new careers begun in the post-war era, this argument fails to stand up to scrutiny.

Over the years, I have received many letters in response to my articles on the youngest Nazi Party members, including one from a woman from Erlangen whose father had commenced his studies at the university there in 1947. Attached to the letter were his de-Nazification documents from the University of Erlangen, including a letter from the rector dated 21 November 1947. In the letter, the rector gave 'some sound advice regarding the completion of future application forms':

Some of the students who the military government had suspected of deliberately concealing their Nazi Party membership, but whom had then [...] been permitted to continue their studies by the University Officer, once again answered the question regarding party membership with *No* when filling out their personal information forms at the beginning of this semester. In the case of a new inspection, this could lead to renewed difficulties. It could then be difficult to defend the assertion that the person in question was unaware of his enrolment in the party.[30]

The rector advised his students to answer the question regarding party membership on all future questionnaires not with a *Yes* or *No*, but instead to enclose an attached piece of paper stating that 'they had not discovered anything definite about their enrolment in the Party during the Nazi era, and had first heard about the existence of a membership card in their name in the NSDAP index in 1947, but that according to a notification from the military government of Schweinfurt, there was no documentation in the files of the NSDAP Schweinfurt branch in their name.'[31]

Armin Nolzen's analysis of the 1947 publication 'Who Was a Nazi', in which the Americans compiled their knowledge about party members and admission processes, and which served as a guidebook for the de-Nazification process, also contradicts Frei's claim that Broszat and others became unwitting party members:

According to this, early 'party comrades' emphasised again and again that their organisations were automatically incorporated into the party and that they had become members against their will. Never, the American processors established, had an organisation been transferred into the NSDAP in this manner.

This also applied for the HY and BDM, whose members had been transferred neither collectively nor automatically. On the contrary: only a minority of the members of these youth organisations had been put forward for membership of the party, and every candidate had to sign his enrolment application personally.[32]

Nor did Frei have any evidence for his allegation that the enrolment procedures had been carried out in a 'sloppy' manner. This contradicted the report by Buddrus cited earlier and the findings of both the researchers in the Federal German Archives and the Americans, who spent 50 years studying the NS files.

There are certainly indications that local, lower-ranking NS officials had a tendency to be zealous when it came to the recruitment of Hitler Youth members into the party. In November 1944, the Reich Youth leadership criticised the alleged 'excess of [the quota by] 50 or even 100 per cent which occurred in some districts with the enrolment of members born in 1926 and 1927'. However, even this does not offer any indication that the Hitler Youth members in question were enrolled in the party without their knowledge.

The name of student Horst Ehmke, for example, is on a list of party applicants including 1895 individuals from the district of Danzig-West Prussia. According to the index card I found in his name, the future justice minister and chief of staff of the chancellery led by Willy Brandt submitted an application to join the NSDAP on 10 February 1944 and was accepted as member number 9842687 on 20 April. 'I didn't know I was included on the list,' Ehmke said to me when we spoke, 'nor did I make an application.'

The Federal German Archives also hold a letter of response from the NSDAP enrolment office dated 20 May 1944, sent to the auditor general in Danzig. It communicates the issuance of only 1892 membership cards. The applications of three Hitler Youth members were rejected 'because they each lacked a signature' — Ehmke's clearly made it through.

Hermann Lübbe, whose alleged NSDAP membership also became a topic of discussion in 2007, could not remember ever having provided his signature. But nor was he able to rule out the possibility of having done so: 'I don't mind if someone says to me that I suppressed the memory,' the philosopher said to me, 'but making use of this category of suppression means cutting oneself off from the realisation of how things really were in the Nazi era.'

Clearly many young people acquiesced in what they felt to be a necessity or to societal pressure; many may have seen their enrolment as a bothersome routine matter, and then forgotten about it. Or they may have been pressured into joining after some rousing speech, for example. 'So, is everyone in agreement? Is anyone against?' — speaking out would have required more courage than can be expected of the average 16- or 17-year-old.

And herein lies the dilemma at the heart of the debate surrounding the membership cards and signatures: today we are further away than ever from knowing how it really was back then for the generation that built up the Federal Republic after the downfall and which has shaped it until the present day.

The sociologist Heinz Bude wrote that their personal history reflects the history of post-war Germany: 'They mercifully escaped the contextual guilt of German history and yet still continue to feel their own involvement in it; they are hopelessly stuck between the two.'[33]

Now the membership cards — cards whose diagnostic value is unclear and which reveal nothing about individual guilt or responsibility or recklessness — are catching up with the *Flakhelfer* generation. The NS bureaucracy functioned well, it would seem, as it is still delivering its archival legacy right up to the present day.

Horst Ehmke discovered that for himself when, on a visit to the Wehrmacht information office, he was presented with his medical files, which included orally and rectally measured temperature data from a field hospital: 'That's the Germans for you, my Prague-born wife said to me. They may destroy the whole world and themselves included,' Ehmke said. 'But the files, oral and rectal, they're all present and correct.'

CHAPTER THREE

The Boys Left Standing

Peeing during the oath to the Führer: Erich Loest

Nineteen-year-old Erich Loest's loyalty to the Führer ended in May 1945 in the same way it had begun nine years previously: with the overwhelming urge to empty his bladder.

His *Werwolf* unit — part of the resistance force working behind enemy lines — had been routed by the Americans, and a farmer had hidden the boys in a barn. They were lying there in the hayloft with their hand grenades and submachine guns, dreaming of the final victory, when the farmer woke them with the news that Hitler had fallen. The world stood still. Hitler was dead — which meant that the war was over and lost.

'Nothing of the kind had ever entered my image of the world before,' Loest said when we met in 2011, thinking back to the start of his second, new life. 'I was lying there, and then I heard life starting up again on the farm. A door slammed, a milk churn rattled. And I urgently needed a piss. So I got up and pissed down the roof beam. And that was life, in its primal form. I went on living.'[1]

Nine years earlier, on 20 April 1936, Erich, freshly dressed in his brown shirt and black trousers, had marched with his new comrades from 'Brownshirt Square' in Mittweida to the shooting clubhouse where they were solemnly accepted into the *Jungvolk*. The ceremony would probably have been more impressive if the ten-year-old hadn't needed to pee, urgently. Eventually, he crept from the ranks to relieve himself: 'I felt happier at that moment than at any moment during the rest of the day,' Loest recalled in his autobiography. 'Out in the hall a hundred boys were swearing loyalty to their Führer, but there in the men's toilet stood little Loest, his willy forced through the leg of his corduroy shorts, and everything was fine again.'[2]

In reality, nothing was fine, of course. Loest chuckled when he told me about his oath-taking — 'how I had to pee during the most sacred moment with the Führer'[3] — but back then it was deadly serious. The lives of the *Jungvolk* did not count for much, except as heroic sacrifices for the Fatherland. 'The flag is greater than death', as the Hitler Youth song went.

Loest, like all Hitler Youth members of his generation, was trained to display blind obedience: they were to be tough as leather, swift as greyhounds, hard as Krupp's steel. A German boy didn't cry. A German boy didn't show physical weakness. The madness of their delusion only melted away with Hitler's death.

How did it all start for Loest? He came from a bourgeois nationalistic household: the father ran an ironmonger's shop in Mittweida; the son was at secondary school. The family was rather apolitical: Loest's parents voted for Hitler, but when his father was offered the chance to take over an 'Aryanised' business at a cheap price, he turned it down. To do so he would have had to join the party. So they were better off without it.

Theirs was a social milieu that quickly came to terms with

the new powers that be; Loest, writing about himself in the third person, 'never heard a word said against the Nazis in his friends' houses'.[4] Most of the fathers were members of the Nazi Party, who had either joined out of conviction before 1933 or afterwards in reaction to the economic upturn. In the spinning mills, quarries, and the metals industry of Mittweida there was full employment, not least because the local factories were stamping millions of metal badges and other Nazi trash to decorate Christmas trees or adorn the clothes of young Hitler loyalists.

In retrospect, Loest sees himself as a 'little time-keeper' who was actually more interested in girls, German popular music, and cigarette cards, and would really have been happiest sitting at home having Sunday carp or schnitzel, rather than eating pea soup from metal bowls at the compulsory state summer camp.

Nevertheless, young Erich soon became a *Jungenschaft* (German Boys' Federation) leader with a Sig Rune (the lightning bolt symbol popularised by the Nazis) on his belt buckle. When he was 13, his *Jungvolk* leader asked him if he wanted to start leading a group of new ten-year-old recruits. 'He immediately said yes, and at that moment his relationship with the Hitler Youth changed fundamentally. He was no longer a mere member of the crowd; he was a little leader, he had responsibility and a lanyard, and had put his foot on the bottom rung of the Jacob's ladder with the Führer at the top.'[5]

Youth leads youth, as Hitler's seductive maxim had it. Ambitious Erich recognised that in this state there was no room for spare wheels: 'There were only keen Hitler Youth leaders.'[6] From then on, he followed the path laid out for him — not always willingly, perhaps, but always dependably.

On 20 April 1939, Loest travelled to Berlin with his father to take part in Hitler's birthday celebrations. The 13-year-old mini-

Führer disappeared in the cheering mass in front of the Reich Chancellery. *Heil, Heil, Heil.* Arms in the air. *Ein Volk, ein Reich, ein Führer* — One people, one empire, one leader. 'He was a part of the power,' Loest recalled.[7]

Even decades on, he couldn't forget how that feeling of power changed him, how he had personally witnessed 'people who had no power, and who perhaps didn't want any, suddenly changing when power fell into their laps, however small that power might have been'.[8] In his uniform and red-and-white Führer lanyard, 'skinny little Loest' was now issuing orders to 35 younger boys and being greeted respectfully in the street by complete strangers.

Five years after the end of the Third Reich, Loest addressed his wartime experiences and the first days in occupied post-war Germany in the novel *Jungen die übrig blieben* (*Leftover Boys*). In it, he writes of the horror of killing, the fanaticism of the young soldiers, and the horrible awakening when they suddenly realised how criminal the call for a 'heroic death' really was.[9] But *Leftover Boys* is first and foremost an anti-war novel. The specific moral and political injuries dealt to boys like himself under Hitler's regime only appear in the margins.

Loest never wrote the novel about the Hitler Youth that repeatedly stirred in him. 'Every writer torments himself with his own blank spots,' he observed.[10] He did, however, write about the uncertainty of his own experiences in the Third Reich in his autobiography, *Durch die Erde ein Riss* (*A Crack in the Earth*).

Today, his unsparing, clear-sighted self-reflection grants us a better understanding of the mechanisms of psychological manipulation in the Third Reich, and the reasons for the subsequent repression of it by those who had been swayed. Many of the young party members from the generation of child soldiers discussed in this book held leadership roles in the *Jungvolk*.

In 1942, Loest donned silver braid, epaulettes, and an officer's cap, and was given command of 120 boys as a flag-bearer. Every year, the district leadership tested the suitability of *Jungvolk* members for future leadership tasks. The toughest, most intelligent, alert, and hard-working boys gathered in a youth hostel so that the future elite of the Reich — 'the Gauleiters and Kreisleiters [regional and county leaders] of the 1970s and 1980s, the Reich Commissars for the Crimea and the Caucasus, for Burgundy and Brabant' — could be inspected.[11]

Loest helped with the selection of the 11- and 12-year-olds, who were supposed to display not only their courage, but, even more, their unquestioning obedience. 'How many of them, if they hadn't been freed from themselves in 1945, would have shot Jews on command?' he mused later.[12]

In April 1945, Loest and his bravery-addicted comrades in the *Werwolf* were still fighting against the approaching Allies. The imagination of Hitler's last heroes didn't stretch to a German defeat: 'They weren't even afraid of imprisonment, misery, hunger and exile; as far as they were concerned, a future without victory was absolute blackness, it would be nothing, nothing would exist.'[13]

If the corruption of youth by power in the Nazi state operated as insidiously as Loest suggests, is it any wonder that the collapse of that state in 1945, the total loss of power of a generation drilled for leadership, set psychological clocks back to zero?

The feeling of shame was immense. But Loest and his comrades were helped by the general desire of all Germans to forget the past very quickly. They were given neither the opportunity to debate nor the chance to reveal their personal guilt. Loest, too, swiftly left the Third Reich behind him, by simply not asking himself any further questions about it: 'Was he still a Nazi? No one asked him.

A scab was already forming: I'm not to blame, and if I am, only a little bit. Overseeing pack drill as a flag-bearer every now and again, a little bit.'[14]

The child soldiers of the Third Reich had followed the path assigned to them as if they were sleepwalking. After their rude awakening, civilian reality was no doubt very different from what these boys, adults by now, had expected. Joining the Nazi Party, which for many had merely been a logical next step at the time, now would have seemed, in retrospect, too shameful to imagine. Adventure games in the *Jungvolk*? That was imaginable. Power and party membership wasn't. But as Erich Loest shows, they went hand in hand from the beginning.

Loest, too, became a member of the NSDAP at the age of 18. 'I must have signed the piece of paper,' he said with a shrug when our conversation in his Leipzig flat turned to the topic of his membership card. He was baffled by the denial of some of his contemporaries: 'That repression business must work for a lot of people.'

It worked for him, too — for a while. Loest is among the few of his generation who not only admit their membership in the NSDAP, but also the fact that they repressed or even forgot it for a long time.

In November 2009, Loest received a letter from the Federal Archives in Berlin which, along with the files of the former American Document Center, had taken over the central membership files of the NSDAP. Following a request from a journalist, the archive informed him, a membership card issued in his name had been discovered. There it was, in black and white: Erich Loest, party member number 9986544, application made 10 February 1944, accepted 20 April 1944.

'So it was true after all,' Loest observed in his diary. Because two years previously, when a few other cases were made public, he had had the uneasy feeling that there was a skeleton locked away in a closet somewhere: 'When Dieter Hildebrandt, Walter Jens, and Dieter Wellershoff revealed or played down their problems in this regard, some memories were awakened in me. Let's see what that journalist makes of them.'[15]

'That journalist' was me, and at first I made nothing of Loest's index card at all. One reason for this was that the publication of the NSDAP memberships of prominent public figures could easily be abused in a sensationalistic way by over-zealous media — either positively or negatively. Either the newly discovered membership was loudly parroted as a scandal, or the news itself was dismissed as an attempted smear. And it didn't matter how delicate I tried to be in my articles about these hidden and forgotten memberships — and even in my interviews with the individuals concerned — the only thing that counted was the scarcity of information.

Since I wasn't interested in grabbing cheap headlines, I decided to explore the issue through further intensive research, and then try to arrange an interview with Loest. So it didn't perturb me when, in 2011, he pre-empted my plans and told his own story in the appropriately named volume of interviews *Geschichte, die noch qualmt* (*Still Smoking History*):

Of course I applied to become a member of the NSDAP, but three weeks later I was enlisted into the military. By then, it was the rule that membership of the NSDAP was frozen in the Wehrmacht. I didn't get a reply to my application. When I came out of imprisonment later on I went to the recruitment office where they kept a list of NSDAP members. I asked if I'd been granted membership. They couldn't find anything. Great, I thought, one less problem to worry about.[16]

Loest couldn't have known at that time that the NSDAP membership files had survived. When he received the message from the Federal Archives, he didn't hesitate for a moment before owning up and explaining his silence: 'So I was a member of the NSDAP after all. I couldn't put it in my books, not even in *A Crack Through the Earth*, because I just didn't know.'[17]

Admittedly, Loest had never said anything about being unable to remember making the application. But he could easily have denied it, like so many others, citing the absence of any signed membership application. In either case, it was a question of formalities; the decisive difference was how the individuals affected dealt with it. By 'dithering' like Walter Jens, as Loest put it in our interview, saying that perhaps he might have signed some scrap of paper or other. Or by soberly admitting to it, as Loest did: 'This fact needs to be made part of my CV.'

Loest went on to sweep away a few current myths about the supposedly hated Nazi functionaries: 'Some of the SA leaders in the city were very well-respected and efficient people.' This wasn't intended as a whitewash. It doesn't alter one's moral judgement of Nazi criminals. But perhaps it does alter one's judgement of all the other Germans from that time who claim never to have had anything to do with them.

In his autobiography, Loest also casts a sober eye on the Nazis who influenced his youth. He shows that even in shades of grey, one can draw clear outlines. Take the headmaster Lehnert, for example. An old fighter, a member of the NSDAP before 1933, a Nazi through and through: 'there's no point retrospectively branding him a follower.'[18] But Mittweida's Hitler Youth leaders, whom Lehnert prepared for party membership with political training, revered him. To them, he wasn't a strutting Brownshirt; he was a role model. 'He wasn't the fat, bawling boozer that books and films show wearing a little cap, or the pub brawler of the Party's early years. He was correct, just, Spartan.'[19]

By rejecting black-and-white versions of history, and the compensatory legends of embarrassing, uniformed cocks of the walk, Loest gives an insight into the dangerous fascination that National Socialist role models such as Lehnert held for young people: 'A whole school went through hell and high water for this man. He was an armchair criminal.'[20] Knowing what we do today does not undo that fascination; it just makes it all the harder to bear.

The foolish reverence that most Germans had for Hitler, for example, may, after decades of educational efforts, have turned into revulsion. But one can never be sure.

When the curators of the German Historical Museum put on the exhibition 'Hitler and the Germans' in 2010, the public in Berlin-Mitte flocked to it in their thousands. Long-unseen Nazi knick-knacks had been dug out from the darkest corners of the museum storerooms: saucers with SS runes, Führer card games, and swastika table-lamps. The excellently curated exhibition juxtaposed the German people's fascination with the Führer with the crimes that they had let him incite them to commit.

But the organisers weren't entirely at ease with the exhibition. In an interview at the time, curator Simone Erpel explained why Hitler's dinner jacket wasn't on display: 'Such relics contain the danger of a Führer cult. Even if Hitler put such things on only once. But the visitors and Hitler should remain at a distance. We're not showing the supposed fragment of Hitler's skull from Moscow either. It wouldn't contribute anything to our knowledge.'[21]

After nearly 70 years of *Vergangenheitsbewältigung*, there clearly remains a danger even today that — where Hitler is concerned — the Germans could prove more susceptible to dark fascination than to knowledge acquired through education.

And that is perhaps one of the greatest paradoxes of the post-war era: we have allegedly learned enough from history to prevent it from repeating itself, but at the same time the artefacts of that very history are considered so dangerous that they must remain locked up safe and sound.

Erich Loest remembers the attraction of Nazi knick-knacks only too well. The Führer never came to Mittweida, but he was still a presence in little Erich's nursery: as a little tin Hitler, 7 centimetres tall, who could even stretch out his arm. 'Ninety per cent of people were like me,' Loest growled bitterly. 'It would never have occurred to us to rebel.' Indoctrinated from a young age, he and his contemporaries in the *Jungvolk* and the Hitler Youth 'were intelligent, energetic, ambitious boys. It was obvious that we would join the party if we were told to'.

Is it really so incomprehensible that talented and ambitious young schoolboys living in a dictatorship should have seen joining the omnipresent state party as a legitimate career option? Perhaps it only seems so in the light of later knowledge, from the point of view of those who never directly experienced the consequences of totalitarian indoctrination.

'And they will never again be free ... for the rest of their whole lives' — that had been Hitler's vision for the country's youth. He was proved right. Even as old men, the echo of the Third Reich still sometimes rings in the ears of former Hitler Youth members. Someone like Günter Grass catches himself humming the HY song *'Uns're Fahne flattert uns voran'* — 'Our flag flies before us' — while shaving. And someone like Erich Loest lies wide awake at midnight after hearing the German national anthem on the radio: 'After a pause of a second and a half he expects to hear the stamping rhythm, as it had continued a thousand times before with the Horst Wessel song [the Nazi Party anthem, which traditionally followed the national anthem during the Third Reich], harsher now, more belligerent, no longer solemn: Tam tam tam tam! The duration of that pause is as ingrained as its continuation. Reason and half a lifetime are powerless to fight it.'[22] It never stops, never.

The major key of conformity: Hans Werner Henze

A hideous storm of brass-band music poured over the audience in the Cologne Philharmonic Hall on 24 February, 1993. 'Brass-band music of the worst kind' — the view not of an angry critic, but of the composer himself. Hans Werner Henze's *Requiem*, being performed for the first time in Cologne, was supposed to go straight to the marrow of the audience, as Henze wrote in his memoirs: 'I wanted to make them aware that the vocabulary of the brutes is still in use, that it poisons hearts, that it drags the concepts of dignity and reflective beauty and fine-minded thinking down into the dirt of generally utilitarian complacency.'[23]

Henze, who died in 2012, and who, as a 17-year-old, was recruited first for labour service and then to the Wehrmacht, never gave the past an easy time. His work, as he repeatedly stressed, was to be understood as a warning against forgetting Nazi crimes, as a musical vindication of peace, justice, and humanity: 'Worldly, multicultural and brotherly.' The phrase 'never again' rings out loud and clear in many pieces by this most famous and influential of German post-war composers. For Henze, composing was, as he explained in a major interview a few years before his death, 'a work of mourning', and memories sometimes came over him like waves of fever or nightmares.

Henze was without a doubt one of the most politically committed German composers after World War II. He supported socialism in Cuba, put student movement leader Rudi Dutschke up at his Italian villa when he was seriously injured after an assassination attempt, and campaigned for Social Democratic chancellor Willy Brandt. He devoted his 9th Symphony, premiered in 1997, to 'the heroes and martyrs of German anti-Fascism'. In his autobiography, Henze, making nimble use of the first person plural, aligns himself with the resistance fighters in Anna Seghers' novel *Das siebte Kreuz* (*The Seventh Cross*), on which his symphony is based: 'We identify ourselves with our compatriots from those days, and erect a new monument to them, the forgotten heroes of the resistance.' While Günter Grass, born in 1927, shook up weary post-war literature with *The Tin Drum*, Henze stirred up the music world. Against the major 'key of conformity' he set his own music: a warning in the minor.

The discovery that I made in a cellar of the Federal Archives in Berlin in 2009 was a discordant counterpoint. In the files stored there, I found a card identifying the composer as a member of the NSDAP, No. 9884828. According to information from the responsible department manager in the Federal Archives, Hans-Dieter Kreikamp, the application was made on 18 January 1944, and accepted according to Directive 1/44 of the Reich Treasurer of the NSDAP on 20 April 1944. There is no signed membership application.

However, Hans Werner Henze, born on 1 July 1926 in Gütersloh, appears on a list of 500 membership cards that were sent by the *Gauleitung* of South Hanover-Braunschweig to the Reich Directorate in Munich on 15 March 1944. In a letter of 7 June 1944 to the Hanover *Gauleitung*, the membership office of the NSDAP Reich Directorate objects to the lack of a signature from one of the 500 applicants on the list. But it is not Henze, 'whose membership application therefore raised no objections', according to Kreikamp. 'Without the field marked "own signature" on the form having been completed, the membership procedure could not have been carried out.'

In a telephone conversation I had in 2009 with Henze, he claimed to know nothing about his NSDAP membership: 'I don't remember ever feeling the desire to join the NSDAP,' the composer said, adding that his 'phantom membership' must have been a birthday present from the South Hanover-Braunschweig *Gauleitung* to Hitler.

Was Henze in fact a 'chosen one' who was granted NSDAP membership without providing his signature? Or could his father, an ardent National Socialist, have filled in the membership application without informing Hans, who had been conscripted into the army? Henze has placed a 50-year embargo on the family correspondence in the Sacher Archive, so we won't be able to discover whether he learned of his party membership in field post letters until 2062 — and perhaps not even then, because those papers might have 'disappeared' along with other unpleasant documents after the war. In his memoirs, Henze mentions rather cryptically that his earliest compositions had already been in existence after the war, 'but had then been lost with various other youthful sins during one of [...] many house moves'.[24] '*Tant mieux*,' he writes — so much the better.

The composer describes his father, Franz Henze (1898–1945), a teacher, as a committed National Socialist who became for his son — a homosexual, left-handed outsider who studied Hindemith scores in secret — the epitome of the totalitarian Nazi regime. 'My hatred of my father,' he writes, 'dovetailed with my hatred of Fascism, and transferred itself to the nation of soldiers that struck me as a nation of fathers.' Even 30 years after Franz Henze's death, his son suffered 'stomach cramps at the memories of my father, which now rise up relentlessly from the big black pool of oblivion'.

Similarly, in 2009, Henze said of the discovery of his NSDAP membership card: 'It feels as though some evil spirits are rising up out of the darkness.' Perhaps long-suppressed memories were resurfacing with the archival legacy of the Nazi state, memories of the tragic complicity of a generation that, in its youth, involuntarily ended up in the service of a regime of terror.

The speech of thanks that Henze gave at the University of Osnabrück in 1997 when he was awarded an honorary doctorate is less ambiguous:

> In 1945, at the end of the total Second World War, we sat on the rubble, counted and buried the corpses, wept over them and regretted our collective failure in the face of dictatorship, our follower status and collective lack of moral courage ... A complete revision of our thought had to take place. It had to begin with the collective admission of collective guilt. A catharsis took place — for individuals, not for everyone![25]

A striking emphasis on individual atonement is revealed here — a theme of salvation that recurs in Henze's autobiographical writing. The end of National Socialist rule, the composer wrote as early as 1963 in the essay 'Music as an Act of Resistance', had meant the start of a new time 'in which the innocent, the pure, and those purified by remorse will be allowed to receive things that are free and distant, slumbering possibilities of nobility unrecognised in humanity'.

Perhaps Henze's life-long musical resistance, his insistent advocacy for peace, humanity, and justice is part of the belated resistance of a whole generation of artists and intellectuals, an attempt at atonement for their own shame and reparation for the injustice of youth betrayed. But when it comes to the supposed party membership of people, such as Hans Werner Henze, who were 17 and 18 years old at the time, it cannot simply be a matter of attributing guilt. It can only be about understanding.

Forgotten, but not in the past: Iring Fetscher

Long before Sigmund Freud, the philosopher Friedrich Nietzsche described how repression works: '*I did that*, says my memory. *I cannot have done that*, says my pride, and remains adamant. In the end, memory yields.'

It is an important metaphor, and one that could serve as the motto of a whole generation of Germans. Political scientist Iring Fetscher, born in 1922, quotes Nietzsche's words right at the start of his autobiography, *Neugier und Furcht: Versuch, mein Leben zu verstehen* (*Curiosity and Fear: an attempt to understand my life*). Fetscher has no illusions about the reliability of his own memories: 'The selection process undertaken by our memory always ends up in our favour, however much we might strive for honesty.'[26]

Fetscher is a gripping memoirist: clear-sighted, wise, generous towards others, and often ruthless towards himself. But for all his openness, here again a great void opens up, circled by the author's reflecting mind. There are many memories of the officer's career and of his enthusiasm for this and that — in which he does not always appear to advantage — but only silence about his joining the party.

Yes, he did feel guilty after the war, Fetscher told me when we met in his Frankfurt sitting-room in 2011. Guilty because at first he was enthusiastic about Hitler's Germany and the war. After the war, he explained, he converted to Catholicism, 'so that I could confess'.

Fetscher spoke openly and clearly about his experiences in the war, and about how one is drawn into such a thing: 'I wanted to have a Knight's Cross of my very own.' Pointing out a framed drawing from 1940 of a young officer recruit in uniform, he said quietly: 'I was always worried that this portrait would be all my mother would be left with if I didn't come back from the war.'[27] Even after 70 years the resemblance was unmistakeable.

In his memoirs, Fetscher admits that he struggled to imagine his way into the emotional world of his 18-year-old self, and to try to understand why he applied for an active officer career: 'Today I find it much easier to understand the little boy who was in love with "Wanda", the elegant tigress at Frankfurt Zoo, than the ambitious officer who longed for military decorations.'[28]

He finds it hard to grasp his 'switch from an ambitious artillery lieutenant to an anti-war democrat'.[29] The formula he found to account for his transformation is that he was dazzled primarily by the splendour of the officer's life, by the heroic stories in the newsreels — not by the ideology of National Socialism.

It is small wonder that Fetscher tries to understand his early development primarily from the perspective of war rather than politics — World War II was the defining event of his early years. The German defeat was also supposed to be his liberation. But, initially, 'of course relief over the end of the killing was greater than the awareness of liberation from National Socialism'.[30] On the last day of the war, Fetscher's father, a Brownshirt and author of a book on 'racial hygiene', was shot by an SS patrol in the ruins of Dresden.

Back in April 1940, Fetscher had been summoned to the local branch of the NSDAP, where membership of the party was explained to him. 'As I had already been accepted as an officer recruit, it was easy for me to turn down this "offer"', he wrote in his memoirs.[31]

A short time later, however, he was registered as a member of the NSDAP. Although Fetscher claims not to remember ever signing a membership application, this is contradicted by the file card issued in his name, with the number 7729137, which I found a few years ago in the Federal Archives. Given that he was born in 1922, Fetscher can hardly rely on the carefully constructed legend of those born later, of having been collectively recruited into the party without consent.

So how did he explain having been a member? 'I don't know.' One possible, albeit extremely unlikely, explanation might be that Fetscher applied to join, but did not get beyond being presented as a candidate because he had joined the Wehrmacht, and at the time party membership and active military service were mutually exclusive. When the suspension of membership for military personnel was lifted after the attempt on Hitler's life on 20 July 1944, Fetscher's NSDAP membership may have become valid. If official notification of this failed to reach him, as it did in many other cases, he could have assumed that his application had been fruitless, and consigned the episode to oblivion.

As a young officer, Fetscher's superiors saw him as 'intellectually arrogant' because he wasn't just interested in Knight's Crosses but in Spinoza and the German mystics, too.[32] Like most young people, he was full of contradictions, which the war made obvious. Every day, Fetscher and his soldiers fired their guns at the enemy. But when the young lieutenant acquired a Polish goose for his crew, they were incapable of slaughtering the creature themselves and had to ask a farmer for help.

Many years later, Fetscher read in Hegel, the great German philosopher of history, that the gun was 'the invention of general, indifferent, impersonal death', a piece of technical equipment that made personal feelings of hatred superfluous. The soldier at the gun becomes a cog in the machine, and the more immature he is, the less concerned he will be about the consequences of his actions. It struck a chord. 'With young people,' Fetscher acknowledged, '"one" can therefore more easily organise modern wars, because they cannot yet grasp concrete and complex connections.'[33] And mass rallies, deportations, and genocide, one might add.

Fetscher revered the Dutch cultural historian Johan Huizinga who, in his classic work *Homo Ludens,* analysed the immature 'puerility' of the day, as expressed in mass rallies of hundreds of thousands of people standing in rank and file as thoughtlessly as tin soldiers. At the time, Fetscher wrote later, he was not aware how infected he himself had been by that puerility.[34] It was the fate of his whole generation to have their adolescent susceptibility to the megalomania of the National Socialists exploited.

In February 1943, Fetscher was stationed in Holland, and decided to use the opportunity to meet Huizinga in person in Leyden. But Fetscher didn't find the scholar at home, because the Nazis had arrested him shortly before. Young Lieutenant Fetscher wrote furiously in his diary about the 'new, terrible recognition of German barbarism'. Instead of talking to his idol, four days later he heard the words of another gifted speaker on the radio: Nazi propaganda minister Joseph Goebbels, announcing total war in the Sportpalast 'with rhetorical brilliance'.[35] Twenty-year-old Fetscher quoted Goebbels' words in his diary: 'Do you want total war? Perhaps more total than we have hitherto been able to imagine? ... Then, nation, arise and charge, break free.'[36] He was impressed — perhaps even intoxicated? The speech had been a 'great spectacle', wrote Fetscher, and one whose 'profound tragedy hardly any of those present understood', capturing on paper his own enthusiasm for the 'brilliant speech of a unique, enhanced national rapture'.[37]

Fetscher studied political science after the war, and became one of the most significant contributors in his field, holding a chair in political science at the University of Frankfurt from 1963 to 1988. After becoming professor emeritus and embarking on his memoirs, he came across his old Goebbels note from 1943. The enthusiasm of his 20-year-old self would not leave him in peace. Fetscher went on to write a whole book about the Sportpalast speech. In it he muses: 'Goebbels must have impressed me. Today I find it hard to understand what I felt at the time.'[38] But there is still no word about his own membership in the NSDAP, no empathy with his former self. It is as if that were a different person.

Or not. Perhaps we, the later generations, are the ones who can't understand how people change and yet must keep everything — good and bad — within a single frame. Goebbels' speech, Fetscher explained to me at our meeting, was still a great rhetorical achievement, 'however horrifying'. Can one say such a thing? Must one perhaps say it over and over again? Are we not making things too easy for ourselves if we dismiss Hitler, Goebbels, and all the other Nazi bigwigs as fanatical, noisy squawkers whom no one in their right mind could seriously have fallen for? Perhaps we should listen more carefully to those who are able to speak from personal experience of the effect that such poison could have, even when it was dripped into the ears of intelligent, refined people.

After our meeting, I read Fetscher's autobiography again, and found a passage that the author must have written as early as 1947, and in which he pursues his ideas about the war dead and the inner peace that still eludes him: 'It's all a long time ago now. But it's only forgotten, it hasn't passed away, it has just been repressed and lost — not overcome, not defeated … Yes, outside there is peace. If only it were inside us too!'[39]

Many of his generation who grew up in the Third Reich

must feel as he does. Intended for death by a criminal regime, they became half-innocent, half-guilty, at once perpetrators and victims.

In post-war Germany they came to terms with their own memories, but the feelings of guilt remained: 'The years pass, and peace doesn't come, and I know that it can't come, won't find a place in our hearts, until we atone in some great, peaceful and moral deed for everything we owe them, the living and the dead, the survivors, friend and foe.'[40]

'I still can't look at flags, even today': Hilmar Hoffmann

The influential cultural critic Hilmar Hoffmann clearly remembers the feeling that came over him when he listened to the speeches of Joseph Goebbels: 'His voice just slipped into you. People still like to listen to him as an example of rhetoric, from the point of view of his linguistic style.'

Hoffmann lives in Frankfurt on the edge of the forest with his dachshund and his house-keeper. President of the Goethe-Institut for many years, he has a lot of stories to tell. On the sideboard are gifts from Willy Brandt and Yasser Arafat. On the walls of Hoffmann's study, the shelves bow under the weight of all the books.

One book immediately caught my eye when I visited. It lay open on the long table in the middle of the room: *Africa* by Leni Riefenstahl. There was a handwritten dedication from the author: 'Dear Hilmar, I dedicate this book to you with warmest gratitude. Best wishes yours, Leni.'

Hoffmann grew up with the films that Riefenstahl made in the Third Reich about the Führer and the *Volk*, about the Nuremberg rallies, about the Olympic Games in Berlin in 1936. For the young people of the time, Riefenstahl's films were like opium. Her artfully choreographed images of mass rallies and homages to Hitler showed the complete absorption of the individual into the mighty collective.

The schoolboy from Bremen succumbed to this mass intoxication, too. 'We wanted to be like the blond drummer-boy on the screen,' Hoffmann explained. 'We wanted to be part of this movement and the attitude conveyed through it.'

It's impossible to imagine today, he acknowledged, grimly raising his massive eyebrows: 'Today Hitler's voice sounds like the devil in person. But at the time it was a voice that intoxicated us.'

Like so many others, young Hilmar Hoffmann followed the path set out for Hitler's heroes. According to his membership file, the 17-year-old applied for party membership on 1 April 1944, and was accepted on 20 April, with the number 9596961.

When he learned of the existence of this file, Hoffmann was shocked. 'I was a convinced *Jungvolk* leader but not a convinced Nazi,' he said. He has never concealed his youthful illusions. Even as a prisoner of war in the Rocky Mountains, he said, he and his comrades believed in the Third Reich — right to the end.

Hoffmann has spent his whole life trying to understand the Third Reich, and process his own experiences in it, and has written a brilliant book about the seduction of youth by Nazi film. In it, he describes Leni Riefenstahl as the 'Führer's flag-bearer in fascist film' and 'the Führer's ideological courtesan'.

He has fought for a long time against what she did to him and his generation on Hitler's behalf. 'I still can't look at flags, even today,' he told me, with a look of revulsion. 'But hatred isn't a cure, any more than repression is.

Shortly before her death, Hoffmann met the 100-year-old Riefenstahl for an interview. The conversation remained cordial, but the bitter punchline only became apparent recently: while Hitler's friend Riefenstahl always denied ever having been a member of the NSDAP, today it is Hoffmann who has to explain why he became a member.

So, in a way, Hitler was right when he said that Germany's youth would 'never again be free, not for the rest of their whole lives'. In spite of the terrible end of his rule, a whole generation of young Germans ended up bearing a burden that they still have to carry today. As children, they had Hitler-fever; as young adults, they had to heal themselves, when they still couldn't have known what democracy was. 'I have stuck with democracy,' Hoffmann said at the end of our conversation, 'throughout the whole of my professional life.' But the weight never lifts.

'I ask myself: were you in the NSDAP?': Walter Jens

On 20 November 1942, Walter Jens applied to join the NSDAP, and was retroactively accepted from 1 September 1942.[41] When asked about his membership in an interview with the newspaper *Süddeutsche Zeitung* in 2003, the talented German philologist was dumbfounded: 'I ask myself: were you in the NSDAP?'[42] He couldn't even remember where the local group of the NSDAP was based in his district of Hamburg-Eppendorf. 'There might be something there that I can't remember. You can't confess to something you didn't know about until a few moments before.'[43]

His memory of the 'Spruchkammer' hearings, the German civilian de-Nazification courts after 1945, was as remote as his memory of his membership application, Jens admitted. 'It could be that I unwittingly didn't tell the truth. I don't think so. Neither do I think that I made use of the amnesty when teaching in Tübingen.' The husband of his landlady in Freiburg, 'who had to protect himself', was also a party member. 'It could be that he once took me along. It could be that the Party leader addressed me as a "fellow Party member". I have vague memories of that.'[44]

He had 'no decisive proof against [himself]', Jens argued, but nor did he have any in his favour. He ignored the evidence of the file card on account of the fact that it didn't fit with his own personal truth, which he had worked out in 1945: 'I don't think the truth can be found in file cards.' Certainly not the whole truth. The contradiction between Jens' version of history and that contained in the Federal Archives is understandable: compulsion, corruption, conformity — they are all part of the complex picture that many post-war converts to democracy have had to integrate into their personal histories. For most, that could clearly be done only at the cost of repressing the stigma of party membership. Thus many have adopted as their own the exceptional case of unwitting membership — a contradiction in itself. If Jens really did, as he claimed, receive ten letters a day from people who had had exactly the same experience, the argument that his case was exceptional collapses. Everyone wanted to be an exception, but depended on a collective apology: We were all in the same situation; none of us knew a thing!

The historian Götz Aly defended Jens, analysing his doctoral papers along with other documents. 'From experience, this kind of source is a good way of establishing the ideological burden in the academic climate of the time,' Aly claimed.[45] He then reached the truly surprising conclusion that Jens' dissertation on dialogue in Sophocles 'didn't contain the merest hint of political conformism'. Perhaps Jens' own statements may be more useful if we are to judge the 'ideological burden' that he was forced to carry.

In the interview with the *Süddeutsche Zeitung*, the professor emeritus, confronted with his NSDAP membership, revealed that he had been 'horrified some time ago to discover a speech that I delivered, with macabre innocence, to between ten and 15 members of a fellowship. A speech in which, so indoctrinated was I by the teachers, I used words such as "degenerate literature".[46] Neither did he enjoy reading his school-leaving essay entitled 'Heinrich wins the Reich' anymore. Jens made no secret of the fact that he was temporarily drawn to the *völkisch* (race-based nationalist) ideology of the National Socialists — the foolish but certainly venial sin of a young person seeking his bearings in that totalitarian state.

However, despite Jens' confessions, Götz Aly sees no reason to accept the fact of his NSDAP membership, referring verbosely to documents which, as Aly himself is repeatedly forced to admit, 'are only partly fit to exonerate him'. But this is clearly an argument of convenience: on the one hand, unreliable documents are used as a defence; but on the other, unreliability is used to call into question the strict acceptance procedure for NSDAP membership.

How, for example, can we explain the fact that Jens was accepted as a member in November 1942, even though there had been a total block on NSDAP membership since February of the same year? The first of September 1942, to which Jens' membership was backdated, was the cut-off date for the transfer into the party of individual members of the Hitler Youth born in 1923–24, who had to make their own handwritten applications for this to take place.

It was clearly both possible and desirable for certain individuals to join the party even before the block on membership had been lifted. In Jens' case, former membership of the Hitler Youth constituted an exceptional state of affairs such as this. It is obviously understandable that people could have joined the party in response to external pressure, and without any genuine conviction. The German philologist Karl Otto Conrady, born in

1926 and also listed as a member of the NSDAP, has spoken of a generation of young people who 'found their way into the regime as if into a natural, appropriate, correct form of state and society'.[47]

Jens explained in his *Süddeutsche Zeitung* interview that it was his teacher Bruno Snell who converted him into a republican democrat, adding, 'But I hadn't yet got there in 1941–2.'[48] In a lecture he gave around this time to National Socialist students, the rhetorically talented Jens had disparagingly described his future idol Thomas Mann as a 'littérateur' outside of the *völkisch* ideology. But by his own admission, Jens borrowed his copy of Thomas Mann's *Lotte in Weimar* from another teacher, Walther Rehm. He wasn't a fervent Nazi either, but he joined the NSDAP in the same year as Jens.[49]

One cannot reproach Jens for temporarily succumbing to the ideological temptations of Hitler's state. On the contrary — he responded as many young Germans did. All the more remarkable, therefore, are the small acts of resistance — not heroic deeds, but signs of incipient emancipation. Jens showed that he had the courage to step out of line with the predominant doctrine in a later lecture about Thomas Mann in Freiburg and in a statement he made to the Gestapo when they interrogated him about his Latin teacher.

Nevertheless, the question remains: Why is it so unlikely that a young, ambitious person such as Walter Jens should have deliberately joined the NSDAP in a time when great ideological and political forces were brought to bear on the nation's youth? And why did the revelations of his NSDAP membership and the 'cringeworthy questions about the decades of silence of a moralist who didn't always keep his mouth shut', as his son put it in his book *Dementia: farewell to my father*, leave Jens speechless?[50] When the old scholar was informed about the existence of his file card in 2002, he kept the discovery a secret from his own family. 'He was so ashamed that he didn't even tell the woman he had lived with for more than half a century.'[51]

Jens' wife, Inge, told *Der Spiegel* that she didn't believe that her husband had unwittingly joined the NSDAP, but suggested that it was 'probably an unconscious repression that had happened in his early years'. Her husband had 'simply erased' the memory of such embarrassing events.[52]

That the revelation of a long-forgotten or repressed Nazi Party membership was liable to pull the 'ground away from under Jens' feet'[53] may have something to do with the unambiguous moral criteria with which we sit in judgement over the behaviour of young people in the Third Reich. But haven't they sat in judgement over themselves all their lives; haven't they always struggled to learn the right lessons from their youthful mistakes and pass them on to future generations? And haven't they managed, by and large, to lead successful post-war lives?

The fury of silence: Dieter Wellershoff

The war had been over for seven years, but the traces of devastation had still not disappeared when 26-year-old Dieter Wellershoff climbed to the viewing platform of Cologne Cathedral in the spring of 1952. At his feet, he saw a desolate landscape of debris and badly cleared streets.

For the young generation, the hope of a new beginning lay in ruins. And slumbering in the ground were the bombs 'which for some reason hadn't exploded, and which would only be discovered when the further reconstruction of the city needed deeper foundations'.

That is how Wellershoff, one of Germany's most influential

writers, described it more than 50 years later in his essay-memoir 'The Post-War Period — Conformity or Learning Process', venturing that it was the same in the realm of the mind: 'Too much was hidden there, and would only come to light much later.'

Wellershoff was right: German history is a minefield, even today. In the city of Cologne alone, bomb-disposal units find several dozen bombs from World War II every year. And just as explosive, but even more difficult to defuse, are the findings from the basement of the Federal Archives in Berlin.

'Oh, my God — that was what I always thought when we heard about the Nazi Party membership of Eich, Höllerer, and Jens,' Wellershoff said when we spoke on the phone. 'I was actually shocked by it. I felt a kind of mixture of "I wouldn't have done it" and a sense that I was lucky to have been born late.'

Wellershoff was born on 3 November 1925 in Neuss, but eventually the past caught up with him, too. He received a letter from the Federal Archives in Berlin: a card issued in his name had been found in the membership files of the NSDAP: Dieter Wellershoff, member number 10172531 of the NDSAP.

A high number — one of the last to be issued. Obviously the NSDAP were still recruiting leaders for the period after the final victory.

'I was totally flummoxed when I found out about the card,' Wellershoff said on the phone. 'We were at war at the time, and thrown back on our bare existence.'

A few days later I met Wellershoff in his pre-war flat, where he spread out documents and photographs on the glass table before me. There was a certificate of discharge from a British prisoner-of-war camp, along with a family photograph album from the 1930s and 1940s. And a copy of Wellershoff's NSDAP membership card, sent to him by the Federal Archives.

Did he ever sign a card? I asked. 'The card is there in the space, and the fact that the card exists is an inexplicable phenomenon. But the scene that should go with it is missing,' Wellershoff said, tapping agitatedly with his fingers on the arm of his chair.

'It took me completely by surprise, and I can't remember ever signing anything. I would never have thought I had anything to do with it,' he continued. 'But it has to do with the fact that, deep down, I always thought that if you were a *Jungvolk* leader you didn't automatically join the party.'

He added: 'All I felt when I saw those Brownshirts was revulsion. I have always had such an aversion to the political that I didn't even join the German Party [a conservative political party in West Germany after the war] as a young man.'

Wellershoff joined the *Jungvolk* at the age of ten, and he later became a *Jungvolk* leader. 'In Grevenbroich I was up at the top, no one could tell me what to do.' After Reich Labour Service he volunteered for military service with the Hermann Göring Tank Division, 'to escape the Waffen-SS recruitment officers'. On 13 October 1944, he was wounded in East Prussia and spent several months in a field hospital in Bad Reichenhall. In the spring of 1945, at his own insistence, he was sent back to the front, but soon ended up as a prisoner of war, first with the Americans and then with the British, and was released in the summer.

Was the 18-year-old Wellershoff really accepted into Hitler's party without any action or knowledge on his part? Did an eager local leader perhaps put his name on the list and forge his signature? After all, Martin Walser, Dieter Hildebrandt, and Hans Werner Henze all insisted that their membership was nothing more than a 'birthday present for the Führer'.

'I imagine,' Wellershoff said, 'that the Düsseldorf Gau [the local administrative division] was a year behind because of bomb damage or something of that nature. And then they just named 368 people who had declared themselves willing to join the party, back-dating it to 1943.' The reason for the long back-dating of the membership emerges from a letter of 6 May 1944 sent by the Reich leadership, in which, taking into account the 'special conditions in the Düsseldorf *Gau*', the leadership declared itself willing, on an exceptional basis, to accept and process membership applications that had not yet been handed in, 'following the conclusion of this year's Hitler Youth membership drive'.

The 'special conditions' in the Düsseldorf *Gau* may have referred to difficulties meeting party-recruitment quotas in the largely Catholic Rhineland. Wellershoff was unusual in coming from an educated Protestant household. But the 'membership drive' certainly doesn't refer to the automatic enrolment of whole age groups, as a number of historians have confirmed.

Wellershoff was very believable when he said that he didn't remember. 'Whether I was in the party or not has no bearing on the fact that I feel personally appalled that something like that should have happened and that I was involved. It's something that you can't sweep under the carpet or minimise — war and the extermination camps, the bombing of the cities.' And why should someone whose appraisal of the Third Reich is otherwise unsparing keep such a detail secret?

No, the repression lies elsewhere, and has to do with an alienation of experience between the generations, Wellershoff believes. In a real dialogue between the generations, the author said, the young generation should think about how it was possible from an anthropological point of view for people to get involved in something like that. 'This good feeling of "No, we're different people", that's a repression mechanism as well.'

Obviously, we needed to talk. The testimony of eyewitnesses is indispensable, even if historians claim otherwise.

And Wellershoff was ready to talk, with remarkable openness. He spoke about his youth in Grevenbroich, the flagpole outside the front door of the parental home, which his father, as a district architect, had built according to his own plans. Wellershoff described his father, Walter Wellershoff, as a man with a weakness for smart uniforms. The family photograph albums showed a tall, gaunt man, smiling, surrounded by his family. Walter Wellershoff was in the NSDAP, 'but he was a completely apolitical person,' his son said.

Walter Wellershoff may have been a small cog in the machine, a follower. But his commitment to the Nazi state does not seem to have been quite as casual as his son remembers, if we lend credence to the statements that Walter himself made on his de-Nazification form: 1.5.1933, joined the NSDAP. 1.11.1933, joined the SA (which, contrary to his son's memories, he didn't leave, and which promoted him to *Rottenführer*, section leader, in 1937). 1934, joined the Reich Air Defence Association, the NSV (the NS People's Welfare organisation), and the NS Association of German Technicians. 1.10.1936, joined the NS Reich Warriors' Association. 1.4.1937, joined the Reich Colonial Association.

'I'm not surprised that your father was in so many associations,' Wellershoff's wife Maria called from the next room when she heard of all her father-in-law's commitments. 'He wasn't a hero; he was a conformist.' And it occurred to Wellershoff that he had once heard his mother goading his father and telling him he could go even further in the National Socialist state. Ambition, opportunism, conformity — the attitude of Wellershoff's parents was typical of many adults in the Third Reich. But was it typical of the young people, too?

Listening to Dieter Wellershoff, there was a big difference:

'Hitler Youth and *Jungvolk*, one could accept that, we were those things ourselves. But the party was something quite different.' Where did the difference lie? 'It was the adults in charge of this system, who were often stuffy conservatives and opportunists. You have to believe us young people when we say we didn't act out of opportunism.'

All the greater, then, was the shock when their vision of the world imploded soon after the end of the war. Thinking back to when he found out about the concentration camps, Wellershoff said: 'I was completely aghast that we had put our lives into the service of this kind of thing. A monstrous betrayal of our own generation, a monstrous betrayal. We felt abused. Unbelievable. We couldn't believe in anything anymore.'

But who was responsible for that abuse?

'The Nazis.'

The Nazis?

'Yes, the ones who did it, the party. Of course there were accomplices, in all the other countries.'

How do you distinguish Nazis and non-Nazis, Herr Wellershoff?

'You can tell the Nazis by the fact that they had the ideology which said we have to eradicate a particular sort of person.'

Were all the people in the NSDAP Nazis?

'No, no, no. Many of them just conformed, of course. My father, for example, said he had to ensure that houses were made decent. Not that Jews were to be murdered, but that the houses were to be made decent.'

Houses, autobahns, full employment — that was the story of the adults. Who can you trust when that story unravels and you are confronted with the incredible accusation of having been drawn into something about which you were completely ignorant?

Wellershoff shook his head. You can only trust yourself, be an individual, rebel. 'Don't look at me, our generation said. We could only trust ourselves.'

Knowledge and truth have always been important for Wellershoff. Few people have described the bedazzlement of his generation so openly and so soberly. A generation of young people doped up on lines from Hölderlin and addicted to the idea of a hero's death, who 'grew into the torch-smoke and the sea of flags of the Nazi Reich, and then, as war turned inexorably to total defeat, paid their bloody tribute as participants and more or less co-perpetrators of a terrible moral disaster that could not be cast off'.[54]

Wellershoff has spoken openly about his youthful enthusiasm for Hitler's Wehrmacht, and his desire to fight as a soldier at the front. In the 1990s, he took a spa cure in Bad Reichenfall, where he had been treated as a wounded soldier half a century before. Little there reminded him of the former field hospital. In the subway, someone had sprayed 'Welcome to Zombie-Town' on the wall, and only the increasingly sparse survivors still had their memories of the war. 'But do we not become inhabitants of Zombie-Town by forgetting?' Wellershoff wondered. 'It's always the forgotten that comes back in an altered form.'

What reasons could there be today for concealing a party membership that can hardly be held against an 18-year-old who had grown up in a criminal system? Was it 'regrowing shame', as Günter Grass described it, referring to himself? Or a piece of repression by young men who had just escaped with their lives?

After the end of the war, the members of that young generation of *Flakhelfer* were repeatedly confronted with the moral consequences of a catastrophe for which they weren't to blame, and forced to justify themselves — first by the victorious

Allied powers, then by a young generation in their own country. How could they deal with that without succumbing to self-denial and self-hatred?

Even today, one can sense the feeling of rage with which these men, now over 80, defend themselves against moral reproaches and generalised judgements. In his 2007 book of memoirs, *Der lange Weg zum Anfang* (*The Long Journey to the Beginning*), Wellershoff condemns the 'general suspicion among the generation of '68 that the silent fathers, who immediately set about rebuilding the country and their own lives after they came back from the war, were all Nazis in disguise'.

Lurking behind this anger there may be the fear of one's own achievements being devalued by the 'shaming odium of having been a follower', as Wellershoff put it; that the party insignia would stick like a stain to the careers of people who were really model democrats. This is illustrated by an unfortunate event that Wellershoff recounts in his novel *Der Ernstfall* (*The Serious Case*). After coming back from a prisoner-of-war camp to his home town of Grevenbroich in the summer of 1945, he absent-mindedly greeted an old teacher in the street with the Nazi salute: 'It just slipped out, a stupid slip of the tongue, as compromising as stained clothing. The stain stuck to me and made me look ridiculous. I couldn't just wipe it away with some quick and assiduous correction.'

CHAPTER FOUR

The (Former) Lives of Others

I t is said that former politicians have to learn to drive all over again after the loss of their staff cars and chauffeurs. If that was the case with Hans-Dietrich Genscher, then he did a good job. The former Free Democratic Party minister for home affairs and long-term minister for foreign affairs had his 250 PS Audi firmly in hand as we sped towards Bad Godesberg on a journey back into the past: to the Friedrich-Nietzsche School in Halle, where in 1942, at 15 years of age, he was struggling with an essay on the Austrian poet Grillparzer.

Genscher still knows some of Grillparzer's verse off by heart. 'Just one thing is happiness here on Earth, one alone: a heart peaceful and unburdened, a chest free of guilt,' he proclaimed as he accelerated. 'Greatness is a peril, glory an empty game; what it gives, nothing but shadows, but so much more it takes away.'

He told me that he had always carried the leitmotif of Grillparzer's words with him, especially once he became a politician. But for a teenager in the Third Reich, it was a dangerous topic. If internal values are really the most important, asked the young Genscher in his essay, then why is everyone in Germany running around in uniforms?

Genscher was lucky — that's how he tells it today. When the

written test was handed back, the teacher explained to him that he threw the essay away after his inkpot ran out. Laying his hands on Genscher's shoulders, he said: 'So you see, my boy, now there are only two people in the whole world who know why it was for the best that I threw your work away.'

The 15-year-old learned an important lesson back then: knowledge is power. It was the first time Genscher recognised the importance of secrets — and the power they give you over others. It was a tremendously useful lesson for life in the young, forward-looking Federal Republic, where looking back would have reminded the majority of Germans of their own secrets, whether they were small or large.

Even in the early post-war era in Germany, there was an urgent desire to bury the past as much as possible. In 1964, the Free Democratic Party (FDP) chairman Thomas Dehler announced at a party conference that anyone who was shocked by someone having been a formal member of the NSDAP 'denies a generation of young people who had to live under very particular circumstances from being able to live their lives, and in particular from being able to have any impact politically'. By then, Genscher was already on the podium as national secretary of the FDP, having been brought into the Bonn FDP fraction by Dehler in 1956. And there was a secret in his past, too, a number: 10123636. That is the number 17-year-old Genscher was given when he was accepted as a member of the NSDAP in 1944 — without his knowledge, as he assured me: 'I didn't sign any enrolment form.'

It is true, the Federal Archives where the NSDAP card index is now stored contain no such enrolment form — although there is an index card in Genscher's name that shows the application date as being 18 May 1944 and records his enrolment as taking retroactive effect from 20 April 1944, Adolf Hitler's 55th birthday.

But Genscher's name also appears again: in a 'name-checked list' of the enrolment notes that were sent from the *Gauleitung* in Halle on 23 August 1944 to the NSDAP Reich leadership in Munich.

Genscher claims that he only found out about the existence of his membership card in the early 1970s. By that time, he was already minister for home affairs in the social-liberal coalition under Willy Brandt. A colleague gave him the tip-off that there was a 'certain document'. 'After that, I had it looked into by the Home Affairs Ministry, and then they sent it to me,' he said.

Genscher kept the information to himself. His membership card was removed from the main card index of the Berlin Document Center, and then disappeared — along with those of other top German politicians — into the safe of the American director.

'Keep your enemies close, but your party comrades closer' is the old piece of political wisdom. But Genscher's 'comrade' didn't betray him. Not in West Germany, at least.

In East Berlin, however, a senior lieutenant of the Ministry for State Security (MfS) sat down at his desk on 4 September 1970 and composed a memorandum for Aktuelle Fragen, the in-house task group dealing with current political questions: 'It has become apparent from information provided by the Central Evaluation and Information Group Nr. E 8125/70, that according to files from the Document Center of the USA in West Berlin, Home Affairs Minister Genscher was transferred from the Hitler Youth into the NSDAP on the 20.4.1944.'[1]

The Ministry for State Security's Central Evaluation and Information Group (Zentrale Auswertungs und Informationsgruppe, or ZAIG), was brought into being after the 17 June 1953 People's Uprising in order to keep the SED (Socialist Unity Party) leadership up to date on the political situation. From the 1970s, if not before, it was the 'central hub in the state security apparatus'.[2] The information that ZAIG collected from operative processes — or, in common parlance, espionage — was also used by the MfS's 'agitation department' for propaganda campaigns against West German politicians.

Dieter Skiba, a former MfS officer whom I interviewed in 2012, acknowledged that, politically speaking, membership in the NSDAP or SS could certainly have been relevant 'for those individuals who may have been undesirable'. And also for intelligence, of course — 'So that one could say: Listen, we'll keep our mouths shut.'

The secrecy surrounding the NS past of many East Germans served the party leadership and State Security service (Stasi) as more than just a useful means of exerting pressure. When young Günter Guillaume's party membership was discovered by his superior at the Volk und Wissen publishing house after he told a fib, the Stasi pressed him into collaborating with them. Guillaume had been accepted into the NSDAP on 20 April 1944, the same date as Genscher. Three decades later, Stasi spy Guillaume was a close adviser of Willy Brandt, Home Affairs Minister Genscher, and Günther Nollau, also a former NSDAP member from East Germany and the president of the Federal Office for the Protection of the Constitution.

But not even the Stasi revealed Genscher's NSDAP membership. 'This is a common ploy in the secret service,' Dieter Skiba explained. 'To want to know everything, then pull something out of the bag now and then when necessary. We stockpiled a lot of information.'

It would be another two decades before the NSDAP membership cards were passed into the hands of the German Federal Archives, in the summer of 1994. A few weeks later, the public found out about Genscher's card. 'Beforehand, the FRG

[West Germany] didn't want to know,' Skiba asserted, 'and as we always said: If I don't actually possess the information, I don't need to know about it. If I don't have the files, then I'm not responsible for making them public or dealing with them. For the FRG, that was an easy way of saying: Us? No, sorry, we don't know anything about that. The Americans are dealing with it.'

Of operative importance: when the Stasi tried to spy on the BDC

Clearly, West German academics weren't the only ones interested in the Document Center's files and NSDAP card index — East Berlin's Ministry for State Security was, too. Long-standing BDC director David Marwell believes that the Stasi were repeatedly able to access information from the Berlin archive.[3]

Thanks to a source in the Document Center, the MfS acquired detailed information about the building, employees, and organisation of the secret US department as early as 1960. The 'IMs' (unofficial collaborators) 'IM Bolz' and 'IM Alexander', who were 'directly active in the enemy object' supplied the MfS not only with the telephone numbers of BDC director James Beddie and various departments, but also the names and personal information of about half a dozen German workers, including the later acting director, Egon Burchartz.[4]

Until 1952, German Democratic Republic (GDR) authorities occasionally received information about material on fascist organisations and former members of the Nazi Party that was being stored in the BDC. But once the Cold War intensified, the Americans battened down the hatches. The reason was obvious: it was hardly in the US's interest to give the East German government authorities access to still red-hot Nazi files, the contents of which could be used in East Berlin for propaganda campaigns against the Americans.

From the 1960s onwards, the Stasi endeavoured to systematically collect information about the pre-1945 career paths of prominent FRG citizens using the files on hand in the East German archives. In 1967, the central MfS department IX/11 was founded with the aim of finding incriminating evidence, evaluating it, and putting it at the disposal of other departments in the ministry. The processed information was published from 1965 onwards in the 'Brown Book', which was subtitled 'War and Nazi Criminals in the Federal Republic'. At the height of the student uprisings in West Germany in 1968, the third edition of the 'Brown Book' was released, in which the GDR propaganda machine named and shamed former National Socialists in the FRG's political, economic, administrative, military, legal, and academic fields.

On 3 July 1965, *Neues Deutschland* reported on a press conference with Politburo member Albert Norden in East Berlin:

Twenty-one ministers and State secretaries from the Federal Republic, 100 generals and admirals of the Bundeswehr [armed forces], 828 high-ranking judicial officers, lawyers and judges, 245 leading officials of the Auswärtiges Amt, Bonn ambassadors and consulates as well as 297 mid- and high-ranking officials from the police force and the Federal Office for the Protection of the Constitution were influential pillars of the Hitler dictatorship.

MfS operatives, meanwhile, were patting themselves on the back for their successful investigative research. In a memo sent from the 'agitation department' to State Security Minister Mielke, they politely listed their points of achievement:

The 'Brown Book' came into being with considerable support from the MfS agitation department. Materials and information were supplied by the MfS agitation department for all sections of the article, and the sections 'SS murderers from A to Z' (page 75), and 'Members of the Gestapo, the SD and the SS in the West Berlin police force' (page 91) were compiled almost exclusively from our materials.[5]

The substantial propaganda effort conducted under the leadership of Albert Norden to uncover the Nazi pasts of prominent West Germans cannot be allowed to detract from the fact that, 99 per cent of the time, these sensationally presented allegations corresponded to the truth. The manipulation of documents about West German Federal President Heinrich Lübke did, admittedly, contribute to the fact that the 'Brown Book' was quickly written off in West Germany as deceitful propaganda and even impounded at the Frankfurt Book Fair. But on the whole, the facts presented in it are now regarded as verified and dependable.[6]

The Document Center was seen as the Holy Grail for Nazi hunters in both East and West Germany. But while the Stasi's researchers were struggling to collect from the GDR's archives the remaining files on East Germans who had fled to the FRG, the Americans had much quicker access to the information, which had been arranged alphabetically by name immediately after the takeover in 1945. The NSDAP membership index and other files held in the BDC were also much more comprehensive — almost complete, in fact.

From the beginning, the Americans made an effort not only to safeguard their knowledge about their alliance partners, but also to use it. The already mentioned IM intelligence report of 1960 reveals that there was another reason why the Americans carefully protected the powerful information they held: 'IM Alexander' informed his leading officers that 'the American secret service were exploiting the object's criminal activity against the GDR by scouting out documented circles of individuals and priming them for propaganda.'[7]

The MfS also had an interest in forcing West German individuals to collaborate in espionage with the help of compromising files from the years predating 1945. But the attempt to obtain information from the Document Center via IMs ran into difficulties after three years. In 1963, the connection to 'IM Alexander' broke down and could not be re-established. The material that had been processed until that point was not enough to enable East Berlin spies to penetrate the American government department. For this reason, they decided to shift to formalities for the time being and have the BDC premises observed by the Mitte border command.

According to MfS officer Skiba's report on a conversation he had in 2012 with his former boss Wolfgang Schwanitz, who was the leader of the MfS's East Berlin district administration in the 1960s: 'We had it under close observation back then, photographing from the outside, trying to get the names of the individuals who were working there. But we didn't have direct access to the archives or the card index. That rankled with us, of course; we would have loved to get a foot in the door in Ludwigsburg [the location of the Central Office for the Investigation of NS Crimes], too.'

In 1968, the informer 'IM Horst Meyer' reported the external dimensions of the Document Center and stated that it was 'a flat-roofed building of 15 by 12 metres, predominantly guarded by an American duty station and surrounded by a wire fence topped with barbed wire'.[8]

By 1970, however, IM reports revealed that the building had expanded to 50 metres in width and that it allegedly contained 13 subterranean levels. Perhaps the thought of vast piles of Nazi files caused the spies' imaginations to become overactive. Either way, the intelligence was so contradictory that those in charge of the operation decided to discontinue the collection of information on the BDC premises.[9]

Two years later, a West German state lawyer from Osnabrück was observed going into the Document Center and coming out again three hours later. On the same day, the director of RIAS (Radio in the American Sector) was also on site, with numerous boxes of film in his possession.

In 1974, the Stasi obtained drawings and detailed descriptions of the Document Center. From the wooden hut that housed the American guard posts to the subterranean concrete bunkers and flat-roofed stone buildings (which, according to MfS sources, served as the storage facility for the *Völkischer Beobachter* [the Nazi Party newspaper]), the spies continued to map out the obscure object of their desire, situated in the midst of allotment gardens on Berlin's Wasserkäfersteig.

Seven years later, 'IM Horst Fischer' succeeded in siphoning off officers from the US Army's Guard Battalion at the BDC. In the process, the East Berlin spies found out that the BDC would no longer be guarded by the Americans after 1 August 1981, and that the handover of the Nazi files to the FRG authorities was allegedly being planned. As the MfS no longer had a relationship with the Document Center, those responsible were unsure whether the 'FRG authorities were to take over the object and guard it themselves, or whether the files would be taken and stored in the FRG'.[10] This, admittedly, was equally unclear in Bonn and Washington — and would remain so for a number of years. In

East Berlin, it was presumed that the Nazi files had passed into the 'hands of the Federal authorities'.

'Research has to be done'

For Bundestag President Karl Carstens, November 1978 was an opportunity to reminisce about his time as a junior lawyer in the Third Reich. For days on end, the Christian Democratic Union (CDU) politician searched through his cellar and loft for personal documents from the Nazi era. 'Yet another leading Christian democrat is hunting for his past', wrote *Der Spiegel* after rumours of Carstens' NSDAP membership from 1940 until the end of the war became public.[11]

Suddenly, Carstens' candidature for the highest position in the state shot out of reach. For 1979 would bring not only the election of a new president in Bonn, but also the decision in the German Bundestag (parliament) to lift the statute of limitations for murder — a decisive step which would mean that NS criminals could be brought to trial even 35 years after the end of the war. Was there now the chance of a Carstens trial? That would have drawn criticism for the conservatives, not just from the rival Social Democratic Party (SPD), and from abroad, too.

Carstens' hunt through his private archive paid off: he was able to produce a de-Nazification court verdict from 3 June 1948 which testified that although he had applied for party membership in 1937 'under pressure from his superiors', he had intentionally handed in his papers incomplete and late, with the result that his application of 12 May 1939 was rejected due to the intake freeze in effect at that time. On account of the fact that Carstens had requested to leave the SA in 1935, and had therefore no longer received the student benefits provided by the state, the court even declared him to be a resister of sorts, who 'in accordance with his powers, had actively resisted the Nazi dictatorship and suffered in the process'.[12] It seemed Carstens' independent research had only led him to exonerating material, mocked *Der Spiegel* in a November 1978 report on his attempt to justify his past.

Carstens himself claimed that although he had not been a true resister, he had taken a hostile stance to the party: a moral tightrope act, perhaps, for in order not to endanger his graduation, the temporarily impeded party member had collected membership fees for the NSDAP between 1937 and 1939, during his time as a junior lawyer. The question is, can someone be hostile to the system and yet help it at the same time?

The Stasi were interested in Carstens' NS past, too, but were unable to provide anything to further incite debate. In their Normannenstrasse headquarters, they were completely dependent on the Western press when it came to Carstens' case, and simply lifted articles from *Der Spiegel* and other media sources. Carstens' Stasi file (under the moniker 'Matrose'), for example, commented that he had been 'particularly burdened by his Nazi past and mentality', that he had been a member of the SA and the NSDAP, and that he had participated in war crimes trials as a judge. Reading between the lines, you can almost hear the sighs of the East Berlin data collector: 'At the present time, there is not yet any documentary proof or internal information that document already-known or new aspects of Carstens' fascist past or which are suitable [for] finding him responsible for further activities or decisively incriminating him. The sources presented are based exclusively on FRG press releases.'[13]

As controversial and accurate as the information on the later Bonn federal president may have been, the fact that it had already been revealed in West Germany meant that it could hardly serve as ammunition for propaganda campaigns such as those in the 'Brown Book'. The democratic press in the West had already uncovered the information — and without the help of the MfS, which was now reliant on them.

Nonetheless, the Stasi didn't let the opportunity to evaluate and comment upon the revelations in the West German media slip by. They stated that, as a member of the SA, Carstens had shown 'his positive stance towards fascist Germany', receiving state financial support for his studies in the process — something which was only granted to students who demonstrated their National Socialist mentality.[14] Meanwhile, the debate in West Germany regarding the NS past of the presidential candidate was also revolving around similar questions.

The crux of the matter was whether Carstens, born in 1914 in Bremen, had been a convinced National Socialist, or more of an opportunistic follower who complied out of career reasons due to the pressure exerted by those around him. Had Carstens really ostentatiously worn the party symbol on his Wehrmacht uniform as a trainee in the anti-aircraft artillery school, as many witnesses claimed but he himself vehemently denied? Usually, party membership was incompatible with the Wehrmacht and thus suspended during military service. The Stasi had heard this, too, and therefore constrained themselves to the following comment: 'This assertion cannot be verified; it doesn't normally correspond to the accepted practice at the time.'

Carstens had joined the SA in 1934 and was accepted into the NSDAP in 1940. He filled out the enrolment form back in 1937, allegedly under pressure from his superiors. The Stasi's researchers summarised the further development of his career as follows:

He graduated and sat his second State exam. The chairman officiating at the exam was the Hamburg Higher Regional Court president Rothenberger, later state secretary in the Reich Ministry of Justice, a man of Hitler. He evaluated Carstens' exam performance as 'commendable', the second-best rating that was given. At the beginning of 1940, the membership freeze in the NSDAP was lifted and Carstens' party membership came into effect. The membership had allegedly been on hold from the start, as Carstens was already a soldier in 1939.[15]

But the Stasi's researchers were unable to content themselves with referencing the defamatory material published in the Western media. So the historians of Department IX/11 were given some homework: 'Research has to be done,' they were told, in particular on the war and military court of Bremen and the Reich war court of Berlin, where Carstens was active between 1939 and 1945 as an assessor and defence lawyer. Participation in NS court rulings was a much more serious charge than nominal party membership. This had been made clear shortly beforehand in the case of the Baden-Württemberg minister-president Hans Filbinger, who was forced to step down once it became known that he had participated in handing out death sentences shortly before the end of the war as a naval judge.

But the more detail the Stasi tried to obtain in reconstructing Carstens' past, the less they ended up with. In 1980, an IM from Bremen reported that West German NS-victim associations were planning to publicise new proof of Carstens' former loyalty to the NS during the national election campaign, in an attempt to 'ensure the CDU's defeat'.

For the MfS, any propaganda action regarding the NS past of the newly elected West German federal president remained wishful thinking due to lack of proof. In any case, Carstens' true opponents were not in East Berlin, but in his own party. That's where the rumours about his involvement in the Third Reich started, among his very own — the right wing of the Christian Democrats. That didn't escape East Berlin's attention; they soon noticed that the Bonn debate was not about Carstens' NS past, but a power struggle between the right wing of the CDU and the party leader, Helmut Kohl: 'They wanted to publicly taint Carstens in order to make him look unsuitable for the role of federal president. The real aim was to shunt Kohl out of the picture … the same extreme legal forces who had so far supported such "right-wing" individuals as Carstens would now sacrifice him without hesitation just to get rid of Kohl.'[16]

As long as German politicians kept knowledge about their pasts to themselves, Vergangenheitsbewältigung was much more frequently a means to an end in East and West Germany than the Sunday soapbox oratories let these politicians presume; a tool for intrigue that was used willingly and often.

The cards never lie

At 8.00 a.m. on a Monday morning in 1988, Lieutenant Colonel Dieter Skiba's telephone rang. The leader of Department IX/11 in the Ministry for State Security picked up the receiver and heard a gruff voice bark at the other end: 'Have you read the papers yet today?' It was Stasi boss Erich Mielke.

'Yes, Comrade Minister,' replied Skiba dutifully, 'I've read *Neues Deutschland* cover to cover.'

'I don't care about that, I mean the *Spiegel*,' Mielke replied. 'If there's something in there, let me know.'

Monday was '*Spiegel* Day', even at the Stasi Normannenstrasse headquarters. Skiba just had one problem: How was he supposed to know what revelations the Hamburg-based news journal had decided to cause a stir with this time? The only copy in his sector was with the director of Department IX, which was responsible for research. 'I had to go to the general and wait in the front room until he was finished with it,' Skiba told me.[17]

After waiting for an hour, Skiba got his hands on the magazine and began checking to see whether there was any information from the NS era in his department about the individuals in question. 'We couldn't just call and say: "Comrade Minister — we don't have anything!" That's why we always collected everything, even the newspaper cuttings, in case it came into old Mielke's head that we had to do something.' Mielke was expecting a written report by Monday evening, 'so that by the Politburo meeting first thing on Tuesday morning, he could discuss it in detail with the general secretary'.

One could simplify things by dividing history into winners and losers, in which case Dieter Skiba has been on the losing side twice already, historically speaking.

His state collapsed, his agency was disbanded, and his party renamed itself again and again as it descended into post-socialist irrelevance. Along this route from the SED (Socialist Unity Party) via the PDS (Party of Democratic Socialism) to the socialist party Die Linke, the all-powerful unity party of the GDR lost several million members.

Skiba gave vent to his feeling when we met in the Berlin publishing house of *Neues Deutschland*, the erstwhile SED party newspaper. 'The SED had around 2 million members. Now think about how many of those 2 million are still in the left-wing party now and really identify with the GDR.'

Skiba may have been on the losing side, but he's no opportunist.

And that's not something that can be said about many of his former comrades. 'Twisting and turning like a goat tethered to a rope, all of a sudden they were resisters,' he said grimly, staring at the dove-blue wallpaper of the run-down office.

The Society for Legal and Humanitarian Support (Gesellschaft zur Rechtlichen und Humanitären Unterstützung, or GRH) is based on the 20th floor of the *Neues Deutschland* building, from where, according to its charter, it campaigns for 'rehabilitation, justice and historical truth'. Former GDR head of state Egon Krenz is also a member, which speaks volumes about the GRH's compatibility with the current political consensus of the Federal Republic.

Skiba accepts the fact that critics see the GRH, which he founded with former cadres from the SED, MfS, and the GDR National People's Army, as an obstinate bunch of old reactionaries. But by the same token, no one can accuse him of being a turncoat.

He knows all about turncoats. 'There are always going to be people like that, and that's why I say that mere membership of a party doesn't say anything about the mentality and behaviour of those people. That's why we tried to reintegrate the millions of NSDAP members back into society. In the GDR, you couldn't just say that every eighth person is a Nazi *a priori,* that kind of thing just won't wash!'

The question is, how do you build a Socialist People's Republic with millions of former fascists? Skiba was seven years old when the Third Reich lost the war and Germany was divided. Gradually, the inconceivable extent of German wrongdoing became known, and as different as the two German states were, the governments in Bonn and East Berlin were united on one point: never again could fascist crimes be perpetrated on German soil.

Skiba, a farmer's son, got involved in building up the GDR

— first in agriculture, then with the Ministry for State Security. 'The subject of the Nazis didn't use to hold any relevance for me; after all, I was just a farmer.' He joined the MfS in 1958 and was transferred to the district office in Oranienburg. There, he was to devote his attention to redeveloping the national memorial site of the Sachsenhausen concentration camp. Over the years, Skiba also analysed the trials of SS men in Sachsenhausen and, in 1968, was one of the first to become part of the newly founded central department IX/11 in the Ministry for State Security — 'not a specialist in the field, but already well-versed'.

For decades, Skiba and his colleagues delved into the pasts of their countrymen and women, collecting biographical material from the Third Reich, evaluating it, passing it on. His office was the East German counterpart to the Central Office of the State Justice Administrations in Ludwigsburg, which was responsible for the criminal prosecution of National Socialist crimes in the Federal Republic.

The MfS had held files from the era of the Third Reich ever since its foundation in 1950, Skiba explained: 'They were taken over from the Kriminalpolizei K5, where Mielke was significantly involved in the manhunt for Nazis.' According to Directive 201 of the Soviet Military Administration in 1947, the K5 was responsible for the prosecution of NS criminals in the GDR.[18]

Since 1952, the MfS had included Department XII, the central registry and archive where Nazi files were registered, processed, and archived. Skiba's special unit, IX/11, eventually emerged from this, officially called into life by Stasi boss Mielke with Directive 39/67. Department IX/11 worked in close collaboration with the documentation centre of the GDR Internal Ministry, which was founded in 1964 and also collected files from between 1933 and 1945.[19]

The fact that Mielke's men were intensifying the search for Nazi files two decades after the end of the war was due in part to the big political debates of the 1960s in West Germany. 'It's all connected to the problems with the statute of limitations,' Skiba explained. 'The archive materials had to be prepared for use in the fight against a statute of limitation for Nazi and war crimes in the Federal Republic, and for the support of the committee of the National Front [an alliance of political parties and mass organisations in the GDR].'

As previously mentioned, Politburo member Albert Norden was already making use of defamatory material in the early 1960s for targeted campaigns to discredit West German politicians and officials. Whenever it seemed politically advisable, the Stasi also supplied West Germans like Beate Klarsfeld or Günter Wallraff — anti-Nazi activist and undercover journalist, respectively — with defamatory material about FRG politicians. In 1969, Klarsfeld famously slapped the face of German chancellor and former NSDAP member Kurt Georg Kiesinger at the CDU party conference. When she campaigned for the federal presidency in 2012, it was revealed that she had received a payment of 2000 deutschmarks (at the time approximately $1500) 'for further initiatives' a week after the conference, and she was accused of being an 'SED puppet'.[20] However, Klarsfeld couldn't have known that she had been directly supplied by the Stasi. Officially, the information came from the documentation centre of the GDR's State Archive Administration. According to Skiba, who was present when Klarsfeld was handed the NS files on Kiesinger: 'The fact that the MfS played a significant role in that wasn't common knowledge.'

Keen to continue discrediting its political enemies, the MfS was watching developments in the West closely. Back then, according to German criminal law, the statute of limitations for murder expired after just 20 years. This meant that NS murder crimes could not be effectively tried from 1965 onwards. After a series of heated debates, the Bonn parliamentarians agreed on a compromise: they postponed the beginning of the statute of limitations from the end of World War II to the year that the Federal Republic was founded. In this way, murders carried out under the Third Reich could be legally tried and punished until 1969.

When this deadline was close to expiring, the parliamentarians postponed the statute of limitations problem once more by increasing it to 30 years. It was only in 1979 that the Bundestag lifted the statute of limitations for murder and genocide once and for all with a majority of 255 votes to 222.

The Federal Republic wrestled with the statute-of-limitations question for two decades, and in East Berlin it wasn't just Skiba and his colleagues industriously collecting material. The MfS department responsible for international intelligence, the HVA, was also interested in finding out where West German politicians stood on the statute of limitations question.

In the CDU and FDP, in particular, there were concerns over the potential prosecution as accessories to murder of those who gave orders from their desks.[21] Even within party circles, there were a considerable number in the late 1960s who would have been personally affected — the FDP politician Ernst Achenbach (NSDAP membership number 4789478 from 1 December 1937), for example, who campaigned for the interests of NS and war criminals for decades as a lawyer and Bundestag member. Nor did it escape the HVA's attention that Achenbach's colleague Hans-Dietrich Genscher had supported his draft bill for the statute of limitations on NS crimes in 1968.[22]

Over the course of time, Department IX/11 grew to include 50 workers: researchers, archivists, indexers, analysts, librarians, and technical-support workers. 'Like a drop in the ocean,' Skiba said. 'It wasn't much, if you consider that the Ludwigsburg Central Registry initially employed over 200 state lawyers.'

But the Stasi's researchers weren't just interested in compromising details about the Nazi past of 'enemies of the people' in the West. They were also investigating the former political lives of their own comrades in the Workers' and Farmers' State, who, Skiba asserted, 'we were able to identify as suspect GDR citizens from archive materials'.

They combed through East German authority archives, and procured materials from Poland, Czechoslovakia, and the Soviet Union in the hunt for leads on the Nazi past of their German suspects. Collaboration with Moscow wasn't always easy: 'The Soviets had masses of files, and we got our hands on many of them, but they didn't let us look at everything,' Skiba recalled. 'We would have liked to have all the files about political emigrants from Germany who were convicted and executed in the show trials of the 1930s. But they didn't give them to us.'

By the end, the Stasi historians had amassed 10 kilometres of files and prepared a list of 1.5 million membership cards. Every regional unit of the MfS, every war office or military intelligence unit, was able to lodge queries with Department IX/11: What was the NSFK? What role did the SA play in Pößneck? 'There were several thousand queries every month,' Skiba estimated. 'Statistically, I'd say that we responded to around 15,000 to 18,000 queries a year.'

The file trade

Skiba and his people were always well informed about the readers in the archives. Anyone who wanted to research file material from the Third Reich in the GDR State Archive had to lodge an official application that was passed on to Department IX/11. As long as the applicant didn't seem suspicious to the Stasi, he or she could get access to the files — provided they weren't being used by IX/11 as part of an ongoing trial. If that were the case, 'they didn't get anything'.

It was part of the MfS's Cold War logic that they assumed the enemy would be active and trying to obtain intelligence on the GDR archive. A note in the files from 1983 about collaboration between the Stasi and the State Archive Administration gives the urgent warning that 'enemy attacks on the state archive have noticeably increased in recent years, in particular regarding the investigation of GDR archive holdings as part of complex research topics, ideological attacks regarding the misuse of archive materials of the GDR and the exploitation of opportunities for making contact with archive readers'.[23]

In order to recognise and effectively prevent the 'subversive misuse of the GDR's archival holdings', no-access inventories were to be newly defined, direct contact between foreign researchers in the files prevented, and the State Archive Administration designated as the central authority for the authorisation process.[24]

During the Cold War, Stasi historians officially had no access to Western archives. That also applied to officially traded microfilms of the US National Archives. Skiba's people had obtained a catalogue of the microfilms archived in Washington and made a shopping list. There was just one problem: 'The Americans didn't sell them to us!'

And so Stasi historians tried to get to their coveted information via trades. Skiba recalled: 'We made the following offer to researchers from the West: "You can get a People's Court verdict against this or that person if you get us this and that in Washington."' From time to time, historians from the West would be excused from paying copying costs if they provided archive material in return. This meant that the agents always posed as archive employees.

'With the help of a little avarice, we got them,' Skiba said, without a trace of satisfaction. After all, even his department suffered from constant financial difficulty. In the last years of the GDR, the work of Stasi historians was significantly hindered by the rampant shortage of foreign currency.

When, in the 1980s, original documents from the Document Center came onto the black market in West Berlin, the Stasi soon caught wind of it. 'But we didn't have any money, so we couldn't buy them,' Skiba said.

There's a certain irony in the fact that, by the late 1980s, the GDR's omnipresent secret service wasn't even in the position to acquire the United Nations war-criminals list. Skiba became aware of the list's existence when his department received queries from the West regarding wanted war criminals.

'I wrote to the minister saying that it was important for the GDR to know which individuals were on the UNO's war criminals list, and that we needed 500 dollars in order to snap it up.' Mielke wasn't sure whether the war-criminals list was of importance for the GDR anymore. After some to-ing and fro-ing, Skiba was granted the money. But by then it was too late. 'Things were already coming to an end, so we didn't even need the list anymore.'

A government can't choose its people

One of the myths of East–West German post-war history is that the GDR was a fortress of anti-fascism, while in the Federal Republic tens of thousands of veteran Nazis had already reacquired leading positions in the state and society.

The de-Nazification phase was quickly tied up in the East, too. After the war, the Soviet occupying powers and the GDR's K5 criminal investigation department tracked down suspected Nazi criminals in East Germany. Many thousands of East German citizens were arrested between 1945 and 1948 (when de-Nazification officially came to an end), and interned in special camps without trial. After the foundation of the East German state in 1949, the last remaining inmates of the Soviet camps were condemned in constitutionally questionable circumstances during the so-called Waldheimer show trials.

If *Vergangenheitsbewältigung* were an Olympic sport, the GDR legal system would have finished in front of the Federal Republic's until the very end. Even in 1989, the GDR state public prosecutor listed 12,881 new verdicts passed that year on NS suspects. For the same time period in the Federal Republic, it was just 6485. However, the East German statistic included not only the 4000 verdicts from the Waldheimer trials, but also the numerous de-Nazification trials in which nominal memberships of NS organisations were punished.[25]

'Many individuals had been in the NSDAP or SS,' Dieter Skiba said. 'We placed particular emphasis on preventing former leading figures from the fascist era from getting back into important posts.' But that hadn't always been the case. 'Department IX/11 was simply founded too late.'

It seemed practically impossible in both East and West to create a state without the technocrats and millions of former supporters of Hitler's regime. The Stasi files reveal astonishing parallels: in the GDR, too, not just in the West, former NSDAP members had pushed their way back into leading roles after the foundation of the state. It was only in the late 1960s that — also as a result of the changing generations — a reduction in the number of individuals with Nazi pasts in important societal roles became evident.

'But the kind of exposed Nazi elite that made their way back into exalted positions in the Federal Republic, we didn't have that in the GDR,' Skiba said defensively. 'We didn't have the kind of SS generals who wrote memoirs or who had attended Nazi marches.' After all, it wouldn't have been smart to confess to having been an old reactionary in the GDR, something that was more possible in West Germany due to the culture of freedom of opinion.

In the East, the gap between claims and reality was more of a chasm. Take the church, for example. Stasi researchers generously supplied the 'agitation department' of the SED's Central Committee with compromising details about the backgrounds of FRG church functionaries. This resulted in propaganda actions with titles like 'Clerical militarism in action! SS leaders, Nazis and militarists in leading positions of the West German Evangelical Church'.[26] And yet numerous ex-Nazis had found shelter in the church in East Germany too, as the Stasi knew only too well.

Stasi researchers secretly procured handwriting samples from leading evangelical figures in the East. Using false identities, they spoke with people close to them and compiled intelligence reports.[27] They made long handwritten lists about 'pastors with active fascist pasts', detailing their former roles and memberships of NSDAP organisations in the Third Reich.

The results were devastating. A 1962 analysis of the concentration of former fascist officers in the Evangelical Church of the GDR drew the following conclusion: 'It has been established that all important military and in part also economic roles of our Republic are occupied by former fascists with specialist knowledge, or through rotation in office by correspondingly qualified pastors.'[28]

A large number of the functionaries engaged in the GDR's Evangelical Church at the time — in its governing body, training centres, church organisations, and congregations — were alleged to have been active fascists before 1945. In the church governing body of the jurisdiction of Saxony alone, there were 22 former members of the NSDAP and five of the SA. The level of influence of church men with Nazi pasts can be seen in the example of superintendent Ernst Kracht, born in Rügen on 27 May 1893: Kracht was responsible for 17 congregations, 21 rectorates, and had been a leading member of the SS from 1933 onwards.

The establishing of former Nazis in the regional churches had less to do with intelligence actions on the part of the West than MfS analysts suspected. It was primarily possible because, during the de-Nazification of East German pastors, most of the members of the NS organisation Deutsche Christen had been removed from their roles and replaced with members of the Confessing Church, which during the Third Reich had resisted Nazification by the dictatorship. 'But these supposed cleansing initiatives,' the MfS now realised, 'did not apply to former members of the NSDAP, SA and other fascist organisations.'[29]

A Stasi dossier from 1963 came to the sobering conclusion that 'The majority of church governing bodies consist predominantly of former NSDAP members who, even today, still have an adversarial attitude to the politics of the Party and government.'[30]

At the MfS, the 'sword and shield of the party', they soon realised that even members of the Confessing Church could have been members of the NSDAP or even the SS. But this didn't hinder the Stasi in its attempt to recruit former NSDAP members to infiltrate the regional church of Saxony.[31]

Even in the 1960s, the intelligence services of both German states had few scruples when it came to the selection of agents and 'unofficial collaborators'. Just like the German Federal Intelligence Service in the West, which had no problem employing people like the SS murderer Klaus Barbie, the MfS, too, had few misgivings when it came to selecting suitable henchmen. On the contrary: knowledge of enemy agents' Nazi pasts could come in useful for blackmailing them into betraying secrets and acting as double agents.

The MfS also wooed former SS men and members of the NSDAP, Gestapo, or SD, as the historian Henry Leide revealed.[32] These included NS criminals who had been classified as 'key culprits' by the Allied Control Council Directive 38 of October 1946. At the district offices of the MfS, the instruction was issued to 'prepare' as many of the individuals in question as possible for 'genuine collaboration with the MfS, or to make use of the circumstances available to force them into doing so'.[33] The idea was to smuggle these individuals into the West and use their Nazi past to pressure them into working for the MfS from there.

But surely there was quite a conflict in doing this? Skiba brushed that aside: 'As I always say: Anyone who sits at the table with the Devil is going to need a long spoon. After all, you can hardly plant renowned anti-fascists into West German Nazi networks! That's why we needed former NSDAP or SS or even Gestapo and SD members, in order to penetrate the West German secret service and get to the information.'

When it came to dealing with former National Socialists among their own ranks, matter-of-fact pragmatism prevailed in the GDR, as Skiba was very well aware. He spent years evaluating the files, searching for and finding thousands of former party members, SS members, and Gestapo men who had long since established themselves as People's Comrades in 'really existing socialism'. What happened when the Stasi wised up to them?

Nothing at all. NSDAP membership alone wasn't relevant to us. We passed on the information, of course, when we found a record card showing that someone had been a NSDAP member. But when we talk about Nazis, we have to make sure we clearly define who we mean by that. For us, members of the NSDAP or the Hitler Youth and so on weren't the kind of Nazis we were interested in. When we talked about Nazis, we meant the activists, not just the Nazi Party, but primarily those in the secret services, the Gestapo, the police and legal system, the Ministry of Propaganda. Our definition of a Nazi wasn't about membership of the NSDAP, but the role that someone played during the era of fascism.

However, the fact that membership of the NSDAP or SS didn't present a problem in itself doesn't mean that the MfS weren't interested in finding out everything they could about the pre-1945 pasts of GDR citizens. An instruction stamped 'Secret and Classified' from the Stasi State Secretariat on 2 June 1954 ordered all district offices to submit all their material to their regional offices within two months and to evaluate it 'post-haste'.

It had become clear to the founders of the MfS that the Nazi files distributed among the government authorities were a source of interesting information about their own people. In practice, as the Stasi leaders wrote, it turned out that the evaluation of old files 'could produce important clues for operative work'.[34] For this reason, all NS files then had to be centralised as a matter of urgency.

From then on, the Stasi researchers went to great lengths not only to avoid mistaken identity — for example, where people shared the same name — but also to try to attribute individual culpability to the suspects in question in every case. If they couldn't manage to do so, they had to disappoint their prosecution-hungry comrades in the district offices and call them off the case in question, whether they wanted to or not. Until 1948, suspects could still be interned and condemned within the framework of the Allied Control Council directive. 'But from the 1950s onwards we didn't use this maxim anymore,' Skiba said.

'Membership of the SS or NSDAP wasn't relevant to us when it came to prosecution. Nor could we have locked up a Gestapo or RSHA [Reich Security Head Office] collaborator whom we had nothing on.'

If a query came from a regional service unit, then the workers of Department IX/11 would have to check whether there was any defamatory material on the person in question in their archives. Officially, Skiba's department was responsible for the 'politically operative evaluation and supply of materials from and relating to the time of fascism and their operative utilisation for the activities of various lines and service units of the MfS and its associated research.'[35] But in contrast to the FRG's Prosecution Service, the Stasi prosecutors also employed espionage tactics. 'We could also work with unofficial collaborators, control of written correspondence, telephone bugging, and observation in people's home — all of those means were available to us. We also tried to find and question witnesses, but we couldn't let on who and what it was about,' Skiba explained.

Unlike in the West, suspects were not informed that they were under investigation. They were clueless. 'We always worked on the assumption that if they knew in advance we were investigating them for Nazi and war crimes, there was the possibility that their former comrades would help them to flee.'

If the Stasi came into the possession of personal files on GDR citizens of the relevant generation, they compared the names with the perpetrator lists in the IX/11 archive. When Skiba's people got their hands on the bank-account records of the Ravensbrück Sparkasse savings bank in the late 1970s, an investigation into the customers' places of residence revealed that 84 female former guards of the Ravensbrück concentration camp were still living in the GDR. 'We weren't able to find evidence for a single one of these 84 having been involved in maltreatment, gassing, or shooting. We informed the regional offices of course, saying that Martha so-and-so is living in your region, keep an eye on what kind of woman she is. But when it came to prosecution, there was nothing to be done,' Skiba recalled.

In 1988, a Walter O., born in Erfurt in 1925, came into the Stasi's sights. His military conscription book surfaced during an expansion of their archive material, revealing the GDR citizen to be a former member of the Waffen-SS. However, the Department IX/11 director also informed the district office in Erfurt that no further conclusions could be drawn from O.'s membership alone: 'Given that no information is available pertaining to the concrete execution of duties and behaviour of the person in question within the Waffen-SS, although the documents may prove former membership of the Waffen SS, they do not confirm participation in war crimes.'[36]

And in the case of Rudolf M., a concentration-camp guard born in 1923 in Ehrenberg on whom there was a pending request for information, the Stasi experts were only able to confirm that he was part of the troop in question. Furthermore, they expressly pointed out that 'with regard to individual involvement in crimes against humanity, in particular during his deployment in Auschwitz and as an attendant on one of the "evacuations" from the concentration camps otherwise known as death marches, there was no evidence available'.[37]

After the rigorous cleansings of the immediate post-war era, the GDR, too, soon brought an end to the de-Nazification process. The 'directive regarding measures of atonement' clarified the position of former Nazis and Wehrmacht members in the newly founded GDR. All former members and supporters of the NSDAP or its organisations, as well as officers, non-commissioned officers, and soldiers of the fascist Wehrmacht could from this point on take active roles in the public service and all industries. The only exceptions to this regulation were roles within the People's Police, the justice system, and the inner administration. On the second anniversary of the foundation of the GDR, the last trials following Directive 201 were halted as part of an amnesty action initiated by the president, provided that no higher sentence than a year's imprisonment was expected.[38]

On 2 September 1952, a regulation 'regarding the lifting of restrictions for former members of the NSDAP and its associations and former officers' came into force. It lifted all 'established restrictions of rights for former members of the NSDAP or its associations, including former officers of Hitler's Wehrmacht' and gave them from that point on the same civil and political rights as all other citizens.

The new leading powers' offer of integration to former Nazis was well received. In spite of numerous 'party cleanses' carried out in the mid-1950s, almost 11,000 SED comrades in the region of Erfurt alone were former NSDAP members, as the historian

Sandra Meenzen discovered.[39] Other regions were in a similar situation. These statistics had been gathered at the behest of the SED headquarters, and made the party leaders uneasy. Wasn't that a few too many former Nazis among the comrades?

In some circles, almost all the comrades had 'brown-tainted' pasts, as a 1954 report by the Central Committee warned: 'In the region of Hildburghausen there are key organisations in which almost 100 per cent of the workers are former members of the NSDAP, for example in the party organisation surveying office, where 18 of its 19 members had once belonged to the NSDAP.'[40] And if we take not only Nazi Party membership but also membership of the Hitler Youth and BDM into account, the proportion of SED members in the region of Erfurt with a Nazi past climbs as high as 35.8 per cent.[41]

There were former NSDAP members even in GDR government circles after the war, sitting in the People's Chamber, Council of Ministers, and SED Central Committee — individuals such as Manfred Ewald, Hans Bentzien, and Horst Stechbarth. Even in the 1980s, there were more former NSDAP members in the SED Central Committee under Erich Honecker than there were former SPD members (in the Soviet occupation zone, the SPD was compelled by the Soviets to merge with the SED after 1945). The West German historian and activist Olaf Kappelt had already published most of the names in 1981 in the FRG's 'Brown Book', Braunbuch DDR: Nazis in der DDR, and two decades later he summed up the Nazi past of the old GDR guard as follows:

For more than forty years, until March 1990, the former NS Gau student leader of Thüringen, Siegfried Dallmann, was in the GDR People's Chamber. Professor Heinrich Homann held out in the GDR State Council until the very end; the upper-class

shipping company heir had joined the NSDAP as early as 1933.
Heinz Eichler, the secretary of the GDR State Council until 1989,
was another former NSDAP member. And on 7 November 1989,
the long-standing director of the GDR press office was removed
from his role; he too was part of the old guard of former Nazi
Party members.[42]

Things were no different at the SED party headquarters. And
no wonder, for in 1946 the SED Central Committee had already
lifted the incompatibility directive, according to which former
NSDAP members could not be accepted into the Socialist Unity
Party of Germany.

'Of course we had Nazis in the East, too,' Dieter Skiba
conceded. 'After all, the GDR couldn't pick its own people.' After
the war and the desolation it caused, the GDR leadership, just like
the government of the FRG, saw no other choice but to integrate
the millions of former National Socialists. Clearly it wasn't possible
to build a new state without supporters and experts of the Hitler
state — and especially not without the young people who had
joined Hitler's party at 17 or 18 years of age and who were now
the generation of the future.

'Someone who joins a party at 17 or 18 years of age isn't
necessarily a Nazi, not in the sense we see it,' Skiba explained.

Even in the East German socialist state, people were
increasingly willing to look past the youthful mistakes of up-and-
coming comrades. Anyone who admitted to their own NSDAP
membership orally was not obligated to mention it in the written
staff questionnaire. According to Skiba:

We never concerned ourselves with the individuals who had
been transferred from the Hitler Youth into the NSDAP as

young men in 1944–45 for the Führer's birthday. As early as 1948, there was an amnesty decree from the Soviet military administration in East Germany, after which the Hitler Youth from the age groups transferred in 1943–44 were classified as exonerated. This also meant that they didn't need to declare their NSDAP membership in later documentation.

In general, queries regarding NSDAP membership were included on the cadre questionnaires of both the candidate in question and his or her parents. But it speaks volumes that, as Sandra Meenzen believes, numerous SED members obstinately concealed their earlier NSDAP membership: 'For despite all the SED's offers of integration, public confession against a background of the GDR's omnipresent anti-fascist rhetoric and shifting disqualification criteria with the "party cleanses" remained a risky enterprise.'[43]

In February 1963, for example, the acting minister of agriculture, Karl-Heinz Bartsch, was removed from office and excluded from the SED Central Committee. The party organ *Neues Deutschland* justified this measure with the allegation that Bartsch, born in 1923, had 'concealed his involvement with the Waffen-SS, and by doing so caused the Party considerable harm'.[44] The Central Committee used the Second Conference in April 1963 as an opportunity to have a discussion about 'honesty towards the Party'. The party leaders did not demand disqualification from the party of those who had been NSDAP members, but rather appealed to all comrades to be truthful. This was based on the assumption that there was no reason to conceal or lie about the past, for the SED had 'given all former nominal members of the Hitler party the chance to participate and start a new life'. This applied in particular to the 'youth which had been led astray and brought up in a fascist manner'.[45]

And yet, trust is good, but control is better: The motto of the MfS was 'Be Prepared'. 'There are many important figures in the GDR who we at the MfS had a divided relationship with,' Skiba recalled. 'People who we knew had tarnished stories from their past. But you need to be able to prove it. Afterwards, much of it did turn out to be true.'

The NS pasts of East German functionaries and top politicians became particularly critical when the West got wind of them more quickly than their own State Security Service. In the Federal Republic, the reaction to East German campaigns against West German politicians was to uncover stories about the Nazi pasts of East German top functionaries in turn, and they had the advantage in that they could rely on the help of their American allies and access to the files of the Document Center.

A Stasi memo from February 1969 about the 'suppression of the Western campaign about supposed Nazis in the GDR' accuses the 'Nazi hunter' Simon Wiesenthal of assisting West German efforts in this regard.[46] In the majority of cases, the revelations about the Nazi pasts of East German politicians were researched with just as much care as the information in the GDR's original 'Brown Book'. And so the Cold War ensured that both German states occupied themselves with reciprocal investigations.

When Olaf Kappelt published his 'Brown Book' in 1981, GDR state security minister Mielke was furious. The 'rabble-rousing and shoddy work' of a known anti-communist and Republic traitor was attempting to create the impression that 'there were a number of former NSDAP members exerting active influence over the political and societal life of the GDR'.[47] In the MfS, they immediately assumed that Kappelt had acquired his information from the Document Center in West Berlin. A special unit of workers from departments XX/2 and IX/11 were immediately instructed to check Kappelt's allegations. In a 'strictly confidential' communication of the GDR Council of Ministers from 19 May 1982, the leaders of regional MfS units were reminded that the majority of the individuals named were personalities who 'had been actively engaged in building up the GDR for decades'. The checks, therefore, were to be carried out in a 'strictly internal' manner so that none of those in question found out about it. The possibility that they may not have known about their NSDAP membership was also to be considered. Mielke's people came to the conclusion that, as far as Kappelt's book was concerned, 'the presence of new information could not be denied'.

'We were told to check the book and see whether there was anything of penal relevance in there,' Skiba told me. 'We didn't find anything.' The facts, he conceded, were correct. 'The question was: how did we assess them?'

When it came to assessing party membership, the most important question was how that membership had come about. Was there ever any truth in the much-used excuse that the individuals in question had been transferred into the NSDAP without their knowledge?

In any case, even the MfS didn't want to rule out the possibility that those named by Kappelt had 'concealed defamatory details from their files and therefore given the enemy the opportunity for blackmail and further defamation'.[48] The Nazi past of many individuals remained hidden from the MfS for a long time because as nomenclature cadres, or prominent leaders of the inner political circle, their files had not been accessible to Department IX/11. When the contents of the 'Brown Book' were being checked, the investigators realised that there were 90 such individuals, ten of whom were Central Committee nomenclature cadres and workers of the central party apparatus; 25, in central functions; 31, in local functions; and 24, 'retirees'.[49] In addition, there were 75 individuals who had been members of Hitler's party after 1943. The investigators concluded that, at least when it came to NSDAP admission up to 1942, it could be assumed that those in question had known about their membership and that an omission to declare it in staff files after 1945 meant 'as a general rule [...] an intentional concealment'.

In this context, the MfS investigators also turned their attention to the question of how individuals of the year groups born in 1926 and 1927 had come into the NSDAP. According to a 'memo on considerations relating to the awareness or non-awareness of NSDAP membership', each year, members of the Hitler Youth who turned 19 were transferred into the NSDAP by an 'administrative act of the Reich leadership' on 1 September (and, from 1943 onwards, on 20 April, too), provided they had been members of the Hitler Youth for four consecutive years beforehand.[50] 'Former HY members transferred in this manner,' the MfS concluded, 'weren't always aware of their NSDAP membership, because the completion of individual application forms was waived for the transfer of year groups, despite being required by the general organisational guidelines of the NSDAP.' This applied in particular to youths who had already been drafted into military service at the time of the transfer and whose membership coincided with a time of active service. However, the possibility was considered that those in question could have been informed of the transfer by the local NSDAP group during a period of home leave or a stay in a military hospital.

Whether this was true or not remained the secret of the individuals in question, who tended to plead ignorance both in the East and the West. The possibility that individual application procedures had been waived for the transfer of year groups remained pure speculation — in this case, partly because the efforts of the GDR cadres in question to exonerate themselves coincided with the party leadership's fear of being seen as a melting pot of old Nazis, particularly by the Western anti-communists. 'We always assumed that this collective enrolment was carried out, but we didn't have proof,' Skiba admitted. For this reason, it seemed appropriate to the MfS leaders, even in the case of NSDAP members admitted after 1943, to include personal statements in the files of those named in the West's 'Brown Book' after checking the information in the GDR's documentation centre, in order to expose future falsification of questionnaires.[51]

So, in the end, Department IX/11 was willing to comply with the exoneration strategies of former Hitler Youth members after all. The Americans knew better after intensive study of the NSDAP archives, and had done for a long while. But in ignorance of the NS party files stored in the Document Center, the Stasi's experts continued to assume that entire year groups of the Hitler Youth had been transferred without their own knowledge.

This assumption was not based upon a systematic evaluation, but rather the investigation of a few individual cases in which the persons in question assured the MfS researchers that they had not known of their NSDAP membership.

Skiba recalled a personal conversation with the former GDR defence minister and NVA (National People's Army) general Heinz Kessler, who, according to the files, was a member of the NSDAP from 1943: 'He told me himself that he knew nothing about it.' Kessler claimed to have already been in a Soviet prisoner-of-war camp when his party membership came into effect. This, of course, doesn't rule out the possibility that Kessler could have signed the NSDAP admission form some months earlier — at a time when the young man's perspective may have been very different. According to the MfS's knowledge at the time, Kessler, born in 1920, was not part of one of the younger year groups that were allegedly transferred collectively.

Occasionally, even before the publication of Kappelt's 'Brown Book', the MfS stumbled on inconsistencies during the course of its discreet research. In 1979, the acting director of Department IX/11 turned his attention to a query regarding the 'NSDAP membership of a male individual born in 1927' in Bautzen. The NSDAP membership number of the unnamed individual was 9974320, and Lieutenant Colonel Dr Nieblig from the IX/11 argued:

> It is known that members admitted in 1944 were given membership numbers of over 9 and 10 million. According to the central record office it was not possible to establish a concrete time period for the allocation of membership number 9974320. The place of issue, however, was definitely Munich. The original record cards available (admittedly there was not a complete collection) support the conclusion that the year group of 1927 was transferred in its entirety in 1944 and that the overwhelming majority had the transfer date of 20.4.1944, while a lesser number had 1.9.1944. According to the procedure set out in the material available, a similar practice would also have been carried out in Bautzen, with Hitler Youth members born in 1927 being transferred into the NSDAP on the 20.4.1944. When it comes to the exact concrete form in which this happened and who in particular it affected there is no proof in the available archive material, because the transfer lists from Bautzen are not at hand.[52]

This seemed to bring the case to a close — that is, until two years later, when the 'Brown Book GDR' was published and revealed former NSDAP member number 9974320 to be General Major Helmut Nedwig, who in his post-war career had ascended the ranks to become leader of the GDR criminal police. The investigation that followed revealed that on the questionnaire in his cadre file, he had stated under Point 15 ('membership of political parties and organisations between 1933 and 1945') that he had not been part of any party or organisation back then. In reality, the secret of his membership had already been discovered back in 1948, when the K5 criminal police in Bautzen found NSDAP membership records in which Nedwig's name was listed with the enrolment date of 1 May 1944.[53] Even Nedwig's second wife was on the list. But Nedwig vehemently denied his membership, saying that it wouldn't have been possible at 16 or 17 years of age, and that his parents' approval would have been required. Besides, he added, he was already doing his Reich labour service at the time, and the whole thing was a 'regional measure carried out without his knowledge'.

However, Stasi researchers noted that this depiction of events contradicted the information in the 'Brown Book', according to which Nedwig had been accepted into the NSDAP on 20 April 1944; in other words, before commencing his labour service. Nedwig's speedy ascension of the ranks within the Wehrmacht also made the investigators suspicious: why had Nedwig become a corporal after just three months and a company troop commander after another four?

These contradictions in the career of the GDR's highest-ranking criminal-police official prompted the MfS to commence 'conspiratorial verification measures' in Bautzen in May 1982 in order to obtain further evidence and 'reliable witnesses' who knew

Nedwig in the period between 1940 and 1950.

A short while later, the investigations into Nedwig were abandoned. As the leader of Department IX/11 stated on 3 August 1982, no archive material on Nedwig had been found. 'As a result, membership of the NSDAP cannot be either confirmed or refuted at this point.' In the absence of new results, MfS colonel Stolze recited the assumptions his deputy had made in 1979, and presumed that, in Bautzen, too, all Hitler Youth members of that year group had been transferred into the NSDAP in 1944.[54]

We now know that, in reality, only slightly more than one-third of the Hitler Youth from the 1927 year group were transferred into the NSDAP. Of the 18 million youths who were HY members from 30 January 1933 until their 18th year, in total only 7 to 8 per cent were transferred into the Nazi Party.[55]

For the criminal-police chief Helmut Nedwig, however, the matter was closed. A short time later, he was promoted to General Lieutenant.

CHAPTER FIVE

In Mr Simon's Safe

On 17 September 1987, Daniel Simon, the director of the Berlin Document Center, was expecting an important visitor. US ambassador Richard Burt and his deputy James Dobbins were on their way. After the two men arrived and had been taken on a tour of the archive, Simon brought them to his office. When they were on their own, Burt enquired into the state of return negotiations with the Germans. Simon told the visitors that both sides had agreed the handover could only take place once all the documents had been recorded on microfilm. The Interior Ministry in Bonn had already authorised the necessary funds to pay for the microfilming. But payment would only be made once an official agreement had been reached.

The ambassador nodded, but Dobbins seemed to be unsatisfied. They had already been negotiating with the West German government for years, he explained impatiently. 'Why don't we just tell the Germans they'll get the files as soon as we've finished filming, and be done with it?' Simon replied that no one knew what the situation would be like in five years — 'You chaps in Bonn and Washington can probably judge that better than I can.' The ambassador concurred and indicated that there were more diplomatic implications than were immediately apparent.

Then the two visitors started talking about a delicate matter. They had heard of a 'special list', they said — could they see it? The director went to the safe in the corner of his office, took out a document, and set it down on his desk. 'Incredible,' the ambassador murmured, as his eyes glided across the names of more than 70 leading German politicians who had all been members of the NSDAP. Even Dobbins could hardly believe his eyes.

From Konrad Adenauer's cabinet to Helmut Kohl's, former members of the NSDAP had sat at the table in every German government since the war. Under chancellor Willy Brandt alone, 12 former Nazis served as ministers.[1]

Simon had arranged for the list to be drawn up under conditions of strict secrecy for internal use, and had the NSDAP membership cards of the individuals in question removed from the main card file in order to keep them separately in his safe. Only Don Koblitz, the legal adviser to the American embassy, had a copy.

By the time the visitors said goodbye an hour later, Simon had convinced them that a return of the Nazi files would have devastating consequences for German politics. The director sat back down behind his desk and began to write a memo to the American envoy in Berlin: 'I think the list has made it clear to you that the Document Center is a political millstone around the neck of the Federal Republic.'[2]

The memo from the director of the BDC and the ominous 'special list' are now in the National Archive in Washington. Information about the Nazi pasts of top German politicians was considered so controversial that US envoy Harry Gilmore replied by return of post that no copy should be made available to ambassador Burt and James Dobbins unless they explicitly asked for it.

For the Americans, the files were primarily a diplomatic problem. Again and again, other secret services — as well as journalists, academics, and private individuals — tried to get hold of the information contained within. But the Americans weren't interested in bothering their West German ally in the Cold War with revelations about the Nazi pasts of their political staff. The special list existed so that questions about specific people could be checked, but no information was to be issued to third parties. From the early 1960s until 1991, the Americans repeatedly took the names of prominent German politicians out of the main card file and locked them in the safe of the BDC director. Under the leadership of Daniel Simon alone, the files of around 50 people were secured in this way.[3]

The noteworthy thing is that the staff with Nazi pasts came from the middle of the political spectrum — 27 members of the CDU/CSU, 25 SPD members, nine FDP politicians. Only the Republican Franz Schönbuber was regarded as being on the far right.[4] Apart from politicians, men like Wolfgang A. Mommsen (president of the Federal Archives), Helmut Schlesinger (president of the Bundesbank), and Klaus Bremm (general inspector of the Bundeswehr) were named in the files, as well as the director and several members of staff at the headquarters of the State Justice Administrations in Ludwigsburg, which dealt with the prosecution of Nazi criminals.[5]

But the file cards removed by the Americans represented only the tip of the iceberg. The actual number of people with Nazi pasts in German offices and parliaments was considerably higher. Even in the 1960s, former members of the Nazi Party were probably in the majority in these circles. It is only today that the degree of repression over the decades is becoming clear.

'Destroy upon termination'

This kind of research is only possible today thanks to the Nazi files that were administrated for almost 50 years by the Americans in the Berlin Document Center. But even after their return to the Germans, the question of whose Nazi files had been examined by whom during the US administration was to remain unanswered. According to a list drawn up by the US State Department in the early 1990s, most of the files made their way to the shredder before they could be handed over. Under the heading 'Records of the Berlin Document Center', the State Department decreed in December 1991 that the files of the visa and rogatory letters departments, lists of checked names, and private dossiers should be destroyed: 'Destroy upon termination of US. administration of the BDC.'[6]

But in many cases the archives were not disposed of, and are still in the National Archive in Washington, as evidenced by the signature of a National Archives member of staff made in the margin of a list some time around 1997. The staff member had been producing a finding aid for the BDC files and, in the process, comparing the list with the holdings available in the National Archives. It is not always possible to tell from these handwritten notes what happened, and when, to the documents in question during the crucial years between 1991 and 1997. For example, the personal files ('file summaries') produced by BDC staff on 5 x 7 inch file cards were 'obviously' — to quote the marginal note — destroyed in the Document Center. Dozens of archive boxes full of requests and correspondence, on the other hand, were in fact catalogued. These include comprehensive lists of NSDAP members in Germany and all over the world compiled by BDC staff after the war, as well as an incomplete list of party applicants, including only names beginning with the letters I–K, M, and P–R.

Given the fragmentary nature of the surviving applications, which is clearly down to the availability of original files found by the US Army in 1945, it hardly seems surprising that no applications could be found from Genscher, Wellershoff, Walser, and others. And given that applications were the precondition for party membership, we may assume that they were lost or destroyed at the end of the war.

But it seems contradictory that the Americans should treat the information as top secret if suspected NSDAP membership — as Genscher was quick to assert — had happened without members' knowledge and was therefore insignificant.

In fact, there is much to suggest that the American custodians of the BDC — who, after decades of continuous archive work, were more familiar with the Nazi Party documents than anyone else and considered supposedly unwitting membership to be a fabrication — correctly assessed the controversial nature of the files and made access particularly difficult as a result.

The application forms and personal files in the BDC archives don't just confirm that America was in the know about the Nazi pasts of top German politicians from early on. They also show how discreet the Americans were for decades in their treatment of controversial information regarding their German allies. The hope that many German politicians had of being 'safe from snooping' in the Nazi files was in fact realised under American management. While the German public didn't find out about the NSDAP membership of president Walter Scheel until the end of his time in office, BDC staff had discovered his membership card as early as 1954. The year before, Scheel had been elected to the Bundestag and subjected to a routine investigation.[7] When Scheel became minister of economic cooperation in Konrad Adenauer's cabinet in 1961, his NSDAP membership card was requested once again.

The existence of his NSDAP membership card didn't stop Scheel from presenting himself as a sleuth in his soapbox speeches. As foreign minister, he announced in a document celebrating the 100th anniversary of the Auswärtiges Amt (Ministry of Foreign Affairs) that he was going to launch an investigation into the history of the ministry during the Third Reich.[8]

In the end, he neglected not only to put this planned investigation into action, but also to reveal his own past in the Third Reich. It only became public in 1978 when Scheel, by then head of state, was accused of being a member of Hitler's party.

The reference to the president's NSDAP membership came from an ex-member of Scheel's own party, the former FDP chairman Erich Mende. He had switched to the CDU in October 1970, but was clearly still well informed about the NDSAP membership of his former fellow party members.[9] Like Scheel, Hans-Dietrich Genscher had also learned from a party colleague in 1970 that there was an NSDAP membership card in his name in the BDC.

It wasn't until November 1978 (when the NSDAP membership of Karl Carstens came to light as he prepared to stand as the CDU's presidential candidate) that Scheel decided to take the bull by the horns, and admitted in a strangely convoluted declaration that he, too, had been a member of the NSDAP from 1942 on. He couldn't remember whether he himself had made the membership application, he alleged, but his membership had been suspended during military service. 'Walter Scheel couldn't have given the country a bigger surprise,' *Die Zeit* commented in amazement.[10]

With his preposterous excuse, the FDP politician paved the way for all the others who wanted to play down their NSDAP membership over the decades that followed. The more often the fairytale of unwitting party membership was repeated, mantra-like, the more the people involved believed it. When Scheel was asked about his NSDAP membership in an interview in 2010, he roundly denied it: 'From the day Germany and Frankfurt declared war on one another until the end of the war I was a Luftwaffe soldier. And as a Wehrmacht soldier [translator's note: in this context, the Luftwaffe is taken to be part of the Wehrmacht] one was forbidden to be a member of the NSDAP. Besides, NSDAP membership would have been out of the question as far as I was concerned.'[11]

In reality, soldiers and officers of the Wehrmacht had been granted permission to be party members since conscription was introduced in 1935, but their membership was only suspended during their period of active service. It also casts a telling light on the self-exonerating claims made by younger members of the NSDAP when Scheel, who was born in 1919, suggests that he never made a membership application, and had thus unwittingly joined Hitler's party. Even for those born in 1926–27, no evidence whatsoever has been produced for collective membership without the knowledge of those involved. On the other hand, the cases of Scheel and many others show that from the 1970s onwards it was possible even for older Germans to spread the fairytale of unwitting party membership without subjecting themselves to public mockery.

No more de-Nazification!

The attempts by former NSDAP members to exonerate themselves during the 1970s fell on fertile ground not least because — in spite of the new boom in public *Vergangenheitsbewältigung* — there was a consensus among the representatives of all political parties not to call for a resumption of the de-Nazification process. That consensus dated back to the time of post-war reconstruction, and didn't just involve pragmatists like Chancellor Adenauer (quoted as saying you don't throw away dirty water until you get in fresh). The first head of the SPD, Kurt Schumacher, had himself argued for the rehabilitation of hundreds of thousands of former members of the Waffen-SS, as long as they had not been found guilty of war crimes.[12] The political trench burned between Germans by communism and by National Socialism was bridged in 1966 at the cabinet table of the Great Coalition, at which the former communist Herbert Wehner and the one-time emigrant Willy Brandt sat side by side with former NSDAP members Kurt Georg Kiesinger (CDU), Gerhard Schröder (CDU), and Karl Schiller (SPD).

When Walter Scheel's National Socialist past was made public in 1978, the newspapers reported that Hans-Dietrich Genscher wasn't the only one to leap to his friend's defence. Willy Brandt also backed Scheel, while chancellor Helmut Schmidt and opposition leader Helmut Kohl spoke out publicly against a 'new de-Nazification'.[13]

Admittedly, Germany had embarked on the long journey into *Vergangenheitsbewältigung* from the 1960s onwards: from the Auschwitz trials, through the American series *Holocaust*, Claude Lanzmann's film *Shoah*, and Richard von Weizsäcker's speech on 5 May 1985, to the Wehrmacht exhibitions of the late 1990s and early 2000s. Sixty-five years after the end of the war, the latter led to the establishment of historical commissions. But as long as the political reality of the Federal Republic was determined by people who had lived through the Third Reich, there was a wide consensus beyond party boundaries that it was time to look to the future. The fact that the Nazi pasts of politicians such as Scheel and Carstens become known at all was not because a critical democratic public was crying out for historical enlightenment. Until 1994, the Americans, for fear of 'abuse', ensured that the representatives of such a public — journalists and academics — had no access to sensitive information about senior German politicians.

American and German authorities as well as the government offices of friendly states did, on the other hand, receive information. Some international organisations such as the Jewish Claims Conference, the Documentation Archive of Austrian Resistance in Vienna, and the Simon Wiesenthal Center could apply for information about individuals if legal proceedings had been instituted against them.[14]

In 1985, when the former SS major and convicted war criminal Walter Reder was released from prison in Italy and returned to Austria, the deputy editor-in-chief of the Vienna *Wochenpresse* received personal documents about Reder from the Document Center via the US Embassy, including lists of SS decorations, and assessments of Reder and his career.[15] Reder's return sparked a scandal: on his arrival in the country, the war criminal was greeted with a handshake by the Austrian defence minister, the far-right FPÖ politician Friedhelm Frischenschlager. By releasing information about Reder's SS career in the Third Reich, the American ensured that his crimes — and his courting by members of the government at the time — launched one of the first big public debates about Austria's Nazi past. In general, however, no information was released about people against whom, to the knowledge of the BDC administrators, there was no evidence.[16]

A difficult burden

The Americans did everything they could to prevent a new process of de-Nazification. The political task was simple: information about Nazi war criminals could be issued, but the small secrets of big national politicians were something else — in the 1980s they were still to be protected. 'While we support the legitimate pursuit of Nazi war criminals,' reads an internal memo from the US representation in Berlin, dated 9 September 1986, 'in our view it cannot be justified in anyone's interest or with regard to the private sphere of the individuals in question for us to grant access to journalists and others so that they can go fishing.'[17]

Behind this political target lay the strategic motivation of protecting important political allies in the Cold War against potentially damaging scandals. After all, the Americans still had a vivid memory of the astonishingly accurately researched 'Brown Book' of GDR propaganda, which had attracted a great deal of media attention by unmasking many of the pillars of West German law and politics as former Nazis. The secret memos that went back and forth between the State Department in Washington, the US delegation in Berlin, and various BDC directors in the 1970s and 1980s confirm the impression that the Americans weren't interested in helping to unmask 'ordinary National Socialists': 'To be branded a Nazi is a burden from which one can only cleanse oneself with great difficulty', it says in the internal memo mentioned above. 'We don't want to encourage sensationalist reporting, which would be very likely in the case of open access regulation.'[18] The restrictive caution with which the Americans governed access to the archive even in the 1980s reveals once again that the gentlemen of the Document Center knew very well that they were sitting on 50 tons of political explosives that could still go off at any moment.

The Americans had tried to give most of the captured files back to their rightful owners shortly after the war. As early as 1952, the US government had decided to give most of these files back to West Germany — with the exception of those documents 'which glorified the Nazi regime or had the character of propaganda, or which concerned the administration, the personnel and the functioning of organisations of the NSDAP, unless their return would not endanger democratic life in the Federal Republic'.[19]

A year later the US Army put control of the Document Center into civilian hands, and from then on the archive was run under the auspices of the State Department, represented by the US mission in Berlin. At the time, between 40 and 60 German members of staff worked in the archive under the direction of the Americans.[20] After the Federal Republic reacquired state sovereignty in 1955, the files of the Foreign Office, the Reich Chancellery, and factual files without direct reference to individuals were returned to Germany from the holdings of the BDC. After 1962, the BDC represented above all a personal archive that was regularly consulted by Allied and German authorities on official matters: war crimes tribunals, de-Nazification, pension claims, and state honours.[21]

In 1968, a 'National Archives Liaison Committee' was appointed, which included three American historians who were to advise the West German National Archive on the return of the BDC files. As US senator George McGovern revealed a year later, at that point they were already considering the return of the files to Germany, 'as they were files of German provenance'.[22] The condition was that the complete holdings were first to be filmed, and the original files had to be made accessible to bona fide academics even after they were handed over. The microfilming of the documents was also in line with the fundamental conditions that applied to the return of other German files confiscated by the US.

In 1969, the microfilming of the files of SS officers, the People's Court, and the NSDAP Party Census of 1949 was already underway when the committee reported 'chaotic conditions' in the BDC. The organisation of the archive left much to be desired, and many of the staff members familiar with the files were already reaching retirement age.

The archivist Robert Wolfe recommended that the alphabetically organised personal files be filmed first, as they represented the most sensitive data and would therefore be the first to be returned to Bonn or Koblenz.[23] In 1969, after a four-week visit to the BDC, Wolfe presented the committee with another list of recommendations for handover preparations. In December 1969, the Liaison Committee wrote a six-page report casting the Document Center in an unfavourable light and describing an urgent need for action. A copy of this report, presumably annotated by the then BDC director, has been preserved among the files.

The staff of the Document Center already had their hands full with 4000 requests a month, and there were only three cameras available to microfilm the material, which was in constant use. The filming of the NSDAP membership card files, which was right at the top of the list, would take more than two years. The BDC director complained in a marginal note: 'These would be completed (using the methods of 1969) in 1985.' The detailed statistical analysis of the data in the NSDAP membership card files demanded by historians was also viewed with some scepticism in the BDC: 'What analysis of 10 million cards consisting of name, DOB, residence, profession and date of admitted [sic] to Party?'

Hansen and the hot potato

In 1968, the SPD MP Karl-Heinz Hansen demanded that the BDC be placed under the auspices of the Federal Republic once more. The American government had looked into the future of the BDC only the previous year, and in 1968 the US delegation in Berlin recommended to the State Department that the whole archive, including property and documents, be returned to the Federal Republic. But the West German government had no interest in a new de-Nazification process. Even under the direction of the Americans, there was not always a guarantee that data about the Nazi pasts of leading personalities in the Federal Republic would not be made public. The revelation of the NSDAP membership of chancellor Kiesinger in the same year had, after all, been based on information leaked from files captured by the Americans. Still, the West German government was able to shift all responsibility for the opening of the archive onto its American ally. If the documents had entered German possession in the 1960s, a debate about their content would have been inevitable in view of the considerable public pressure to appraise them.

The American public were also reluctant to hand over the files straight away. By the end of the 1960s, the US administration had only copied three series of archives on to microfilm. There was severe criticism from historians and Jewish associations of the plan to return the files before a complete set of microfilms had been made.

From 1970 onwards, Karl-Heinz Hansen pestered the West German government for eight years with parliamentary requests for the handover of the Document Center. When Hansen paid a visit to the BDC at the end of 1971, its director Richard Bauer assured him that representatives of the Bundestag were also allowed to request information. But when the SPD politician wanted to examine the files of a CDU parliamentary colleague, Bauer informed him that the request would have to pass through official channels.[24]

The answers that Hansen received from the Foreign Office were not very optimistic, either. At the peak of the Cold War, neither the West German government nor its US allies could decide what was to be done with the Nazi legacy. Its return to the Federal Republic, which had been financing it for a very long time, was repeatedly postponed. In 1974, foreign minister Hans-Dietrich Genscher informed Hansen that the handover was solely dependent on the examination of 'questions of finance and funding' and 'questions of the security of the archive against violent attack'.[25] Two years later, Genscher's minister of state, Hans-Jürgen Wischnewski, declared that the West German government considered the continuation of negotiations 'not to be opportune'.[26] The Soviets were unlikely to tolerate the establishment of a further West German presence in the divided front-line city of Berlin. And there were not enough funds for the maintenance of the archive — at that point the Document Center was already being financed by Bonn with 1.3 million marks (approximately US$3.27million) from the reparation fund.[27]

It was not that the West German government was uninterested in the return of the German archive. That was 'by no means the case', declared Karl Moersch, minister of state for foreign affairs alongside Wischnewski, in reply to a fresh request from the stubborn Hansen in June 1976. In fact, the government was very keen on a 'swift and conclusive settlement'.[28]

The SPD left-winger saw another reason for Bonn's hesitant approach, as he explained to *Der Spiegel*: 'To spare former servants of the Nazi Party who are now serving the state again and to protect it against "radicals" from embarrassing revelations about their dark pasts."[29] The average age of the former Nazis recorded in the Document Center was already over 70, the news magazine added, quoting the prognosis of the then president of the Federal Archives, Hans Booms, that the problem would 'have sorted itself out by the 1990s'.

When Hansen levelled accusations against the West German government in a 1978 BBC programme, saying that it 'doesn't want the documents because it wants to hide former Nazis who would find themselves in an embarrassing situation if certain documents were published', his party colleagues were absolutely furious. At a hastily summoned meeting of the Social Democrats, there was — according to *Der Spiegel* — a 'pogrom mood' towards the obdurate troublemaker. Chancellor Schmidt felt personally insulted, and demanded satisfaction. The SPD parliamentary group followed him and did something that had never happened before in the history of the Bundestag: they gave the MP a public reprimand.[30]

Criticism from within its own ranks could hardly have come at a more awkward time for the social–liberal coalition government. In March 1978, the prosecution of Nazi criminals was a very topical theme, one for which the government had planned a documentary report and drawn up statistics: according to these, between 1945 and 1 January 1978, 82,667 enquiries had been made into people suspected of involvement in Nazi crimes. Only 6426 individuals had been sentenced, while those involved in 71,554 cases went unpunished and 4688 trials were still pending.[31]

The papers stored in the Document Center were crucial as evidence in such investigative processes as these. Because of its obvious lack of interest in continuing the handover negotiations with the Americans, the German government was at risk of making itself look ridiculous. Admittedly, during the tribunal in which Hansen was reprimanded, the SPD parliamentary group had stressed that there were justified doubts about whether the examination of 'the crimes of the SS regime' had always been pursued with the necessary vigour after 1945.[32] On the other hand, former chancellor Willy Brandt was forced to admit that during his time in government he had simply forgotten that the Document Center existed.[33] Possibly not quite by accident. 'We would lose all our best people,' Brandt is supposed to have raged at the session, 'if we [...] now start rolling out all over again something that more or less came to an end 35 [sic!] years ago. That won't advance us so much as an inch in domestic political terms.'[34] Schmidt, as head of the government, defended himself, saying that no one had ever informed him about the problem of the handover of the BDC.[35]

As the Foreign Office files reveal, Schmidt had his memory jogged a few days later and wrote a letter to foreign minister Genscher, minister of the interior Maihofer, and justice minister Vogel, in which he asked his cabinet colleagues for enlightenment: 'According to my information, the handover negotiations had been commenced back in 1967. I have never been able to work out why it wasn't possible to conclude the negotiations.'[36]

He had also learned, Schmidt continued, that some of the papers in the Document Center 'were stored in a special way', and asked for a review of whether these papers were also accessible to German criminal prosecution authorities such as the Ludwigsburg Central Office for the Investigation of National Socialist Crimes.

It is possible that, with this rather cryptic formulation, Schmidt was referring to the documents pertaining to prominent German politicians that were sealed specially in the safe of the BDC director to keep them from falling into the wrong hands.

In the papers of the American National Archive, there is an inventory listing the contents of Mr Simon's safe. These included not only SS badges, Hitler signatures, and original documents on Adolf Eichmann, Alfred Rosenberg, and the conspirators of the 20 July 1944 assassination attempt on Hitler, but also 'Information on Government Officials born in or before 1927'.[37] But plainly this information could no longer be found in 1997, as an archivist had crossed out the entry. Was it removed before the Document Center was returned to Germany?

It is still clear that the US also considered it important to investigate the Nazi pasts of those German politicians who had belonged to the generation of the very youngest party members. People didn't believe the legend, invented by the Germans themselves, that these men's NSDAP memberships were based on a mistake and had happened without their knowledge. Why else should the NSDAP papers for those born in the years leading up to 1927 have been kept particularly secret?

'Burn it!'

But even in the 1970s and 1980s, a far greater number of German politicians were affected than the public assumed. Sometime around 1980, the Americans had the whole of chancellor Helmut Schmidt's cabinet investigated in the Document Center. The American State Department operated with extreme discretion. In July 1979, Robert D. Johnson of the State Department sent a list of names to BDC director Simon with the request that it be investigated. Johnson used vague terms to express what the checks were about: 'I don't want or need the information itself, just an indication of whether certain documents exist. In the course of this investigation please show your renowned discretion, as the names will make it clear what is at issue here. You can use your own code for direct hits and negative reports, I am only interested in the following: 1. Party membership; 2. Any SS activities; and 3. Any other, less sensitive category of BDC files.' In true James Bond style, Johnson finally demanded that the recipient destroy the letter after reading — 'Burn it!'

But Simon didn't follow his instructions. In the same bundle of files as the letter, there is also a list of the members of Schmidt's 1980 cabinet. The names of foreign minister Genscher, agriculture minister Josef Ertl (FDP), and chancellor Schmidt are crossed out. In the Document Center, Ertl and Genscher are listed as NSDAP members. Why Schmidt's name was crossed out when no such information about him had been forthcoming is not clear.[38] So far there is nothing to indicate that the Americans had any more information about the chancellor at the time than we know today.

When I spoke to Helmut Schmidt in Hamburg in December 2012, he told me that he didn't know why his name was crossed out, either. 'I'm not surprised that they checked us. I wouldn't put any kind of secret-service nonsense past the Americans.'[39] Schmidt claimed never to have known that Genscher and Ertl were former members of the NSDAP. He was also surprised by the NSDAP membership of his fellow SPD party member Karl Wienand, son of a communist father. 'Didn't know, first time I've heard of it,' the former chancellor growled. 'And it never interested me anyway.' Probably even Genscher didn't know, Schmidt suggested.

Of course, as he told me himself, Genscher had known about his file card since the early 1970s. But why did he and most of the other people involved, in spite of all appearances and without any proof, persist in denying that they had ever been NSDAP members?

'Tell a lie and stick to it,' Schmidt said, without referring specifically to Genscher or other fellow ministers. 'They lied at the beginning, and they haven't shifted.' Wasn't it possible for those leading democrats to admit to a comparatively harmless youthful indiscretion such as joining the NSDAP? 'It isn't easy to admit in public that you've lied,' Schmidt suggested.

Under lock and key

'There was plenty more in the poison cupboard,' *Der Spiegel* chuckled in 1994 after Genscher's Nazi papers came to light. But it would be more than 15 years before two other names emerged from Mr Simon's safe. In 2011, on behalf of the democratic socialist party Die Linke, the historian Hans-Peter Klausch investigated the Nazi pasts of Hessian Landtag MPs between 1946 and 1987 in the Federal Archives. Klausch found out that over 20 times as many former NSDAP members as was officially known had sat in the parliament of the state of Hesse, and that they were represented in almost all the parties. In some parliamentary groups the former Nazi Party members were, at times, even the majority.[40]

In the course of his work on the Nazi files in the Federal Archives, the historian also made a curious discovery. The Federal Archives takes special care with original documents, and where possible offers researchers only microfilm copies. So, for his research, Klausch had been given access to the microfilms made by the Americans before the handover of the Document Center, of which there are copies in both Washington and the Federal Archives.

Looking through the microfilms, Klausch found two regional politicians for whom, instead of NSDAP membership cards, there were photographs of handwritten placeholders, each inscribed with the name and date of birth of the person concerned alongside the reference 'SAFE — MR SIMON 1976'.[41] The two men in question were the CDU politicians Alfred Dregger (1920–2002) and Otto

Zink (1925–2008). By the time the cards of the CDU politicians disappeared into the safe of BDC director Simon, Dregger and Zink were no longer in the Hessian Landtag, and were now in the German Bundestag. Klausch concluded: 'It was in 1976 that the CDU waged their Bundestag election campaign on Dregger's slogan "Freedom not Socialism". In that politically tense situation it would have been far from helpful for the CDU if the former NSDAP membership of two senior representatives of the regional and national CDU had come to light.'[42]

We can only speculate about the circumstances under which the cards of the two politicians found their way into the safe. At any rate, the BDC files confirm that for decades the Americans routinely investigated German politicians as soon as they rose to higher office. That included Bundestag seats, and ministerial, parliamentary group, and government offices. The fact that Dregger and Zink were in the Bundestag may have been enough to put them in the special security of Mr Simon's safe.

The CDU politicians were in very good company there. But even today it remains unclear whose NSDAP files were kept in the safe. The last BDC director, David Marwell, told me he couldn't remember any individual names apart from Genscher. But Marwell did give me one more reference when we met in 2011 at his house in College Park, Maryland. The microfilming of the NSDAP central card file had taken place at a time when some of the file cards were still in the safe. But the membership cards stored in the safe were re-catalogued in the central card file before the documents were transferred to the Federal Archives. The placeholders photographed by chance were the only reference indicating which cards had once been in the safe.

After the conversation with Marwell, with a rather queasy feeling in my stomach, I set about the task of finding a few dozen placeholders among the 10.7 million file cards photographed on hundreds of rolls of film. But, by a stroke of good fortune, I discovered something among the archive documents that spared me months of work: a copy of the list of papers in Mr Simon's safe had been preserved, hidden among the administrative documents.[43]

The list includes the names of 134 Germans about whom there was original or copied material from the Nazi era or from post-war Germany. They range from prominent Nazis such as Hitler (41a), Himmler (39), and Martin Bormann (9), via Hans Globke (25), Kurt Georg Kiesinger (48), and Walter Scheel (80), to Hans-Dietrich Genscher (110), Karl Carstens (114), Erhard Eppler, Friedrich Zimmermann, and Alfred Dregger (all 115).[44]

Not all the people listed were filed as NSDAP members by the Americans. The names of chancellor Konrad Adenauer, president Gustav Heinemann, and CSU head Franz Josef Strauss are also listed. Neither is the list exhaustive; missing from it, for example, is the former justice minister and chief of staff of the German chancellery Horst Ehmke. But all those named have one thing in common: the papers referring to them were assessed as 'politically sensitive', and therefore stored in the safe of the BDC director. Thus, for example, the names of prominent people such as the conductor Wilhelm Furtwängler or the archivist Wolfgang A. Mommsen are also on the list. The latter was an NSDAP member, and had worked in the occupied Soviet Union in archive protection before 1945.[45] In 1967, Mommsen was appointed president of the Federal Archives and thus chair of the West German authorities who would be responsible for the card index of NSDAP members after the files were handed over by the Americans.

Protection against snooping

While the bilateral negotiations between the US and Germany progressed very slowly in the 1970s, renewed consultations in Berlin and Washington in 1980 led to a diplomatic agreement to hand over the BDC definitively once all personal data had been microfilmed. It was agreed that the documents in Berlin and the microfilm copies in Washington were to be used in line with the rules applying in the respective archives. 'As both archives protect individual rights,' it says in the draft contract, 'it is established that the protection of individuals includes state of health, family relationships and other issues from the private sphere, questions of property and general assessments.' But the paper was never signed. In Bonn they plainly only ever gave the appearance of haste; behind the scenes, Auswärtiges Amt staff were obstructing any attempts on the part of the Americans to finally bring the negotiations to an end. The minutes of a Foreign Office discussion from 1986 include the ominous view that 'another 6–7 years will go by before the actual return, and then things will be unproblematic'. Might 'things' have meant the foreign minister's file card? What was to be done with that and other Nazi documents? In the Auswärtiges Amt, they acted according to the motto 'Let things take their course'. A senior ministry official noted on the same document that it would do no harm 'if another few years pass before we take over the BDC'.[46]

When a reporter from the Berlin *Volksblatt* newspaper visited the Document Center, he was surprised by 'the paradoxical situation whereby American or Japanese historians in Zehlendorf opened doors to one another, but German researchers — particularly doctoral students — could not openly view source material about the history of their own country'.[47]

Admittedly, historians and journalists were allowed to research in the files of the Document Center. But, as we have seen, information about living people was only given out to private individuals and researchers if the individuals in question had been sentenced for war crimes or were prominent Nazis. And not all requests were treated the same way. While foreigners were able to apply to the Americans to view the files, German citizens had to obtain authorisation from the minister of the interior in Bonn. Researchers from West Berlin had to turn to the senator of the interior in Berlin, who made his decision according to opaque criteria and was often more rigid in his decision-making than the Ministry of the Interior.

As a justification for this restrictive authorisation process, the German authorities referred to data protection, which was supposed to protect the personal rights of individuals. The publication of a simple membership application for the NSDAP only occurred with the permission of the person in question or, if that person had died, their next of kin. In the case of 'prominent National Socialists' this rule no longer applied, but it was the senator of the interior in Berlin who decided who qualified as a prominent Nazi. In 1984, the SPD parliamentary group in the Berlin House of Representatives demanded the immediate lifting of rules of access for academic research in the Document Center — rules which the group saw as 'making arbitrary decisions possible, preventing actual use and serving to protect former National Socialists'.[48] The spokesperson for the senator of the interior dismissed the politicians with a reference to the de-Nazification law which served as a legal foundation and granted no privilege to academic research.[49] In the meantime, handover negotiations with the Americans, as one might have guessed, had so far been without success.

The main clients of the Document Center were German authorities, who made between 4000 and 5000 applications to the archive every month, even in the 1980s. These included insurance companies, state prosecutors' departments, and citizenship offices dealing with the nationalities of immigrants.

But secret services, such as the Federal Intelligence Service and the Federal Office for the Protection of the Constitution, and federal ministries sometimes wanted to cast an eye on the Nazi pasts of their staff in the context of security investigations — although not, of course, in the public eye. 'Academics shout everything from the rooftops,' the Volksblatt wrote, quoting a German official. 'For us it works perfectly. We get everything.'[50]

In 1984, the *Welt am Sonntag* newspaper reported: 'Bonn is making a grab for the "Berlin Document Center".'[51] According to the article, the Germans had made 'a final offer' to the Americans, and proposed shouldering the expenses for the microfilming, estimated at 4.5 million deutschmarks. The author of the article, Mainhardt Graf Nayhauss, also mentioned the rumour that German politicians with Nazi pasts preferred to leave the material in the hands of the Americans, since the Americans were 'less willing to divulge information than German authorities, so protection against snooping was better'. If a breakthrough was imminent, suggested Nayhauss, who had been provided with dependable background information by interested parties in Bonn, it was entirely thanks to foreign minister Hans-Dietrich Genscher, who was advocating 'promptly, emphatically and urgently' (January 1983) in handwritten memos an 'immediate solution' (July 1984).[52] That Nayhauss declared Genscher to be the driving force behind the transfer negotiations may be down to a small error on the part of the experienced capital-city correspondent: 'having been born in 1927', Genscher, Nayhauss claimed, was 'too young for the

NSDAP, and only a sapper' during the war. In fact, the handover of the NSDAP membership card files would be protracted for another decade. When it finally happened in the summer of 1994, Hans-Dietrich Genscher's NSDAP membership card was one of the first to be found and made public. The ex-foreign minister had stepped down from the government two years previously.

'Avoid national embarrassment': the Périot case

One person who refused to give up, and who drove the guardians of the Nazi files almost to despair for a decade with his constant requests, was the French journalist Gérard Périot.

He set his sights particularly on the CVs of West German politicians, smuggling their names into long lists of GDR notables on whom he requested information from the BDC. But the staff at the Document Center didn't fall for it, and refused to tell him even whether there was any material available about these individuals.[53]

When making his requests, Périot adopted a scattergun approach. In 1972, he sent the Americans a list containing the names of 25 politicians, including Theodor Heuss, Horst Ehmke, Herbert Wehner, and Theodor Oberländer.

The deputy director of the BDC, Richard Bauer, immediately passed the list to US minister Klein and warned him that it contained the names of numerous leading personalities of the post-war era who had no connection whatsoever with the NSDAP — 'So it should be assumed that Mr Périot is using the Berlin Document Center for his own political advantage.'[54] It cannot have escaped Bauer that in many cases, such as those of Ehmke and Oberländer, Périot was quite correct, since their names actually did appear in the NSDAP card files.

When Périot was personally received at the BDC in the spring of 1972 — thanks to the intercession of French government bodies, whose support the ever-inventive Périot had managed to obtain — the diplomatic situation came to a head.[55] Within a very few days he had ordered up more than 300 personal files, one-third of which concerned leading personalities in the Federal Republic. The BDC staff immediately informed the US mission in a letter marked 'Sensitive' that each individual request had to be carefully checked 'to avoid national embarrassment'.[56]

Périot had requested, among other things, the papers for Martha and Emil Kuhlmann, chancellor Willy Brandt's mother and stepfather.[57] He also wanted to see the personal files of a certain 'Herbert Ernst Karl Frahm'. The Americans knew that this was in fact Willy Brandt's birth name. Many of Brandt's cabinet colleagues were also on Périot's list: foreign minister Walter Scheel, trade secretary Schiller, interior minister Genscher, justice minister Jahn, and defence minister Helmut Schmidt.[58] Also on the list were opposition leaders Rainer Barzel and Kurt Georg Kiesinger, as well as many others. 'These files were not shown to Mr Périot', it says in the papers. If each individual name on which Périot wanted information was not first checked, there was a danger that 'German–American relations would be damaged'.

Now the Americans were in a political quandary: on the one hand, they wanted to prevent any possible abuse of the files and spare their German allies embarrassing revelations. But, on the other, the French were putting on the pressure, and Périot himself kept threatening to publicly accuse the US of preventing the investigation of the German Nazi past. As internal correspondence from the Document Center shows, the Americans were aware of that risk. Périot even claimed that US minister Klein had informed him that the Nazis were 'very nice people', and that some of his best friends, such as minister Karl Schiller, were former party members.

At the BDC, they considered such statements unthinkable, but warned that Périot might use any correspondence from Klein against the US in public: 'Mr Périot said that the publication of his book, in which he is going to unmask people like Foreign Minister Scheel, will cause a scandal in Germany, and that this scandal, should the Americans refuse to cooperate with him and put the files at his disposal, will become an American scandal.'[59]

But Périot went too far when he repeated, in a submission to former US secretary of state William Rogers, his accusation that the Americans were protecting former Nazis in the BDC. On a copy of the letter, a visibly furious US diplomat wrote in red pen:

> That is an insult to the USA. Question to Mr Périot: Who saved France? How many Americans collaborated with the Nazis compared with the French, for example Laval, Déat, Pétain etc. etc. Who appointed Mr Périot as supreme judge over the Germans? What criteria does he use to define 'Nazi criminals'? What is a Nazi criminal? Does Mr Périot want to have a new deNazification process in 1972? What political interests does he represent?[60]

In the meantime, Périot even approached an adviser to president Carter. But the Americans continued to freeze him out. It was important, an internal BDC memo noted, to remain polite, but 'we must not and will not tolerate any nonsense from Mr Périot — whether he complains or not'.[61]

In fact, this just turned the Americans into a censoring authority that decided which information from Nazi files should be kept secret for political reasons and which should not.[62] The BDC went on processing Périot's requests, but steadfastly refused to give out 'sensitive' information about German politicians, or even to tell him if information was available. In this way, the Americans hoped to prevent Périot from drawing indirect conclusions about possible party memberships. Admittedly, no Nazi papers had been found on minister Hans-Jochen Vogel, a BDC memo from 1975 noted. But despite having requested access to such papers, Périot was not to be informed of this fact, so that he couldn't draw any conclusions if he asked about Genscher and did not receive the same answer.[63]

The example of Périot shows that the Americans controlled access to the Nazi files in the Document Center according to restrictive but understandable criteria that, for the most part, were consistently applied. The tightly limited access for individual applicants made it effectively impossible for information to reach the German public directly via journalists. That would have required the help of influential people, and it was not forthcoming.

'Slowly getting fed up' — the delaying tactics of the men in power

The only actual abuse of information from the Document Center was to do with power politics, and was carried out by interested parties in German politics. After all, only parliamentary or government insiders were able to access information from the Document Center through the Americans — and some of them clearly had no qualms about using that information for political ends, either to exert pressure or to leak the information to the public at opportune moments.

The Nazi revelation about Karl Carstens, for example, who had not yet been officially chosen as the CDU's presidential candidate, was the result of a deliberate political plot: 'Carstens has become the victim of political opponents,' *Die Zeit* reported in November

1978, 'presumably from his own party, which threw a pebble into the pool to scupper his presidential candidacy before it had even been decided.'[64]

When it came to light at the end of the 1980s that the theft of valuable documents from the BDC had been going on for years, pressure grew to find a definitive solution. A German member of the Document Center staff had pilfered a large number of files — particularly the autographs of prominent National Socialists and files of leading SS men — and sold them on the military memorabilia black market. There was a well-publicised trial against the perpetrators, but no political motivation could be identified for the theft of the files.[65]

In the wake of this scandal, the US State Department replaced Daniel Simon, the director of the BDC for many years, with the young historian David Marwell, who had made a name for himself in the Office of Special Investigations for his involvement in the prosecution of Klaus Barbie. When Marwell took office as director of the Document Center in 1988, the staff were still working more or less as they had since the end of the war. The first thing the young boss did was step up security measures and ensure that the microfilming of the remaining Nazi documents went ahead at full speed. By the end of Marwell's tenure, the Americans had produced more than 40,000 rolls of microfilm.

Marwell also drew up a 'BDC plan' designed to restore the reputation of the American archive and its custodians, damaged by administrative chaos and theft. Marwell hoped that the 'decades of neglect of the BDC and the unhappy events of the late eighties' would be forgotten if a carefully organised and strictly run archive was handed over to the Germans.[66]

He introduced computers and simplified the system of requests and checks. In 1992, the files of the SS, the Reich Chamber of

Culture, and the Race and Settlement Office, as well as party correspondence and various other collections, were stored in the internal computer system. The storage methods and training of the staff were to be organised in such a way that the administration of the archive could easily be taken over by the Federal Archives. Thirty thousand archive boxes and 85,000 acid-free archive files were purchased, and 690 metres of shelves renewed. Daily measurements of temperature and humidity were instituted.

In 1988, the Green Party in the Bundestag called for the immediate return of the Document Center, the lifting of privacy restrictions on the Nazi files, and the establishment of a National Socialism research institution modelled on the Munich Institute of Contemporary History.[67] Green MP Ellen Olms picked up the arguments of SPD maverick Karl-Heinz Hansen and accused Hansen's party colleagues Brandt, Schmidt, and Vogel of having dragged out negotiations for years. A 'tacit, stifling consensus' that the documents should be kept secret had prevailed, Olms said, criticising the 'decades of German-American complicity' in the suppression of personal responsibility with reference to National Socialism. Green MP Antje Vollmer suspected that this was based on an attempt to 'stabilise post-war West German society'.[68]

In response, the home affairs select committee decided to press the West German government to resume negotiations with the US with a view to achieving a return of the BDC even before the microfilming was completed. The application to lift privacy protection for Nazi perpetrators was a resounding failure, however, because even the social-democratic opposition was not prepared to lift the term of protection. FDP member Wolfgang Lüder warned against making the files 'the basis for determining a revival of de-Nazification'. The spokespersons for the government parties responded by attesting that West German governments had always striven for the return of the files of the Document Center.[69]

That information was incorrect. In fact, the Americans had for some time been growing increasingly frustrated with the delaying tactics of the West German government. In 1987, when German government representatives had once again stated how dear to them the idea of the speedy return of the files really was, the BDC director had exploded. In a memo to the legal adviser of the US Ministry in Berlin, Daniel Simon gave vent to his fury: 'I'm slowly getting fed up with them always, always publicly holding us responsible for the delays. And I have no doubt that they would refuse it [a return of the files] if we offered them the BDC tomorrow with no strings attached.'[70]

Shortly after this, it would become apparent how right Simon had been in his assessment of the German negotiating position. As American files reveal, even in the early 1990s, the West German government had set in motion diplomatic efforts to delay negotiations, and called upon the US for help.

The 1989 parliamentary resolution initiated by the Greens had put the government under pressure. But rather than taking the opportunity to press for the return of the archive, Bonn went on playing for time.

In a confidential despatch from October 1989, the US Embassy in Bonn informed the State Department in Washington 'that the Foreign Office is clearly asking for the resumption of negotiations in order to meet the political pressure of those calling for a speedier return of the BDC'.[71]

Early in 1990, informal preliminary discussions took place between the director of the BDC and German delegates from the Federal Archives in Berlin. The Americans were forced to admit that the German delegation had no interest in a swift return of the files. In fact, the emissaries of the German government had been given the task of performing a diplomatic charade. In February 1990, the US envoy in Berlin, Harry Gilmore, informed Washington that the German delegation would uncompromisingly demand the immediate return of the Document Center — but only for show. The Auswärtiges Amt delegation expected to be able to return to Bonn with a clear refusal and to be able to inform parliament accordingly.[72]

The Americans, relying on diplomatic cooperation, went along with the horse-trading and thus enabled the West German government to shift the blame onto their ally, and on technical problems with the microfilming of the archive.[73] The strategy paid off: 'West German government in Washington in bid to release Document Center,' German newspapers announced shortly afterwards, reporting that Washington had refused to release the archive so as not to impede current investigations into Nazi war criminals.[74] It was a watertight alibi, because the West German government was able to assume that American critics and the Jewish World Congress would agree.

It would be another two years before negotiations for the return of the Nazi files could be concluded. In 1992, the US ambassador to Germany, Richard Holbrooke, had it confirmed to him once more by the historians Fritz Stern (Columbia University) and Michael Berenbaum (US Holocaust Memorial Museum) that there were no academic reasons to prevent the archive being returned. In the same year, Hans-Dietrich Genscher returned unexpectedly as foreign minister after 18 years. On 18 October 1993, the US and Germany finally set the seal on the return of the Document Center with an international agreement.[75]

Handover

Shortly before the definitive handover in summer 1994, an article by the journalist Gerald Posner published in *The New Yorker* caused something of a furore. Posner suggested that the Federal Archives Act, which had come into effect in 1988, made it possible to keep Nazi documents under lock and key for up to 110 years after the birth of the individuals named in them.[76]

But the clause in question was a discretionary ruling: for documents about people who had been deceased for no longer than 30 years, or who were born less than 110 years before, the term of protection could be shortened even without the consent of those concerned if their 'use is indispensable in order to carry out specified scholarly research projects or to pursue legitimate concerns'. For persons of public interest and 'office-holders in pursuance of their duties', the Federal Archives Act allowed a shortening of the term of protection 'if the legitimate concerns of the person are taken into consideration appropriately'.[77]

As it would later transpire, the Americans had already broken off negotiations at the end of the 1960s because the conditions of use for private academics suggested by the Germans appeared too restrictive.[78] The negotiations of 1980 had also been unproductive because the US was unwilling to concede to Germany's demands that, in the case of relevant requests from researchers, the NSDAP membership of living individuals be kept secret.[79]

The crucial question in 1994 was: How would German archivists apply the law? The critics invoked by Posner feared the worst. BDC director Marwell, on the other hand, informed his superiors that the Federal Archives had, over the previous few years, often made use of the possibility of shortening the period of restricted access for academic researchers.[80]

In response to criticism of the imminent handover, there was a hearing in the US House of Representatives on 28 April 1994. Tom Lantos, chair of the Foreign Policy Committee, and a Holocaust survivor, expressed 'extremely serious concerns' about access to the files. He stressed that the authorisation practice of the German government — unlike the liberal access granted by the Americans — had blocked researchers from using the Document Center or made it possible only under restricted circumstances.[81]

This scepticism on the part of the Americans was shared by many German archivists. After all, it was not their decision but the result of political regulations that access to personal data from the era of National Socialism was restricted in the Federal Republic. But according to the ethics of their profession, archivists are not only responsible for the preservation of the documents entrusted to them; they also have an interest in opening up their treasure troves and making them accessible to researchers. In 1997, after the handover of the Document Center to the Federal Archives, senior archivist Dieter Krüger expressed his sympathy with the earlier American scepticism: 'German archivists were expected to keep the contents of the documents away from the public rather than helping the public to evaluate them … In actual fact access to the BDC was difficult, particularly for Germans but certainly for West Berliners.'[82]

While critical voices were raised in the US about free access to the records, the West German political establishment worried that, in taking over the archives 50 years after the end of the war, they might be opening a Pandora's box. After all, the names of over 8 million filed individuals presented enough material for a new debate about personal responsibility with reference to National Socialism.

For the archivist Robert Wolfe, who had travelled to Hitler's defeated Germany immediately after the end of the war as a captain in the US Army, the return of the Nazi files to the former enemy was a matter of democratic sovereignty. No archivist in an open democratic society could do his duty to preserve its cultural memory if he did not have access to the material records in their entirety.[83]

And in any case, what option did the Americans have but to hand over the documents to their allies sooner or later? It was impossible after all, Wolfe believed, to either protect the archive with bayonets at the ready, or to transport tons of documents away in the freight trains of the withdrawing US troops.

In the last weeks leading up to the handover, BDC director David Marwell and his staff worked around the clock to ensure that the microfilming of the files was completed in time. Some of the administrative records were destroyed, and the rest were shipped to Washington along with the microfilms.

On 30 June 1994, the American military police took down the Stars and Stripes that flew over the Document Center and formally handed the flag to Marwell. Standing beside him was 88-year-old Kurt Rosenow, who had been the first director of the Document Center almost half a century before. Marwell passed the flag on to his elderly colleague: 'I can't imagine a more worthy owner of this flag than the man who was there when it was first flown over the Document Center.'[84]

The Americans then celebrated with the German delegation until midnight, when Marwell climbed a ladder and personally unscrewed the administrative sign from the building on the Wasserkäfersteig. Almost half a century after the end of the war, the last building occupied by the Allies closed its doors.

A quarter of an hour to deal with the past

In December 2010, Die Linke's parliamentary group, led by MP Jan Korte, presented to the government a large catalogue of questions about the institutions of the Federal Republic and their response to the Nazi past. It concerned personal continuities in ministries and authorities in the country and the regions, as well as the prosecution of Nazi crimes, reparations, and the financing of memorials.

The questions could have been drawn up for a historical seminar about *Vergangenheitsbewältigung*, and the government clearly wanted to come across as a model student. The Ministry of the Interior requested an extension of the deadline twice, and finally presented an 85-page report in December 2011.[85]

It contained, among others, the names of 26 government ministers and a chancellor who had been members of the NSDAP or other Nazi organisations such as the SA, the SS, or the Gestapo before 1945, including Horst Ehmke, Walter Scheel, Friedrich Zimmermann, and Hans-Dietrich Genscher.

Their NSDAP membership had already been made public, thanks to the research of academics or journalists. But it was often disputed, even among historians. The individuals in question claimed never to have signed an application, and to have become members of Hitler's party unwittingly.

The government made a point by including former ministers such as Genscher and Ehmke in the list anyway. Since then, regardless of their own views on the matter, their NSDAP membership has been officially recognised even though the government expressly indicated 'that mere membership of the NSDAP does not allow us to draw definite conclusions about a deeper fundamental National Socialist attitude'.[86]

The German government referred in its report to historical research suggesting that 'the very fact of Party membership tells us little about the behaviour of officials in the Nazi dictatorship — apart from the fact that it makes a considerable difference at which point someone joined the NSDAP'.[87] Research into perpetrators had also shown that not all individuals involved in Nazi crimes had belonged to Nazi organisations and that, conversely, not all members of the NSDAP or other Nazi organisations were involved in crimes. So evidence of Nazi guilt could only be established by considering cases individually.

A huge amount of research needed to be done: the documents listed in the report run to hundreds of thousands of personal files for former officials. Research in the Federal Archives took an average of between 30 and 60 minutes per person, government rapporteurs calculated. Even simply comparing a name against the NSDAP membership card file took 15 minutes.

A quarter of an hour doesn't sound like much when it comes to dealing with the past, but it mounts up. So it's understandable that the German government should have limited the research to spot checks, and apart from that referred only to future research.

But it remains a mystery why the rapporteurs clearly didn't even take the trouble to check the data in a prominent case like that of Genscher's. The date of his NSDAP membership is given as 1945, as indeed it is in Wikipedia, while the year given on his file card in the Federal Archives is 1944.

The German government didn't want to say anything at all on the matter of former NSDAP members of the Bundestag in the 1950s and 1960s. They had no cause to carry out research into other government bodies, they added brusquely.

In contrast, the list of dismissals carried out on grounds of Nazi guilt was highly informative. In the Auswärtiges Amt, some 34 per cent of whose senior members were former NSDAP members, a grand total of three officials were fired on the grounds of their past in the Third Reich. In the Federal Ministry of Justice, it was one.

On the other hand, during the 1950s, officials who had previously been sacked on the grounds of their activities in the Nazi state were industriously recruited into the civil service. The basis of these reappointments was a piece of supplementary legislation to Article 131 of the Constitution, according to which minor offenders could be re-employed. The figures are startling: by 31 March 1955, 77.4 per cent of posts in the Ministry of Defence were occupied by '131ers'; 68.3 per cent in the Ministry of Finance; and 58.1 per cent in the press and information office of the federal government.

The 12 years of the Third Reich may by now be one of the most thoroughly researched periods in German history, as the government report on the subject, with its hundreds of references, suggests. But that is only taking into account the post-1945 examination of the Nazi period, which was carried out all too often by individual special-interest organisations, academics, and the media. It is no surprise that commissions into the investigation of individual authorities such as the German Foreign Office, the Federal Intelligence Service, or the Federal Office for the Protection of the Constitution have only recently been put into action.

Given the sobering results of such research, the finding that perpetually recurs in the government report sounds almost like a magic spell: in spite of all continuities in staff, we must not forget 'that the unconditional normative state rejection of National Socialism shaped the construction of all state institutions in the Federal Republic of Germany'.[88]

A Nazi past for institutions in the Federal Republic, the government argued, could not possibly exist, because these institutions had only existed since 1949. That may be the case in a formal sense, and in terms of state policy, but the argument looks somewhat contrived given the fact that, even in the new institutions, the redeployment of the old workforce could lead to an intellectual continuity.

The Federal Intelligence Service and the Chancellor's Office could no longer ignore this insight when, in 1963, the double agents Heinz Felfe and Johannes Clemens were accused of spying for Moscow. These two senior members of the Intelligence Service already knew one another from their time working together for Himmler's Reich Security Headquarters, and they were part of a network of former Gestapo members working in the intelligence service of the Federal Republic, as a strictly secret government report from August 1963 makes clear. According to this document, 'the former members of the SD [the SS intelligence service] felt very strongly their connectedness and obligations to one another' and 'the equality of the methods of Bolshevism and National Socialism and the affinity between the two systems was plainly such that individuals with pasts in the SD and other areas of Nazism stuck together and were susceptible to recruitment bids by the Soviets'.[89] The fact that the organisation, under its first director, Reinhard Gehlen, had employed many former Gestapo members after 1945 — not only because of their expert knowledge, but also because of their anti-communism, clearly apparent during the Nazi era — plainly counted little with regard to this argument, concerned as it was with exoneration.

'Not everything is in the files'

In spite of such cases, the development of the Federal Republic of Germany is a democratic success story. But the federal government's report about the examination of the Nazi past of the state pushes the cardinal question back to the forefront: How did it manage to build up democratic institutions with undemocratic staff? How could a national community compromised by the constraints and temptations of 12 years of dictatorship end up as an open, democratic society of a sort that had never before existed in Germany?

Certainly the 're-education' program of the Western Allies wasn't the only factor involved. The country's rapid economic success was likely to woo even diehard reactionaries to the young republic.

But for one generation, 're-education' also meant 'self-education': Erich Loest's 'leftover boys' had to de-Nazify themselves in the courtroom of their own conscience. Again and again.

We Germans are notoriously unyielding in our moral judgements, and equally harsh in our condemnation of those selfsame judgements. Perhaps this is the reason why many prominent Germans still portray their party membership as a matter of chance when confronted with their NSDAP file cards.

What began as a tragedy is thus repeating itself as farce. The most recent highlight was a bizarre appearance by the former Baader-Meinhof terrorist Stefan Wisniewski in the Buback trial. (German attorney-general Siegfried Buback was murdered by Baader-Meinhof terrorists in 1977, and important details of the crime are yet to be satisfactorily resolved.) At his hearing before the Stuttgart Regional Court in 1981, 57-year-old Wisniewski wore a black hooded jumper with the Polish inscription 'Follow this trail' and the numbers '8179469' — Siegfried Buback's NSDAP membership number.

The Nazi Party membership of the former attorney general is a well-known fact by now in Germany. But in 1977, his murderers couldn't have known any more about it than they did about the membership of his successor, Kurt Rebmann, who had joined Hitler's party on 1 September 1942.

More recent research indicates a greater number of hidden former Nazi Party members than previously supposed even in German parliaments, right up until the 1980s and 1990s. While the official biographical handbook of the Hessian regional parliament lists only three MPs with Nazi pasts, a study commissioned by the president of the Landtag and published in February 2013 reached the conclusion that there were points in time during which one-third of all MPs were former NSDAP members. Apart from the communist KPD, all parties represented in the Hessian parliament had former Nazi Party members in their ranks. Overall, the historians found 92 former SS members and 26 former members of the SA. Between 1954 and 1970, about 60 per cent of the FDP parliamentary group in the Landtag were former Nazi Party members.

There are as yet no reliable figures for the Bundestag and the federal ministries; but here, too, researchers believe that there are many unreported cases. In years to come, the file cards will yield up long-guarded secrets: about life in the Third Reich and coming to terms with it all in the Federal Republic. But they will reveal nothing about the guilt and involvement of young people.

'Files can lie, too, when they reproduce lies,' Hans-Dietrich Genscher said at the end of our meeting in Bad Godesberg, going on to add, 'Not everything's in the files.' Genscher knows what he's talking about. In his long years in power, he always remembered the lesson that he once learned as a schoolboy in Halle: Knowledge is power. Sometimes, so too is ignorance.

CHAPTER SIX

Last Ink: Günter Grass

It was an unusual birthday party, and not just because of the guests in attendance. On the evening of 14 October 2012, a former German chancellor, a writer, an academic, an artist, and members of the public from the city and the countryside all gathered at the Günter Grass House in Lübeck to celebrate the museum's namesake.

It was not meant to be a formal occasion, but rather a joyous celebration to coincide with the opening — for the first time in ten years — of a new long-term exhibition in the Grass House. In the decade between his 75th and 85th birthdays, the restless author had not only published at least half-a-dozen new books, but had also led the election campaign for the SPD once more, campaigned against atomic energy and for Europe, and revealed his former membership in the Waffen-SS. In other words, just like old times, he had been causing all kinds of uproar.

This much was clear: even at 85 years of age, Grass was still the most influential German-language writer, and as incapable as ever of restraining himself from getting involved. With a well-placed comment he could still make newspaper headlines all around the world, and this was an ability he gladly made use of now and again.

On this cold autumn evening, the mass of people crowded into the rear courtyard of the Grass House. To start with, everything went swimmingly. Speech, speech, fanfare, applause. After the speeches, Grass and Schröder — the former chancellor in attendance — gave a few interviews, then retreated to the function room upstairs. There, in front of a select audience, the second and more interesting part of the event began. But then something unusual happened. The temperature plummeted when one of the evening's speakers, Eva Menasse, began with the observation that she was standing here before Günter Grass in spite of 'the Israel poem', which she forthrightly declared to be a 'piece of folly'.

Grass had published the prose poem 'Was gesagt werden muss' ('What needs to be said') in the newspaper *Süddeutsche Zeitung* just a few months earlier, and had since incurred not only international criticism, but also an official travel ban from the Israeli government. In the poem, Grass, 'grown old and with his last ink', had criticised Germany's U-boat deliveries to Israel and accused the Israeli government of threatening fragile world peace through the 'purported right to have the first strike'.[1]

Even more so than the revelation of his Waffen-SS membership — but nonetheless in its wake — this commentary put Grass on the outer in public opinion, and many seized the opportunity to allege that the poet's criticism of Israel was in fact the deep-seated anti-Semitism of a former member of Himmler's hordes.

Even seasoned commentators accused the writer of having twisted the facts with his criticism of Israel. After all, they said, it was the Iranian president, Mahmoud Ahmadinejad, who kept threatening the Jewish people with extermination, not the other way around. But Grass stubbornly stuck by his statement and leaned upon the considerable support of the private individuals, clubs, organisations, and internet forums which had reached out to him from both home and abroad since the publication of the poem.

Although Grass, too, had always willingly dealt out blows himself, this time the attacks must have hit him harder. In a private memo in May 2012, he declared to his correspondents all over the world that 'the intensity of the insults and intentionally hurtful allegations' had far exceeded his expectations.[2]

The Germanist Heinrich Detering admitted in his speech at the Grass House opening that the poem gave him difficulties, too. But he also backed Grass up against the 'scandalously alienating' attempts to make him, of all people, into 'a kind of life-long SS man, to imprint him with the stigma of the swastika and denounce his life's work as being infiltrated by simmering anti-Semitism'. After all, he said, it wasn't like Grass had styled himself as an anti-fascist resistance fighter from childhood; and by recording the history of mentalities in Federal Germany, he had created a life's work of 'admirable moral earnestness'.[3] One could add, there can be no moral earnestness if you are not personally affected.

And yet, had such a thing ever happened before — a Nobel Prize laureate being accused at his own honorary celebration of having been a fool? It was impossible to ignore the idea that an epoch of literary history came to an end right at that moment.

It's simply the way things are, said Eva Menasse, that the Germans punish their moral torchbearers all the more harshly when they make a mistake. But then again, what does moral authority really mean? Menasse continued:

Today that kind of talk is often accompanied by sneers of disgust, but back then people wanted it that way, they needed it, as urgently as they needed bread and water. Back then, a country which was paralysed by guilt, divided in two, intellectually

injured, politically cautious and outdated looked up to artists like
him with the very same fervour with which they read the riot
acts to their own people, creating something new and unheard
of, something which could go out into the world as a new and
completely different German culture.[4]

Throughout all of this, Grass's expression was deadpan.
Eventually, he clomped over to the podium and told Menasse that
he wished she were right that his poem was a folly. Then he read
another.

That is how Günter Grass is: a teacher who cannot be taught.
One could take his stubbornness, his energetic self-importance, as
a personal character trait, but it may also be a generational trait. I
noticed this vitality, this ambition and ability to put oneself at the
centre of things, many times during my encounters with former
Flakhelfer.

Banished from paradise

Günter Grass belongs to a generation whose representatives rose
to become the moral authorities of the Federal Republic. To this
day, they have defied their successors, who, like every younger
generation, have the right to their own representatives. But this
existentially tested generation of *Flakhelfer* seem to insist that their
service is for life. And so they stand in the way of the planned line
of inheritance. It's a little like Prince Charles and Queen Elizabeth:
he wants to ascend to the throne at last, but she's still sitting on
it. Like her Majesty, who celebrated her diamond jubilee in 2012
and has seen numerous prime ministers come and go, so too the
great writers of Grass's generation seem to have been there forever.
They, too, have been setting the tone for 60 years. When the 1968

student protests turned the Federal Republic upside down, they were already well established. They didn't need to embark upon the long march and ascend through the institutions; they already *were* them, and remain so until this day.

Grass made an early start combating German idealism, and shook his fist threateningly in the direction of those bourgeois sons who became politically motivated again in the 1960s, wanting to save the world with the help of their microphones. 'I sullenly pull out the weed of German idealism, which is a lot like plantain, but it grows back relentlessly. How they continue to pursue a matter — even if it's Socialism — for their own sakes ...'[5]

This comment reveals the pragmatism typical of the *Flakhelfer*; the aversion to total ideologies, to the dominance of 'ideas' and idealism. These individuals won't allow themselves to be led astray again; they don't want to be promised another paradise on this Earth. 'The word paradise makes my snail anxious. It is immensely afraid of the forerunners of paradisiacal circumstances,' writes Grass in *From the Diary of a Snail*. Why is the snail afraid of paradise? 'It knows how total the expulsion is after un-paradisiacal behaviour.'[6]

In *From the Diary of a Snail*, Grass tells the story of Augst, a man who fell for a total ideology and never escaped it again. This part of the novel is based on real events. The man whom Grass calls Augst appeared at a reading the author gave in Stuttgart in 1969, and the story fictionalises what transpired there.

Augst speaks incoherently, becoming entangled in the undergrowth that is his formulae of selfless victims and absolute loyalty, pulling himself together only at the end of his 'stammering sell-out' for a dramatic, final act: 'I'll be provocative now and greet my comrades from the SS!' Then he takes a swig of cyanide from the little bottle he brought along with him and collapses. He dies on the way to hospital, and the newspapers the next day bear the headline 'Ritualistic Protest'.

Grass highlights the ritual character of the scene, comparing the speech and suicide of the former SS man to a passion play where 'knowledge of the plot is presupposed' and in which the unconscious is 'passed around like a handkerchief'.[7] The belaboured phrases of the SS 'comrade' may have been ringing in Grass's ears, too, for he knew them only too well from his own wretched experience.

Grass ends the story abruptly, announcing that Augst was survived by a wife and four children. One of these children, Ute Scheub, became an author, and picked up the thread of the story decades later, when she wrote a book about her father entitled *The Wrong Life*. She knew Grass, who had visited her family in Tübingen after her father's suicide and announced that he wanted to create a 'little literary memorial' for him.[8] Scheub had just turned 13 at the time of the suicide, and she tells the story from the perspective of the daughter of an SS man who finds a suicide note in the loft, decades after her father's public death. The mother had kept it a secret from the children — as she had kept secret problems within the marriage, the father's bouts of depression, and a suicide attempt. 'The consequences of silence,' Scheub wrote, 'are worse than the consequences of truth.'[9]

No wonder the younger generation rebelled in 1968. If they had not, they would have suffocated beneath the immense weight of the silence in their families. As Scheub put it: 'It was a rebellion against a world of bunkers. Against the fathers with bunker souls. Against the bunkered past.'[10]

Something was buried beneath the war ruins in Grass's novels and novellas, too, something that not even his own children knew about. The author only ever told them half the truth, if his

1979 text 'Wie sagen wir es den Kindern?' ('How do we tell the children?') is to be believed. In it, Grass recounts how his children confronted him towards the end of the 1960s with questions about concentration camps, Kiesinger, and the Third Reich, including the all-important question: 'And what did you do back then?'[11]

In his answer, Grass condenses his war experiences into one sentence, the kind that is appropriate for a child: 'It was relatively easy to explain my past, that of a Hitler Youth member who was 17 years old at the end of the war and who became a soldier during the last call-up: I was too young to be guilty.'[12] But Grass kept something to himself. His wife was the only one who knew that he had served in the Waffen-SS, albeit only briefly.[13] He was innocent, and that had to be enough. But he knew this innocence might also have been a matter of chance. What, the children asked him, if he had been older? The sobering answer was: 'I couldn't say for sure.'

When I visited him in 2011 in his studio in Behlendorf, Grass referred once again to the mercy of his date of birth. If he had been 'a ludicrous five or seven years older', he said, he would not have been able to avoid taking part in the immense National Socialist crime. He didn't want to participate in the cheap, belated anti-Nazism of his generation, preferring to identify himself as someone who could have been guilty if he hadn't been so young.

But can those who were born in 1926 or 1927 really see their comparatively late birth dates as a mercy without suppressing all that which, by any measure, was merciless about their fate? The manipulation from the early days of childhood onwards? The poison of Nazi ideology, to which they had barely any resistance at such a young age? War instead of play? Experiencing the complete destruction of the world at just 17 or 18 years of age?

With hindsight, Grass's words sound like an evocation of the betrayed innocence of his generation. It is this innocence, at least, that he wants to get back, by emphasising how young he was at the time and thereby creating distance.

For the innocence of youth, he is prepared to spend a lifetime in the role of admonisher, representing the elder generation's repentance, which never came. It is the suppressed stigma of his guilt — the SS stripes on the uniform of the 17-year-old boy — that turns Grass into the representative of German guilt. The feeling of having indeed been part of it all feeds his frenzy, his intense writing mania, his blustering authority.

Grass preaches to society about guilt, but at night his own anxiety catches up with him, in restless dreams 'in which I experience myself as a failure, guilty'. That's how it goes when you suppress things: eventually, everything surfaces again. In Grass's case, this clearly happened when his children began to ask him about his past in the late 1960s. During the 1969 national elections, he felt that the 'present was ailing from the past'. And Grass knew that he was not the only one to have been infected by this past. In a letter Grass wrote to the economics minister at the time, Karl Schiller, he had urged him to give a public account of his NSDAP membership. About his own, he remained silent; it was only in private notes that he tackled his own involvement: 'The dubious luck of belonging to the "right year of birth" expresses itself in the stuttering sentences which fill my diary against the backdrop of my children's questions.'[14]

Unlike Augst, Grass didn't suffocate on his silence. The agonising 'forcing out of the truth' that Grass claimed to have observed in Augst on that summer day in Stuttgart in 1969 would, in his own case, draw out over many decades and books. In his 2002 novella *Crabwalk*, Grass writes: 'History, or to be more precise, the history we don't deal with, is like a blocked toilet. We flush and flush, but the shit keeps coming back up.'[15]

When he finally spoke openly about his past in 2006, he explained his decades of silence as follows: 'I thought I had done enough with what I was writing. After all, it enabled me to go through my learning experience and take action from that. But the stigma still remained.'[16]

After all, Grass never hid the fact that he was led astray as a young man. But for a long time he preferred to speak in general terms about the fate of his generation, of those born in the same year as him. During a trip to Israel in 1967, Grass made the following statement during a speech in Tel Aviv: 'My birth year says: I was too young to have been a Nazi, but old enough to have been influenced by a system that, from 1933 to 1945, first stunned the world then plunged it into horror. So the man speaking to you is neither an established anti-fascist nor a former National Socialist, but rather the accidental product of a generation born partly too early and partly too late.'[17]

Even when Grass was criticising others, he was always writing about himself. After he publicised his membership in the Waffen-SS, critics accused him of inconsistency. But his shame had been there in his work the whole time, being processed again and again but never forgotten.

Drumming along

Another one of the myths about the *Flakhelfer* is that they were all delivered to democracy in May 1945 in one fell swoop. In fact, the learning process took much longer, and the detoxification process was tough. 'Like many others of my generation,' Grass said, 'I emerged from the Nazi era mentally weakened.'[18]

Hilmar Hoffmann, who became a prisoner-of-war in 1943 and spent the last years of the war in a prison camp in the Rocky Mountains, celebrated the Führer's birthday with the other German prisoners-of-war even on 20 April 1945, with defeat looming. He later wrote: 'The camp [...] was disbanded without delay. To me, this commanded exit from the ideological anachronism of conspiring elite units behind barbed wire, from the ghost camp of ideological delusion, was another important, consciousness-awakening step towards the end of the war.'[19]

They had survived, and in May 1945 the sun seemed to be shining more brightly than ever before. But it wasn't over yet. From now on, these 17- and 18-year-olds had no other choice but to pull themselves out of the ideological quagmire of their youth by their own bootstraps. Günter Grass, like many of them, was keen to do so.

In Grass's case, it was only when Nazi youth leader Baldur von Schirach testified at the Nuremberg Trials that he realised the crimes committed by the Germans weren't a fabrication of Allied propaganda. That was in 1946.

The more they discovered in those post-war years, the more pressing became the need to address the guilt. 'In the beginning, I may have tried again and again to dance around it with my various aptitudes and abilities,' Grass said in 2006, explaining how his best-known work, *The Tin Drum*, came into existence, 'but the basic substance of the subject was always there, waiting for me, and I had to face up to it.'[20]

Grass had begun a stonemasonry apprenticeship and then studied at the Dusseldorf Academy of Art before turning his attentions to literature in the 1950s. It offered him a form of expression for the crowd of characters and things he had collected within him: 'It's not the kind of thing you can want, it wasn't a choice; it was unavoidable.'[21]

The most famous of these characters, even to this day, is the hero of *The Tin Drum*, Oskar Matzerath, who is born with the mind of a grown-up, but stops growing at the age of three. That age was not chosen by chance: in the novel, Oskar is born in Danzig in 1924, so his physical development comes to a halt in the year when his creator came into the world in the very same place.

Also in 1927, Oskar is given a tin drum as a gift, and from then on he is able to tell stories of events that he himself is not directly involved in. It is no accident that the red-and-white striped drum, which can also be seen on the cover of the novel, bears a resemblance to the drums of the Hitler Youth. It is *the* cipher of a generation robbed of its childhood by the state and the war, forced into a climate of guilt from which it struggles to escape.

Despite their achievements as adults, the members of the *Flakhelfer* generation carry the moral burden of having drummed along as children, the full enormity of which could only be realised once the extent of the crime committed in their name became clear.

'As a child, I witnessed everything happening in broad daylight,' Grass stated in 2006. 'And with enthusiasm and approval, even. Of course there was a degree of seduction involved, without a doubt. As far as the youth are concerned: many participated with enthusiasm. And it's this enthusiasm and its roots that I want to explore, as I did while writing *The Tin Drum*, and now again once more, half a century later, in my new book [*Peeling the Onion*].'[22]

It is, of course, significant that in *The Tin Drum*, Oskar is in a care institution in 1954, as he tells his story and that of the Third Reich. But Oskar is not just a victim of his era. He is a perpetrator, too, and he reveals that he has committed three murders. But Oskar's confessions don't show genuine regret and repentance, as the Germanist Hermann Kurzke has pointed out. According to Kurzke, the novel is 'written around a guilty conscience that is playfully confessed, but the moral gravity of which is sealed off'. In the deformed Oskar Matzerath, Kurzke sees the personification of a bad conscience, which 'during the NS era, conceals itself behind childhood, and which after the NS era lingers on as a hunchback'.[23]

Oskar's never-relenting drumming makes the past present, while at the same time drowning it out. In the din, even 'ancient, hard-boiled sinners become thin and moving little children singing Christmas hymns'.[24] As payment for his supposed penance, Oskar gets a record deal, which brings him fame and riches.

On the one hand, this could be interpreted as a criticism of penance-hungry post-war society in the era of the economic miracle; on the other, the author may also have been referring to himself. Grass would have been aware that his literary ostracism of the German past made him, too, affluent and famous.

The hope for redemption referenced in the novel through all kinds of mythological-religious ascension motifs (such as the long escalator journey from the Parisian Metro up into the world of the living) ultimately remains unanswered. In spite of everything, Oskar remains a survivor with a stigma. The biblical motifs, the clichés of the Maria belief and the Jesus analogies, as Kurzke argues, are no longer logical. By playing with these clichés, Grass both reveals and conceals them at the same time. Not without good reason, Kurzke suggests that 'the personal guilt of having supported the Nazis as a young man could well be hidden in the labyrinth of broken fragments which makes up this accomplished work of art' — a suggestion that equally applies to the life's work of many *Flakhelfer* such as Martin Walser, Hans Werner Henze, and others.[25]

Grass's *Tin Drum* is, like his other works, representative

of the *Flakhelfer* generation's attempts to come to terms with the past. They write, compose, research, and engage with the world untiringly, and by doing so seek to assuage their partially suppressed consciences. At the end of the day, it's all there; you just have to look closely.

For Kurzke, the true moral of *The Tin Drum* is a 'blank space circumvented — danced around, even — by a number of artistic measures', and one which Grass concealed until his book of confession, *Peeling the Onion.* 'That which I accepted with the dumb pride of my younger years', Grass writes, 'I wanted to conceal in the post-war years due to my growing sense of shame.'[26] In this text, Grass didn't just reveal his long-concealed membership of the Waffen-SS, but also the lasting shame that 'unwittingly, or rather, not wanting to know, I had taken part in a crime that refused to diminish even after many years, one that refused to grow old, and one that still ails me'.[27]

But what could have healed him? The 17- and 18-year-olds had to find their own strength after 1945 in order to be able to make a new start. The war was over, the Reich a thing of the past, and more and more about the German crime was being revealed. Soon, the guilt was gnawing away at them as relentlessly as the hunger of the post-war era. 'The hunger only affected me occasionally', Grass admitted in 2006, 'but the shame, on the other hand …'[28] Is it any wonder that a new life only seemed possible to these young people at the price of suppressing certain details from their past?

'Eternally itching scars'

This suppression process interested me. After the uproar over his membership of the Waffen-SS had died down, I wrote Grass a letter asking him about it. He answered in detail, expressing his surprise that someone from my generation would give thought to the 'wounds of [his] peers and their eternally itching scars'.[29] These scars — it seemed clear — would never fade.

After all, Grass belongs to a generation who, as young adults, weren't given the kind of instruments that could have helped them with a moral reorientation. Instead, they had drums pressed into their hands, were drilled in practice, and sent off to war, the hymn of the Hitler Youth on their lips: '*Uns're Fahne flattert uns voran*' — 'Our flag flies before us'.

The extent to which the past continued to occupy Grass was evident when I paid my first visit to his studio in Behlendorf. I told him that even when reading *Crabwalk* in 2002, I had got the impression there was something lurking beneath the surface — four years before the revelations about his membership in the Waffen-SS. The first-person narrator, Paul, seemed more communicative than his creator back then, when he said: 'Nothing absolves us. You can't blame everything on your mother or narrow-minded moral code.' Was the author questioning not only the self-disclosure of his entire generation, but also his own pattern of explanation, practised for decades on end? His duty-bound engagement in serving 'the good cause'? His committed service to democracy? The good conscience of the nation that had no clean conscience itself?

Crabwalk reads like the intimate account of an artist who, despite considerable discipline, can no longer keep up the suppression. The tightrope walker of memory, having played so skilfully with the past in works like *The Tin Drum*, is now threatening to tumble down from the roof of the tent. Looking straight ahead is the key; never look down or allow yourself to be distracted. The narrator in *Crabwalk* is already wobbling, even if the audience hasn't noticed it yet. Even his own son knows nothing of the fear of toppling into the abyss of the past: 'What a good thing it is that he has no idea of the thoughts creeping around the left and right sections of my brain against my will, making horrifying sense, revealing fearfully protected secrets, exposing me, with the result that I feel shocked and quickly try to think of something else.'[30]

I told Grass that I detected in the words of his narrator a fear of exposure, one that I believed may not have been unknown to him on a personal level. After all, a speech he gave in 2000 struck a very similar tone. 'I remember,' Grass stated there, 'or I am reminded of something that stands at odds with me, something which has left its scent behind or which is waiting to be remembered in aged letters with treacherous words.' He also suggested that there were memories he hadn't yet formulated into words or processed: 'Speechless objects crash into us; things we thought had been surrounding us in silence for years, but which now start wanting to divulge their secrets: embarrassing, embarrassing! And then dreams in which we encounter ourselves as strangers, unfathomable, in need of endless interpretation.'[31]

I read another extract from *Crabwalk* out loud while Grass filled his pipe and listened in silence: 'What is to be done when the son reads the father's forbidden thoughts, thoughts which have long suffered under house arrest, then all at once possesses them and even translates them into action? I have always taken pains to be politically correct, at least, to not say anything wrong, to seem correct to those around me. Self-discipline, this is called.'[32]

Does that not precisely describe the situation into which Grass manoeuvred himself by putting his membership of the Waffen-SS under spiritual house arrest, keeping it a secret even from his own children? By letting one opportunity after another to confess pass him by — and instead upholding with iron self-discipline his role as the nation's good conscience? Why did the hope of being able to shunt aside the guilt by means of a never-tiring writing process prove to be so baseless?

Grass put down his pipe, fixed me with his alert gaze, and said quietly that the suppressed memories had never let him go. While shaving, for example, he once caught himself singing Hitler Youth songs — something which he said shocked him immeasurably.

When I read his new volume of poetry *Eintagsfliegen* in 2012, I discovered the verse in which Grass processed this experience:

When shaving,
un-bidden thoughts often ambush me,
then evaporate with the foam.
I hum songs too, which — when I was young —
full-throatedly proclaimed that the flag meant
more than death.
After a moment of shock, and a last glance in the mirror
I return to my age here and now, and try to start the day.[33]

Writing may offer the poet relief, but it doesn't redeem him. Nor can his heroes — all the Matzeraths, Materns, and Mahlkes — save him from the conflict. Eventually, the whole story resurfaces. The past can be processed, but never conquered. 'Doesn't it ever stop? Does the story always start from the beginning again?' asks the narrator in *Crabwalk*, and the answer in the novella is: 'It doesn't stop. It never stops.'[34]

Grass created a life's work 'whose frolicsome black fables portray the forgotten face of history', as the Nobel Prize jury announced in 1999. But to this day, even Grass has been unable to overcome the shame of having been corrupted by the Nazis as a young man. Hitler's promise to Grass's generation that they were Germany's future didn't miss its mark. Following the principle of 'Youth leads Youth', the National Socialists lured children with games and adventures, aiming to transform them into little soldiers who were willing to sacrifice themselves. The principle might as well have been 'Youth corrupts Youth'. Serving as Luftwaffe helpers, Grass once wrote, was misunderstood by his generation as being 'time-off from school'.[35] The Nazis were 'genial dogs', he said, grimly remembering the state-organised adventure holidays and events which enabled young people like him to break out of the boredom of their small-town existence.

When I visited him a second time in Behlendorf in November 2011, Grass was once again occupied with these 'dogs'. We spoke in the small library for a few hours about the novel *Dog Years*, which he had written half a century before. Then Grass led me up the steps to the loft of his studio.

On the floor lay the fresh etchings he had been preparing in the preceding months for the anniversary edition of *Dog Years*: copulating black mutts with drooling chops, enormous dogs standing over the smoking ruins of destroyed towns, pale faces on the gallows, skeletons, impaled rats, and ghoulish scarecrows in SA uniforms marching relentlessly across the paper. None of it bore any resemblance to the images of peeled onions and filleted fish with which Grass had illustrated his earlier works. This was a horrific procession of ghosts, like something from a nightmare.

This last part of the Danzig Trilogy, published in 1963, never achieved the public success of *The Tin Drum* or *Cat and Mouse*. And no wonder: *Dog Years* is a highly complex literary novel; mythological, historical, and political themes are broached, narrative layers intersect, characters change frequently. If *Dog Years* were a play, it would be declared impossible to perform. In its complexity, it is reminiscent of the multi-layered second part of Goethe's *Faust*, which likewise leads a niche existence on the theatrical stage.

'I see *Dog Years* as my most important work,' said Grass. Dogs and scarecrows are the ever-present supernumeraries of the novel, and at the same time allegories of the Third Reich. Over the many decades that the novel spans, Grass tells the story of Eddie Amsel and Walter Matern.

Amsel, classified as a 'half Jew' in the Third Reich, uses his natural talent for scaring birds to build artful scarecrows. These serve as a way of representing people caught up in National Socialism:

> Of course one could say that any human being can be made into a scarecrow, for when it comes down to it, and we should never forget this, the scarecrow is made in man's image. But among all the peoples who live as scarecrow templates, it is chiefly the German people, even more than the Jewish people, who have it in them to one day provide the world with the ultimate scarecrow.[36]

Matern supports Amsel in his artistic activities at first, but their ambivalent relationship descends into hate and violence when Matern joins the SA and, along with his comrades, beats his friend. Meanwhile, several generations of dogs appear in the novel, their family tree recounted up and down the hereditary line as a satire of National Socialist racial politics, for even Hitler's dog Prinz is included: 'Senta created Harras; Harras sired Prinz, and Prinz made history.'[37]

And yet Grass doesn't portray the main characters as one-dimensional templates, but always ambiguously. For example, it is Amsel who encourages Matern to join the SA because he needs uniforms for his scarecrows. After the war, Matern processes the

Germans' National Socialist past as a radio actor in hard-hitting radio plays, but remains silent about his own guilt until he is exposed on the radio himself.

There is no clear black and white in *Dog Years*; Grass portrays history in grey tones which, to witnesses from the time, appear to be the only legitimate form of representation: 'It was a matter of renouncing absolute parameters, the ideological white or black, of dispensing with belief and placing importance on doubt alone, on that which makes everything seem grey-toned, even the rainbow.'[38] Grey is the colour of those who know that guilt and innocence cannot always be neatly separated.

Followed by Hitler's dog Prinz, whom he renames Pluto after the Greek god of the underworld, Matern eventually meets Eddie Amsel again in Berlin. Amsel has become a successful businessman by the name of Brauchsel, and is selling wonder glasses that enable young people from the ages of seven to 21 to make adults' pasts visible. At the end of the story, Brauchsel/Amsel leads his old friend Matern down into the tunnels of his immense mine, in which he manufactures scarecrows in industrial quantities.

The two friends' descent into the mine is a hellish journey into the Hades of the German past. Matern turns his head away in shame 'because the collected stock of scarecrows, as he knows, is remote controlled and, as he says: "soullessly automatic …"' having sworn an oath to the company Brauxel & Co.'[39]

The reference to the author's own experiences is obvious: 'Silenced with dogma and appropriately groomed for its idealistic aims,' as Grass recalls in *Writing after Auschwitz* (1990), 'that's how the Third Reich released me and many of my generation from its vows.'[40]

Never having been down into a mine before, Matern's eyes are opened here for the first time, and he is sickened. He rushes to get back up to the light, flooded with horror. He hopes against hope that the lift will get them both back to the surface more quickly, and 'every prayer pleads that the rope stays intact, so that light, daylight, the sun-warmed May can once again ... [arrive]'.[41]

But the happiness of the young survivors will never again be as unclouded as in May 1945, when the war was over and their eyes had not yet been confronted with the images of German crimes. That great panorama of horrific pictures that Grass absorbed into his novel half a century ago and which he is now recreating on copper plates shows that his generation could never avert their gaze from their own past, a past in which images of uniformed marches flow together with images from concentration camps like Bergen-Belsen.

The children wearing Brauchsel's wonder glasses can't just see the past of the grown-ups, but they can look in the mirror, too. By bringing these images into the present, Grass not only gave German guilt a face, but at the same time crept deep down into the tunnels of his own, long-suppressed, shame. There is no escape from that mine, and never will be until the end of his days. 'The underworld is up above,' Brauchsel says — no one can escape it, not him and not anyone — 'and who is still to call them Brauchsel and Matern?'

Having made their way up to the surface, the two men take off their overalls and each take a bath in order to get clean. And that is how the story ends.

On the floor of Grass's studio, among the dozens of etchings, is an image of two people standing next to one another with their heads shaved, their faces hollow like the figure in Edvard Munch's *The Scream*. Shower water pelts down over their heads. But 'not even soap washes clean', as Grass wrote in *Dog Years* and quoted again many years later in his 1990 speech *Writing after Auschwitz*.[42]

In this, he said that after *Dog Years* he stopped writing prose for a while: 'It wasn't that I was tired of writing, but I prematurely believed I had written myself free of something that must surely now lie behind me, not resolved, admittedly, but nonetheless concluded.'[43]

When I left Grass on that November evening, I understood why he initially believed he had done enough with what he had written. In the artful labyrinth of his novels, he had publicly explored his own shame and yet at the same time hidden it in the thicket of letters.

Like many of his generation, who on account of the year of their birth could feel like both victims and perpetrators simultaneously, Grass's way of doing penance was to engage in a trade of indulgences with memory, and yet in the end he still wasn't able to overcome it.

Ultimately, it may have been the sting of suppressed memory that drove him to portray the forgotten faces of history in his works of art again and again — works which, in spite of the professed untrustworthiness of their author, offered Germans both old and young the opportunity to explore their own conscience. It is clear that, by 1990, Grass sensed that his works didn't give him enough room to hide what he had suppressed, even from himself. He implied back then that at some point a clear confession would have to be made, an 'extra-literary interjection'. He spoke of the inadequacy of 35 years of writing, meaning not a lack of success, but the inadequacy of silence: 'Something that hasn't yet come to expression has to be said. An old story has to be told in a completely new way. Perhaps the two sentences will make it after all.'[44]

And yet I believe that Grass would have liked to relieve his conscience even sooner, and that it was not just laziness and dogmatism that stopped him from doing so. A few weeks after the big scandal of Grass's Waffen-SS membership was revealed, the *Frankfurter Allgemeine Zeitung* published two newly discovered letters that Grass had written to Karl Schiller, the economics minister at the time, provoking considerable scorn.

In the first letter, Grass encouraged Schiller, a friend of his, to confess his past as a member of the NSDAP and SA (which was already known to the press). The post-war generation, Grass said, to emphasise his point, only knew appeasements and downplaying, like those of former federal chancellor Kiesinger, who claimed that he had become a member of the NSDAP neither out of conviction nor as an opportunist. During the 1969 election campaign, Schiller had attacked Kiesinger on account of his past. Grass now took this as cause to call his friend up on his own past: 'I think it would be good if you were to openly admit to your mistake. It would be a relief for you and for the public, too, like the sensation after a cleansing storm.'[45]

Following the disclosure of Grass's own Waffen-SS membership, concealed for decades, this latest revelation must have been seemed an expression of outrageous double standards. After all, in a second letter to Schiller (who hadn't followed his advice), Grass rebuked the 'notorious pride of those in the know' and at the same time declared in a convoluted way that this material was not 'unfamiliar to him'.[46]

But there is another way of reading it. A way that doesn't just explain Grass's silence, but that of the many other members of his generation who concealed and suppressed their NSDAP membership for such a long time, until it was revealed by others. In this reading, Grass and his peers were looking for a way of coming clean about the whole truth without being thrown into the pot with the generation of Nazi 'father-perpetrators'.

Grass may have hoped that Schiller, now a chastened democrat, would lead the way, bringing a kind of 'cleansing storm' to the discussion about formal National Socialist membership that would make it possible for others of his generation to confess. After his plea to Schiller fell on deaf ears, Grass explained in the second letter how he had imagined it: 'I pleaded with you to reveal your own explicable relationship to the NSDAP organisations voluntarily and at the right time; not with grand *mea culpa* gestures, but much more in your own sober yet not over-simplified tone.'[47]

The fact that Schiller was not prepared to do so must have shown Grass that, in all likelihood, he, too, had missed the right moment. The spiral of silence had begun a long time before, and the more that became known about the crimes of the Third Reich, the greater the stigma of having been part of it. Today, this stigma is so great that, as we have seen, even those who were proven to have been members of the NSDAP claim to have been party comrades without their own knowledge.

But you have to give Grass credit for one thing: he revealed his secret on his own initiative, instead of waiting for his membership to be proven by a third party and then hiding behind the myth of unwitting membership. It was also Grass who explained to us how it was possible to be surprised by one's own decisions back then. For example, regarding voluntary enrolment in the Wehrmacht: 'That is a strange thing, too: I joined, probably at the age of fifteen, then forgot the whole thing. That's how it was for many of those born in the same year as me. We were doing our labour service, and then all of a sudden, one year later, the call-up order lay on the table.'[48]

One could allow the benefit of the doubt for those born in 1926 and 1927 who claim to have forgotten their NSDAP membership, and assume that their experiences could have been similar to

Grass's enrolment in the Wehrmacht: forgetting about it, being surprised by the notification, later suppressing it. But the guilt remains, and so does the need for justification and atonement, lest the stigma that seems to belong to another person from another time should stick again. After all, these men had gone through their learning experiences and devoted themselves to serving 'the good cause' unconditionally. In 1990, Grass remembered the Easter marches he had taken part in: 'Always part of it and yet at the same time against it. The stubborn horror of the seventeen-year-old who didn't want to believe had evaporated and given way to a resistance based on principle.'[49]

But how hard is it to live with the secret? In fear — varying to a greater or lesser extent — that the facade of post-war life with all of its merits could crack and tumble down? And how much harder is it because those in question could genuinely claim that they weren't guilty of a crime and that they had been politically exploited? After all, theirs was not the brightly whitewashed facade of the perpetrators and those winking upright citizens who soon found their way back into their old careers and acted as though nothing had happened. Instead, they had always appeared to be affected by the crimes carried out in their name in the Third Reich, and always knew, according to Grass, that 'although we may not have belonged as perpetrators, we were still in the same camp as the perpetrators for the Auschwitz generation, our biographies were still written amidst those customary dates, the date of the Wannsee conference.'[50]

And how hard is the confession?

For many of Grass's generation, death spared them from having to explain why they remained silent for so long. Others experienced the danger of trying to survive in a second dictatorship after being compromised because they had survived the first. All of this applied to Oskar Pastior (1927–2006), a Romanian-born writer of German descent. A few years after Pastior had been honoured posthumously with the Büchner Prize, it was revealed that for years he had been a spy with the Romanian Securitate secret service.[51]

Grass included a poem for Pastior in his 2012 collection, *Eintagsfliegen*. It speaks of the deeply felt emotion of sharing the fate of that 'disreputable year of birth'.[52] There can be no doubt that Grass is speaking from his own experience — for example, when he writes of the 'enclosure of syllables' into which Pastior was driven by his fear of repeated imprisonment. 'Pupated, encapsulated, sheltered by an assortment of invisibility cloaks — becoming invisible even to yourself — you nursed your suffering / As if it were your very last possession.' Suppression was the price of survival, one which could not be paid in instalments and which could only be concealed in art. Fear of the closely guarded secret being exposed is expressed as paranoia:

> Nothing could be allowed to come to light, no clue to come close to you,
> to bring you harm.
> Hidden away in the lining of the all-enveloping overcoat, the shame and its source:
> the ever-alert suspicion of casually presumed disgrace.

In the end, perhaps all that remains is regret. The poem ends with a gesture that would probably never have been expected from Grass, of all people. He takes his dead comrade of fate in his arms, and 'silently weeps'.

CHAPTER SEVEN

'The need to spell out our lives': Martin Walser

In 1998, the well-known author Martin Walser accepted the Peace Prize of the German book trade in the Paulskirche (St Paul's Church) in Frankfurt. In his address, he delivered some thoughts on the subject of remembering the Holocaust. No one worth taking seriously could deny the murder of the Jews by the Nazis and the horrors of Auschwitz, the prize-winner stated firmly: 'Everyone knows the historic burden we bear, the everlasting shame, and not a day goes by when we are not reproached for it.'[1] But by now, he said, there was a routine of accusation in the media, and memory had long since become a superficial ritual of atonement.

Auschwitz, Walser declared, was being used as a routine threat, a tool of intimidation to be deployed at any time, or a moral cudgel: 'What comes into being through such ritualisation is mere lip service.'[2]

At the same time, he warned against an 'instrumentalisation of our shame for contemporary purposes', referring not to the victims, but to the descendants of the perpetrators. He defended himself against the 'soldiers of opinion' in the media, who forced him, as a writer, into the service of opinion 'with their moral pistols extended'.[3]

Walser accused these moral guardians, who felt responsible for the consciences of others, of using the 'eternal shame' of the German people in order to put themselves on a level with the victims. 'Could it be that the intellectuals who reproach us, by holding up our shame before us, are momentarily succumbing to the illusion that because they have laboured once more in the grim service of memory they have relieved their own guilt somewhat, and that for a moment they were even closer to the victims than they were to the perpetrators?'[4]

Not so Walser: 'I have never thought it possible to leave the side of the accused,' the author admitted. In the heated debate that flared up after his speech, did anyone hear that sentence, take it seriously, examine it, search it for secret hidden drawers?

The audience applauded at first — in the words of the philosopher Peter Sloterdijk, 'ten years ahead of themselves for a few minutes'. But shortly afterwards the first furious voices arose. In the din, Walser's confession — quiet, and all the more significant for it — was drowned out. The debate about phrases used by Walser in his speech — such as 'looking away', 'moral cudgel', or 'drawing the line' — revealed how apt his analysis of superficial rituals of atonement in the media had been.

At the same time, however, the hubbub distracted from the actual question that seemed to preoccupy the author, namely: What am I to do with my conscience? 'Conscience can't be delegated,' Walser declared, adding firmly: 'A good conscience is none at all. Each person is alone with his conscience.'[5]

How can one examine one's conscience in front of an audience, and yet maintain one's interpretational sovereignty? Walser did it by referring to his role as a writer who takes responsibility only for himself. He sets the course with words; he writes the timetables and determines where the story goes. Anything is permissible, except being at the service of public opinion. Service was something from long ago, at the anti-aircraft gun, serving the Reich, with the military police of the Wehrmacht. After 1945, there was no more service apart from the service of language. For Walser, 'the need to spell out our lives' became the foundation for a new start as a writer after the war.[6]

From that point on, he felt obliged only to language, and sometimes yielded himself to it:

> [T]hen I hand myself over to language, I pass it the reins, regardless of where it may lead me. That last part isn't true, of course. I grab the reins when I start worrying that it's going too far, that it's giving away too much of me, revealing too much of my unpresentable side. Then, fearful and cautious, I mobilise all kinds of linguistic concealment routines.[7]

Walser's speech in the Paulskirche was a game of hide-and-seek between revelation and concealment, of the kind that he plays so often in his writing. The purpose of his address, he announced that day, was 'that the audience, once I have uttered the final sentence, know less about me than they did when I said my first'.[8]

Routines of concealment

How, as a neutral observer, does one approach the life of a person who reveals himself with each word he utters, while at the same time withdrawing himself from view? How does one speak with such a master of aesthetics, an artiste of memory, about his membership of the National Socialist German Workers' Party, which was discovered in 2007 among the Nazi files in the Federal Archives? Back then, I interviewed Walser on the telephone and asked him whether he could remember applying for membership of the NSDAP on 30 January 1944. Walser explained that he had been made a party member without his knowledge. The thirtieth of January, the date of Hitler's seizure of power, was symbolic, and he had 'entered the festival calendar of the Nazi state with his own biography'.

One thing is clear: a membership card is meaningless in itself. All it tells us is that the NSDAP listed Walser, born on 24 March 1927 in Wasserburg, as a member. The interesting thing about Martin Walser's NSDAP membership card is how he dealt with it, and the role that his membership plays in the process of memory that inspires his literature.

In 2007, Walser declared that he had never signed a membership application. He had neither taken part in a membership celebration nor received a party membership card. 'I am supposed to have made my application on 30 January 1944. I don't know where I was on 30 January 1944; I was sixteen years old. Nobody wants to join a party when they're sixteen.'[9]

Today, the thought that a 16-year-old might willingly become a member of a criminal political party does seem far-fetched. But can one simply judge past decisions from the perspective of the present? Hasn't it been driven home time and again by eyewitnesses that past situations can't be judged by contemporary standards? I put this to Walser when we met in August 2012 on the shores of Lake Constance, where Walser grew up and is now spending his twilight years.

Walser shook his head, threw his hands in the air, and waved dismissively. 'For a 17-year-old, the party was not an option,' he said. 'A political party was a ridiculous idea. The mounted SA or the motorbike thing or the Marine Hitler Youth, that you can understand, but the party was a completely faceless thing that wouldn't even have been impressive as a powerful authority.'

But from a contemporary point of view, isn't it equally unlikely that a 16-year-old would volunteer to join a brutal, aggressive war instigated by Germany? That was exactly what Martin Walser did, as he revealed in a 1998 interview with the influential journalist and *Der Spiegel* founder Rudolf Augstein, disallowing in the same breath the drawing of any conclusions about the political convictions of his younger self: 'If you think that the people who joined up voluntarily were automatically Nazis, then you're mistaken ... When people joined up voluntarily for that war it had nothing to do with politics. The very fact that Hitler instigated the war ensured that his cheap, shoddy ideology vanished in the fog of patriotism.'[10]

Walser here provides the best argument for why a 16-year-old volunteer fighter might have been seduced into joining Hitler's party — out of a false sense of patriotism. The recognition that the party in question was the epitome of evil — both true and, for most Germans, late in coming — may not have been accessible to a German boy whose mother had joined the party even before the Nazis came to power.

And in any case, what business would a writer have joining a party? Even Günter Grass was, notwithstanding decades of electoral support, a member of the SPD for only ten years. Party membership cards aren't literature, and writers are too individualistic to modify their language according to party statutes. Walser has seldom been easy to pin down where Germany and party politics are concerned. He flirted with the communist DKP and, later in his conversation with Rudolf Augstein, admitted that his opposition to Franz Josef Strauss, a prominent Christian Social Union politician, had been an error, and 'an example of

[his] flightiness or irresponsibility'.[11]

As a writer, Walser is obligated only to language, which cannot be placed at the service of any organisation for propaganda purposes. As a consequence, he has had to defend himself against accusations of retreating into the apolitical and the aesthetic since the start of his career: as early as 1957, *Ehen in Philippsburg* (*Marriages in Philippsburg*) was criticised on the grounds that none of the characters had been in the Hitler Youth; in his very first book, from 1955, *Ein Flugzeug über dem Haus* (*An Aeroplane over the House*), Germany's past was said to have been airbrushed out. His response: 'That these were, in 1955, Kafkaesque parables in which it would have been difficult to place the Hitler Youth doesn't matter. Aesthetics doesn't matter, the only thing that matters is the demand for political correctness, and as far as I'm concerned that's horribly patronising.'[12] Walser's reply doesn't express a lack of interest in politics any more than his rejection of party memberships might.

When the newspaper *Der Abend* asked Walser in 1964 whether he had been in one party or none, he replied:

What would I be doing in a party? Rephrasing the statutes? Making propaganda? Becoming a candidate? Writers act through language (if they try to act anywhere else they become dilettantes). Politicians act in organisations. Organisations have to work tactically. That ruins language. It's there for the opposite. It doesn't want to make the right impression, but to find the right expression. If newspapers or writers belong to a party, their language degenerates into jargon. The further a writer is from a party, the more use he can be to it. Distance justifies criticism. You don't expect the doctor to go to bed with the person he's treating. There's such a thing as infectious diseases.[13]

The medical metaphor is telling. Walser returned to it in his conversation with Rudolf Augstein when he discussed the question of whether the Germans still represented a danger half a century after the end of the Third Reich. Once a population had been through what the Germans had, he said, such things could never happen again: 'That's how it is. It's an immunisation.'

Anyone who rules out the possibility of the Germans relapsing into Nazi barbarism must first have been through the same process himself. Only someone who's been cured knows what illness means.

Christoph

In 1946, Walser was studying at the University of Regensburg, where he met Ruth Klüger, a fellow literature student, and Auschwitz survivor. The two struck up a friendship that was to last for decades. Walser advised me to take a look at Klüger's bestselling memoir, *weiter leben* (*going on living*). 'I appear in it under the name Christoph,' he said, 'and I don't come out of it well.'

In her memoir, Klüger describes ignoring the past as something that she and Christoph/Walser shared in 1946. She wants to get away from people who have had to go through experiences similar to her own. He gives her poems by Stefan George and verses of his own, and dismisses discussions of Luther's anti-Semitism as ludicrous. 'We were all involved in the repression of the past, former prisoners less so than those who had remained free, admittedly, and former perpetrators most of all.'[14] They are only confronted with the past sometimes, for example when they find an NSDAP membership badge by the side of the path on one of their walks together, and Christoph thinks she's shocked: 'as if I would be that easily scared'.[15] Years later, when we spoke in 2012,

Walser confessed, 'I must have seen her Auschwitz number, and I didn't ask what it was.'

Once, when they are discussing the causes of the Holocaust over breakfast, Christoph denies Ruth — who sees National Socialism as the product of a high civilisation and not, as he does, as the result of a primitive fear of the Other — any capacity for judgement. In his opinion, as a survivor of the camps she can't make an independent judgement of current threats to civilisation, because for her 'everything is disastrous from the start'. She counters his well-intentioned superiority with the not entirely unfounded suggestion 'that perhaps the capacity for judgement of Hitler Youth members in the old days was compromised by their education'.[16]

Klüger brought their long friendship to an end when she publicly distanced herself from Walser after the publication of his 2002 roman à clef, Tod eines Kritikers (Death of a Critic). In an open letter, she accused him of using anti-Semitic clichés when describing the critic in his novel as a 'Jewish monster', and thus wounding and insulting her. Anticipating Walser's objection that his book isn't at all about anti-Semitism, she compared it with Wilhelm Raabe's 1864 novel Der Hungerpastor. Raabe didn't see himself as an anti-Semite either, she said, and he later wrote in a few 'thin Jewish women characters' by way of proof. Klüger gave no more credence to that attempt at compensation than she did to the assertions of either author. In the end, she maintained, the texts speak for themselves, and the damage that they do in the heads of their readers cannot be healed at a later date, although, 'The self-evaluation of the poets and their inscrutable souls is a different story.'

Today, when Walser speaks of his ruined friendship with Klüger, it is immediately clear how hurt he is. Others may have levelled accusations against him, but never has he been so close to someone who went on to do so. He can't understand his old friend's rejection of him, and the most incomprehensible thing of all is her accusation that he spread anti-Semitic ideas. 'When you know someone for 30 years, you know whether they're anti-Semitic or not. You can just tell, always. And Ruth knew me and us, and then the novel comes out ...' However, Klüger's reaction couldn't have come as a complete surprise to Walser. He had read her memoir chapter by chapter in manuscript in the early 1990s, and even recommended it to his publisher. In one passage, the narrator accuses Christoph of having an anti-Semite inside him, in spite of his protestations to the contrary: 'He thought about that for a long time and disputed it, saying he was very interested in Jewish intellectual life.'[17]

I asked Walser whether it was possible that he studiously ignored this passage, even knowing that it was about him, so that it came as a surprise when Klüger publicly criticised him after the publication of *Death of a Critic*. He paused, and reflected for a moment. 'I know I didn't agree with the way I was portrayed. But I just saw it as literature.'

'Transforming life into language'

'My early years in the Hitler Youth became a fragment of legend a long time ago,' Martin Walser warned me when I contacted him to arrange a meeting. 'I don't remember anything I could tell a historian.'

Knowledge is like that: it can be repressed, hushed up, or simply forgotten. Günter Grass kept his SS membership quiet for 60 years. When I talked to Dieter Wellershoff and Hilmar Hoffmann about their NSDAP membership cards, I genuinely got the impression that, with the best will in the world, they couldn't remember signing an application.

It is actually possible to repress unpleasant events so strongly that the memory of them can be cut away. The literary critic Hans Dieter Schäfer describes this process in his book *Das gespaltene Bewusstsein* (*The Divided Consciousness*) with reference to many post-1945 intellectual biographies, and reaches the judgement: 'Presumably in a lengthy engagement with the past one cannot speak of a deliberate lie; it is more a psychopathological reflex with which the facts have, out of shame, been re-evaluated with astonishing ease.'[18]

Lies are banal; moral judgements, two a penny. But repression and re-evaluation are informative phenomena, not least when they are carried out between the covers of a book. The divided consciousness of the early Federal Republic found its artistic expression in the novels of authors like Martin Walser and Günter Grass. They don't lie, they don't even repress; they just bring what is subliminally present more clearly to light than any historical chronicle of the Federal Republic could ever do.

Walser's essay 'The Human Theory of Warmth' is a playful meditation on the essence of secrecy. It was published in 2004 in the magazine *Cicero* — two years after Günter Grass examined the guilt and silence of his generation in *Crabwalk*. Reading Grass's novella today, one cannot help having a sense that even then an urge to confess was forcing its way between the lines. Likewise, reading Walser's essay, one cannot help feeling that here, once again, a hermeneutic safety net is being stretched out in case the author falls in the middle of his memorial acrobatics.

At the same time, Walser seems to sense that secrets cannot be kept for ever: 'There is a fear that you might suddenly be unable to hold back what you have been keeping silent, that it might come pouring out of you. Too soon. Right now. At the wrong time.'[19] Walser wants — as Grass did when he publicised his SS membership himself — to determine the moment of his own confession. Unlike Grass, he didn't succeed, because his party membership was made public in 2007 without his intervention — his only option was a defiant denial.

Hard-line literary critics disdain the idea of drawing conclusions about the author from the work. In the hierarchy of literary genres, the *roman à clef* occupies one of the lowest ranks, near the potboiler and the thriller. It must be clear even to the most clueless of interpreters that too assiduous a search for direct matches is always going to end in failure. At the same time, one might be justified in asking why a body of work like Martin Walser's should have nothing to do with the life of its creator.

At any rate, Walser's biographer Jörg Magenau states that the author is 'constantly busy transforming life into language. When something happens to him, he replies with literature'. According to this view, his novels are a chronicle of his emotions, and thus the most intimate source of biographical information.[20]

You don't have to perform an inquisitorial 'hermeneutics of suspicion', as Magenau puts it, to find the traces of great sublimation in Walser's work.[21] You just have to follow the reading instructions of the author himself. 'Narrative and the narrated are one. In any case and always,' Walser said in an interview in 2002. 'And if one of them has to disguise himself in order to say how ashamed the other one is, then this is merely the usual theatre of possibility required by all human expression.'[22]

So we are not doing Walser an injustice if, in the 'fragment of legend' of his time in the Hitler Youth, we listen between the lines of remembering and follow the trail of consciousness.

By the mid-1960s Walser had already considered writing a

novel about his family in the Third Reich. He was preoccupied with the project, which had the working title *Matrosenleben* (*A Sailor's Life*), at the time when he attended the Auschwitz trial in Frankfurt. Traces of this can be seen in Walser's diaries. In April 1963, he outlines some of its content: no Jews were to be driven out of Wasserburg ('Although there is hatred for the Jews'); the visit of the Race Commission from Tübingen University to the village is to be described, along with how the professors from Berlin join in with the changes that are to be made to the village. 'And the two Jewish villas, well, yes, sacrifices must be made.'[23] The local group leader is harmless, Walser notes in his diary on 18 April 1963, 'just a by-the-by party member' — a clumsy term for somebody who somehow ended up in the party.[24] He was also planning to give an account of the execution of a Polish forced labourer at the midsummer fairground. 'Almost all of it is hearsay,' Walser writes at one point. 'I didn't experience it myself, like so much that I will relate.'[25]

So even back then Walser was trying to reconstruct village life in the Third Reich with the help of his own memories and things he had been told, a mixture of facts and suppositions: 'Fragments from that time, admitted gaps. Sudden, quite concrete efforts, then it breaks off again. Then you have to take a leap.' But nothing came of this novel, at least not at first. Perhaps it was the immediate impact of the Auschwitz trial that made a depiction of childhood in the Third Reich, amid all the cruelties passed down from that time, seem impossible. 'All memories of those days are Saturday sweetness,' he confided in his diary in 1963, 'but now we know it was a time of murder, so we have no sweetness any more. That's the worst thing. And yet sweetness wins.'[26]

The fountain of memory would only leap three decades later, when Walser linked the story of his own childhood with that of another 'by-the-by party member', his mother, in the novel *Ein springender Brunnen* (*A Leaping Fountain*). In it, Walser describes life in the Third Reich entirely from the perspective of his alter ego, the village boy Johann. Johann, born in 1927, grows up in his parents' pub in Wasserburg on Lake Constance. From his sensitive but weak father he inherits his love of language and literature, while his determined mother ensures that the family is able to make ends meet.

Some critics took exception to this treatment. In the *Neue Zürcher Zeitung*, Andreas Isenschmid accused the author of describing his youth in the Third Reich 'with blinkers on'. The word Auschwitz doesn't appear in the novel, and Dachau perhaps three times, Isenschmid calculated, going on to point out: 'He has quite deliberately reduced the knowledge depicted in the book to the knowledge that he had at the time, which is a pitifully small amount, and he refuses, so to speak, to add such a thing as *Vergangenheitsbewältigung* only to show shame about those times.'[27]

In his address at the Paulskirche in 1998, Walser replied that you wouldn't reproach Goethe because the guillotine doesn't appear in his *Wilhelm Meister*, first published in 1795. In notes he wrote for another speech, he mused: 'Never heard anything about the primal law of narrative: perspective. But regardless, spirit of the age comes before aesthetics.'[28]

From the very start, however, in *A Leaping Fountain*, it is aesthetics that counts, not the spirit of the age. 'Saturday sweetness in a time of murder,' Walser said when we were sitting together on his terrace in 2012, 'that's exactly the point.'

The first part of the book is entitled 'Mother joins the party' and relates, among other things, how the lady of the house decided to join the NSDAP in order to save the family pub from the constant threat of bankruptcy. It was only in passing, after 1945, that he learned about his mother joining the party, Walser said in 1998. 'It wasn't as if people said, "Oh, poor Mother. You were in the party." It was a message that seeped through, impossible to say from whom to whom, and without evaluation.'[29] Still, the writer knew the date of his mother's party membership so precisely that in the novel he moved it to Christmas 1932, 'a date that fit compositionally'.[30] In reality, Auguste Walser had joined the NSDAP on 1 April 1932.

Sixty years later Walser was still so preoccupied with the subject that he initially wanted to call the novel *Der Eintritt meiner Mutter in die Partei* (*My Mother Joins the Party*). 'I only wrote the book out of love for my mother.'[31]

One of the book's themes is thus clear, even if Walser ended up using his mother's party membership as the heading for the first part of the novel rather than as its title. In the novel, the mother is persuaded by a local party member to join the NSDAP. At first the strict Catholic has reservations: 'some people said the new party was running after the godless', in response to which the Protestant party recruiter gives her a postcard. It shows Christ on the cross, with two Brownshirts standing in front of it holding swastika flags. The mother has her son Johann read out the caption: 'Lord, bless our struggle. Adolf Hitler.'[32] Indeed, joining the NSDAP would not have been a straightforward decision for a Catholic in 1932. From the beginning of 1931 onwards, all Catholic authorities had forbidden their flocks from joining the NSDAP. On occasion, local priests even refused the sacraments to Nazi Party members.[33] And yet the mother decides — for pragmatic reasons, as the novel suggests — to join the party early on. 'There are still membership numbers below a million,' the party recruitment officer promises, and the mother replies that in future, party gatherings could be held in her own restaurant.

But is it plausible that economic opportunism could have moved such a strictly religious woman to set aside her faith at the risk of being unable to receive the sacraments — even before the NSDAP came to power in 1933? 'She saved us,' Walser insisted.[34] By virtue of joining the party early, Auguste Walser did in fact get a membership number lower than a million.

Another theme in the novel is the process of remembering, which the narrator addresses right at the beginning: 'When something is over, you are no longer the person it happened to.'[35] This sentence has a logical conclusiveness that could mislead the reader into seeing it as a philosophical aphorism. But in *A Leaping Fountain*, Walser does not report the story flatly, but rather teases out the memory in the course of the story. As this happens, things from the past that are not so easily accessible to the memory come to light: 'One's actual past cannot be entered. All we have of it is what it yields.'[36] It is possible here to discern the 'linguistic concealment routines' that Walser mentioned in his address in the Paulskirche — but perhaps they are, at the same time, routines of revelation.

Johann sees the post-1945 fate of those who served the regime all too eagerly in the example of the headmaster Heller: he is made to sit in the window of the local café wearing a sign around his neck: 'I was a Nazi.'[37] A visit to a friend's house, furthermore, allows the boy to see the political opportunism of the followers. The mother of his friend Adolf receives him with the news that her son now answers to his second name, Stefan, and that it would be nice if Johann would 'address him properly' at their first meeting.[38]

Walser's search for the lost past becomes a confession that a successful life, lived in a straight line without a crack, without a gaping wound, is impossible. But that crack must be denied in the present day, when the examination of the past is subjected to an increasingly severe set of norms, and allows no past other than the desirable one. Thus, at the start of the third section of *A Leaping Fountain*, the narrator applies the same critique of history that Walser formulated in his address in the Paulskirche. Today the past is reinterpreted in terms of what is desirable, it says in the novel, producing a 'completely closed, brightly lit, cleansed, authorised past entirely suited to the present. Ethically and politically corrected, through and through'.[39]

So-called *Vergangenheitsbewältigung*, the much-evoked 'overcoming' of past evils, is a contemporary political ritual about which the narrator of the novel is just as sceptical as Walser. The narrator sees the idea that past guilt cannot merely be forgotten but also overcome as a collective self-deception, a gigantic repression: '[W]hatever our past may have been, we have freed ourselves from everything in it that we would now prefer it not to be. Perhaps one might say: we have emancipated ourselves. Then our past goes on to live within us as one that has been overcome. Mastered. We have to come out of it well. But not lie in such a way that we ourselves notice'.[40]

In the novel, Johann is not a resister; he treads the path laid out for boys in the Third Reich. He is a member of the Hitler Youth, and listens with a mixture of queasiness and fascination to SS *Scharführer* (squad leader) Gottfried Hübschle, who conveys to him the Nazi propaganda of the New Man. But to a boy brought up as a strict Catholic, who sees the SS as a 'crowd of godless people', the words sound like 'church phrases'.[41] Johann finds the SS peculiar, and he feels sorry for the SS men 'branded' with runes on their upper arm and advises Hübschle not to replace his tattoo, which was shredded when he was shot in the arm. Hübschle, who introduces Johann to the poetry of Stefan George, does not strike him as a typical SS man. Nonetheless, the boy is too shy to ask him whether there is any truth in the rumours that the SS are shooting prisoners in the East.

What is being explored here is not the guilt of the perpetrators, but the guilt felt by the inactive, the non-perpetrators, those who joined in without questioning or rebelling. Walser — as did many members of his generation — clearly felt that guilt from early on, as for example when he refers in his 1965 essay 'Our Auschwitz' to the idea that the concentration-camp guards accused in the Frankfurt trials had more in common with ordinary Germans than those ordinary Germans might have been willing to admit. He criticises the detached way in which the murderers of Auschwitz are depicted in public and in the media as bestial criminals acting alone, whose crimes had nothing to do with the rest of the German population: 'These trials are not about us … Which of us is a devil, a hangman, a beast of prey?'[42] The Germans, Walser suggests sarcastically, acted as if between 1933 and 1945 they had been living in a different state from the accused. The soothing distance between perpetrators and followers is, in Walser's view, produced by the fact that reports concentrate on the graphic description of acts of cruelty: 'They speak only of deeds that we did not commit, either because we are not among those who made crimes possible but did not actually commit them; or because, when work was being done to make those crimes possible, we were still too young, or clever enough to keep ourselves at a useful distance.'[43]

Walser exempted himself from that self-administered amnesty of conscience as early as 1965. He wrote: 'Anyone who, rather than examining his clear conscience and exploring his feeling of shame, gave any thought to the voluntary and, even more, the involuntary part that he had played in the effects of the collective, could not easily say: the crimes are only the affair of the perpetrators.'[44]

Even decades later, he expressly professes to having taken part involuntarily in the events of the time. 'I never had anything to do with it as a perpetrator. But I was still, and even I don't know why, involved in that filth. And I realise in retrospect, now that it's all too late, that I cannot get out of it.'[45]

Before Walser published his 1965 essay about the Auschwitz trial, he reworked his observations about guilt and complicity in the play *Der Schwarze Schwan* (*The Black Swan*). The title references the abbreviation 'SS', and at the centre of the play is young Rudi Goothein, whose father was responsible, as a concentration-camp doctor and member of the SS, for prisoner transports. After discovering an incriminating letter from his father, young Rudi takes on his father's guilt, and is declared schizophrenic. His father, on the other hand, whose guilt is real and much greater, believes that he has atoned for it with a brief period of imprisonment.

Rudi enters treatment with the psychiatrist Liberé, a friend of his father's and also a former concentration-camp doctor. Liberé, whose real name is the German-sounding Leibnitz, is also incapable of facing up to his responsibility. He has created a new identity for himself and his family, and represses his guilt with displacement activities: 'I have my souvenirs. I had them ... the trappings of atonement, the plaster of memory.'[46] From this critique of superficial rituals of atonement, a direct line leads to the 1965 essay 'Our Auschwitz' and to the Paulskirche address more than three decades later, in which Walser turns against the idea of remembering as a dutiful exercise or a form of lip service.

Rudi, who can no longer bear to keep his guilt quiet, sees his own death as the only way out. First he tries to persuade Liberé's daughter Irm to commit suicide with him in a substitute act for the guilty parents: 'At least we will eradicate the children of the murderers.'[47] But Irm refuses, and in the end Rudi shoots himself, but his self-sacrifice is fruitless. Even after Rudi's suicide, Liberé refuses to go to the law and admit his guilt before the court: 'All I know is: I can't separate myself from myself for the sake of others and say: it was him. I am a poor judge of myself. And I fear there is no better one.'[48] This is the moral paradox of post-war society in the Federal Republic: the parents, who go on living as good people, as if nothing had happened, are the true schizophrenics. Refusing all public responsibility, the parental generation place upon their children, the morally more alert members of the *Flakhelfer* generation, the whole burden of dealing with guilt. Here Walser gets straight to the core of the social and psychological generational conflict of the post-war era, one which would go on to discharge itself violently in the student protests of 1968. By the time of the Auschwitz trials, the collective atonement rituals of the parents' generation will seem like pure mockery to their children.

Walser also stages the Federal Republic's collective exorcism of memory in the 1950s as a play within a play: in the psychiatric institution, Rudi and his fellow patients put on a theatrical performance based around a former concentration-camp doctor who tames the Furies of guilt with his restless activity and readiness to atone. Only as an affluent and successful man can he expiate his guilt as comprehensively as its weight demands. In Walser's eyes, as Jörg Magenau has argued, the dutifully atoning concentration-camp doctor stands for the productivity principle of the Federal Republic: 'Back then he saw how guilt was, to a certain extent, made economically usable. *Vergangenheitsbewältigung* turned into the economic miracle, and reparation into reconstruction.'[49]

In an essay on silence in 2004, Walser even applies the productivity principle of repression explicitly to himself. 'We keepers of secrets,' he writes, are irritable, self-righteous, and intolerant. Why?

Although we are not always aware of it, we are constantly afraid of being unmasked. The outside world might work out why we are so industrious, purposeful, energetic, courageous, uprightly democratic, heartily republican, universalistically consensus-forming, excessively strict and intolerant. All through our lives we try to turn our favourite mask into our face. We must constantly camouflage the difference between mask and face with suspicion, arrogance and pliability. In every inquiry we hear suspicion or even accusation.[50]

It is striking how directly Walser addresses the emotional core of his generation's democratic commitment. The more rapidly his generation rise to become the leading voices of the Federal Republic, the greater is their fear that their pre-1945 past might be unmasked. And the greater the fear of being unmasked, the more frantic the efforts to dodge unwelcome questions.

The Black Swan is not just an early piece of social criticism dealing with the politics of the past. On a subtler level, it is also an engagement with the feelings of guilt of the author's generation, born guiltless and guilty into the age of the Third Reich.

Jörg Magenau has pointed out just how close the figure of Rudi is to his creator. He even has the same birthday as Walser: 24 March. 'Your date of birth alone makes you a fabulous fellow,' Liberé tells his patient.[51] It is the date when his father organised another transport of prisoners to the camp. Liberé's cynical remark makes it clear how directly involved the members of Walser's generation must inevitably have seen themselves to be, by virtue of their dates of birth alone.

Each decade, he returned to the subject of German guilt, Walser told Rudolf Augstein in their conversation in 1998: 'I was never released from that set of problems. But nor have I ever felt reprieved or even exculpated by the mode of treatment practised by the decade in question.'[52] In the 1975 essay 'Auschwitz and No End', Walser writes that one only has to look at a picture from Auschwitz to admit that one hasn't dealt with it. 'Whatever you do with it, you can't delegate it. You can't let someone else manage it. The violence that appears in these pictures came from you, and now it's coming back, to you. It isn't enough to ask your parents and grandparents: What was such and such like? Ask yourself what it's like.'[53]

It would be unfair to accuse Walser of only criticising other people's repression of guilt. Again and again, he has faced up to his own in his plays, novels, and essays. In this respect, the guilt-driven, guilt-driving productivity principle of the Federal Republic also applies to its tireless writer Martin Walser — with one important difference from the conscience-repressers: Walser's examination of his own guilt through writing is productive by virtue of the fact that it becomes representative. His tireless re-examination and re-narration of the past does not serve to repress his own guilt, but rather to present it in artistic form. As with Günter Grass, in a hundred years it will still be possible to read his work as a record of the processes of consciousness of an entire generation that grew up in a dictatorship but created a democracy.

Walser's generation may have been too young in the Third Reich to become perpetrators. But they are the burnt children of bad parents — parents who brought up their children not in the spirit of civic enlightenment and tolerance, but in the tradition of German introspection, remote from politics. 'The thing that rages in Auschwitz also comes in the end from an old school, from bad parents,' Walser writes in 'Our Auschwitz'.[54]

These children were deceived by an idealism infected by National Socialism, like that which Johann encounters in *A Leaping Fountain* in the figure of the SS officer Hübschle. He is, like the doctors Goothein and Liberé created by Walser 30 years earlier, not drawn as an entirely negative character. This gives readers the opportunity to test their own susceptibility to ideological manipulation — a moment of genuine self-knowledge that can serve as an ethical leitmotif for future decisions.

'Ask yourself what it's like' — that appeal to individual memory and responsibility lies at the heart of Walser's writing. In 'Our Auschwitz', for example, he turns the exoneration strategy of ordinary Germans — that the perpetrators acted on their own, the people were innocent — on its head and asserts the opposite: if terms such as state and '*Volk*' (people, nation, or race) are to have any meaning at all, then each individual must enquire into his own complicity in the political crimes of the Third Reich, crimes that were committed in the name of that collective. 'Unfortunately we must assume that we were closer to that state than we wanted to admit in the face of its manifestation in Auschwitz.'[55] Walser is not using the first person plural in a rhetorical way. He is not — and was not even then — concerned with collective guilt, but with individual examination of conscience: 'Then everyone belongs in part to the causes of Auschwitz. Then it would be a matter for each person to find that part. They need not have been in the SS.'[56]

In *The Black Swan*, Walser anticipates his Auschwitz essay, published a year later, in dramatic form. Unlike his father, Rudi Goothein was not in the SS, but he doesn't need to have been a member in order to feel guilty. Walser, observing the trial in Frankfurt, was interested in gaining an insight into how, under certain circumstances, simple people could become mass murderers. In his play, he has Rudi deliver a speech about the function of the individual in the murderous apparatus of the Holocaust:

I probably won't make anything happen. Without the apparatus. It's always been like that: seven angels standing around you. The first says: you look like a victim. The second fetches you. The third dupes you. The fourth reassures you. I bend my thumb. The sixth has already fired up the oven. And the seventh says: so, in you go now. They have always worked in a chain. Each one only said a single word. No one heard the sentence they made.[57]

Rudi's belief that even as the tiniest link in that chain he was indirectly involved in the murder of millions is the cause of his vicarious sense of guilt, something which eventually drives him to suicide. Rudi's identification with his father's crimes seems to be the dramatic correlative of Walser's demand for an investigation into his own responsibility. But it only seems to be so: the author who spoke 30 years later about the 'concealment routines' in his writing may have given his character the same birthday as himself, but not the same year. Rudi was born in 1942 and is thus 15 years younger than his creator. His question about his own role in the Nazi state is thus more hypothetical than that of the author, who was a member of the Hitler Youth and a soldier, and a member of the NSDAP.

In *A Leaping Fountain*, too, Walser speaks both subtly and emphatically about his generation's particular feeling of *having been there*, and by virtue of that fact alone of having shouldered part of the responsibility for the evil of the Third Reich. The description of the safe village world, a world which can only partially escape the Third Reich, need not be read as a confession of guilt. It is also the story of a youth in the collective that followed the preordained paths of religion, education, and state.

That is how Walser's alter ego in the novel experiences it when he is recruited into the Wehrmacht and has to swear the oath to the Führer. 'Johann had imagined that the oath-taking would be more difficult than it was. The repetition of the formulae phrases fell from his lips like the preamble at confession. One more formula. Copying and repeating and promising something that had nothing to do with him. He had nothing against these texts, but they had nothing to do with him.'[58]

That most young people in the Third Reich travelled this path with greater or lesser degrees of enthusiasm doesn't alter the fact that they did travel it: into the church, into the army — and into the party. But most members of that generation deny ever having joined the NSDAP, saying that there would have been no reason for them to do so. Walser expressed himself in similar terms after his membership card turned up in the NSDAP card file. And yet it seems as if here the story knows more than the author. Obviously, it would not take any particular identification with state institutions to be involved in them. 'One more formula' — would that not have applied equally to membership of the omnipresent party to which the author's mother belonged? Is it not likely that Walser and many others of his generation were given an application form to fill in, and obeyed the demand that they join the party? That they signed and promised something that had nothing to do with them? That assumption might come closer to the actual reality of the situation for intelligent and ambitious young people in the Third Reich than retrospective attempts to explain away the existence of the membership cards.

When we spoke again about his membership, in 2012, Walser rummaged around in his memory once more: 'On 30 January 1944 I was 16, and in all probability I would have been skiing at that time of year. And yet that's when I'm supposed to have applied for membership of the party? You don't even need to shrug; it's out of the question.' Only he can consult his memory, and out of the question is out of the question. Hans Werner Henze described his card as a 'forgery'; Walser doesn't see the document from the Nazi bureaucracy as a serious source, either. When I pressed the matter, he slowly started to become impatient: 'And *you*, I shall say now, with the way you're messing about, are turning a piece of Nazi bureaucratic machination into a historically genuine source, and in all honesty I have to say to you that that's quite a bad thing.' For Walser, it is clear that 'only some people did that [forged membership applications], the people who gave Hitler lists of names for his birthday'.

The only question is: Who would have done such a thing? Walser assumed it was the garrison commander, Erwin Kraft. Was this Kraft a convinced Nazi? Walser thought for a moment: 'He was far too young — he was even younger than me. That was his rank. Siegfried Unseld was our garrison commander in Ulm; he was the most important person in that hierarchy.' So Erwin Kraft wasn't even old enough to be a party member. I asked Walser if Kraft were still alive, but he had died in a motorcycle accident just a few years after the end of the war, and Walser had visited him in hospital. So Kraft recruited him? 'My lawyer has the details,' Walser said.

> [Y]ou'll have to read through them, that's generally how it was, and not just in Wasserburg. Generally speaking, the party could hand over whole year groups. Please read upon it at the office of my lawyer, Herr Groth. He has taken a lot of trouble. I admit I didn't read it as attentively as if I were reading Nietzsche. But it made an impression on me, and it also points out how illegal it is to talk about membership in this context.

A case to answer

So let's give the floor to the lawyer. In 2012, in the press chamber of the Hamburg regional court, Walser brought a case against an author, demanding that he retract several statements he had made accusing Walser of spreading anti-Semitic and National Socialist ideas.

The accusations were groundless and require no further attention, but, importantly for this discussion, the trial also touched on Walser's supposed membership of the NSDAP. Walser's lawyers referred, among other things, to the fact that the card in his name bore the wrong date of birth (24 May 1927 rather than 24 March 1927), and that his address was missing. This in itself was not enough to call the membership into doubt, and so Walser's lawyers also referred to an 'expert opinion', or, more precisely, the Federal Archives webpage, about the membership organisation of the NSDAP. According to this source, party membership only came into force legally when the membership card was handed over. And since Walser's actual membership card — the party identification card that would have been issued to him — was not in the NSDAP card file in the Federal Archives, the lawyers concluded that the author had never legally been a member. But this is a false conclusion: the file card that had been found and the membership card that would have been issued to him are two different documents.[59] In addition, there was never a supplementary 'list of members', the absence of which the lawyers presented as further evidence.

Admittedly, it is no longer possible to prove whether Walser was ever given a membership card, thus legally becoming an NSDAP member. But in any case, the formal legal argument missed the heart of the matter: whether the 17-year-old Walser ever signed a membership application, or whether he was put on file without his own knowledge.

This question, still disputed among historians today, had to be resolved before the court because of Walser's statement of claim. His lawyers referred to Directive 1/44 by the Reich treasurer, of 7 January 1944, regulating the intake of members of the Hitler Youth and the BDM born in 1926 and 1927, who could be accepted into the NSDAP as 17-year-olds on 20 April 1944. This directive applied to Walser, who turned 17 on 24 March 1944 and thus, as his file card indicates, could be accepted into the party on 20 April. Walser's lawyers added the document as an appendix to the statement of claim, although plainly without having read it properly. They concluded from the fact that 17-year-olds at the time didn't have to fill in a questionnaire that a certificate of service from the responsible Hitler Youth leader was sufficient for membership, 'so that applications for membership could clearly be made by groups, without the individual member of the Hitler Youth being aware of it'.[60]

That, in fact, contradicts the directive in question. Point 2 does indeed mention a certificate of service, but under point 3 it says: 'The membership application should be carefully filled in by the boys and girls to be accepted into the party, signed in their own hand and passed to the responsible Hitler Youth leader.'[61] Walser's lawyers also neglected to mention a statement from the Federal Archives that directly contradicted their argument: 'In the holdings of the Federal Archives there are reference documents as well as many individual case studies which reveal that the NSDAP party bureaucracy operated highly meticulously, that the membership recruitment process was highly regulated and that, fundamentally, no one could be accepted into the NSDAP without their own participation.'[62]

The court delivered its verdict on 5 October 2012, and partially admitted Walser's claim. As the assertion that Walser had been a member of the NSDAP was likely to diminish the author's social standing, the chamber judged that it was up to the accused to prove Walser's membership. But the court did not recognise Walser's card in the central NSDAP card file as proof of his membership, and accepted his statement that he had never made a membership application. Without a signed membership application, there was no NSDAP membership — that was the essence of the judgement. However, in the Federal Archives only 600,000 membership applications have been preserved, compared to 10.7 million membership cards. Following the logic of the Hamburg judge, one might de-Nazify 10.1 million NSDAP members with a stroke of the pen on account of the fact that their applications no longer exist.

Everything seems to indicate that the intake of selected Hitler Youth members of Walser's age group was carried out in line with party regulations, even in the district of Lindau, where Walser was born. Thus the *Südschwäbisches Tagblatt* reported on 28 February 1944 that 'in all parts of the Reich, the acceptance of the best members of the Hitler Youth into the Fighting Community of the National Socialist German Workers' Party' had taken place the previous Sunday. The newspaper quoted from the speech given by Reich Youth Leader Artur Axmann, to the effect that 'only boys and girls who have notably proved themselves' were accepted into the party.[63] The local news pages covered the membership ceremony in the district of Lindau: 'Yesterday, Sunday, was a great day for those Hitler Youth and BDM girls born in 1926 and 1927 who reported voluntarily to join the party.'[64]

How 'voluntary' party membership was carried out in practice — who was chosen as being among the 'best' and why — is anyone's guess. However, the voluntary nature of the membership was not only emphasised by the party propaganda, but was also prescribed in the membership regulations of the NSDAP. Directive 24/37 stated categorically: 'No compulsion or pressure to join the party may be exerted under any circumstances, since the principle of voluntariness must be fully maintained as one of the most valuable and essential qualities of the movement!'[65] According to the aforementioned Directive 1/44, concerning those born in 1926 and 1927, successful candidacy required, apart from the application form completed in the applicant's hand, a written assurance from the Hitler Youth leader responsible to the effect 'that the candidate has voluntarily declared that he or she wants to join the party'.[66] And the applicant's service certificate had to be presented to the responsible *Ortsgruppenleiter* by 12 February 1944 — in time for the membership ceremony which, regardless of the symbolic entry date of 20 April, was carried out on 27 February.

The last chapter of Walser's *A Leaping Fountain* bears the plain title 'Prose'. It begins with the telling sentence: 'Read all the hot summer long.'[67] He had been reading *Atta Troll* by Heine at the time, Walser told me, and Faulkner and Strindberg. 'Today one cannot imagine what an explosion of joy that was, and one didn't give a thought to what had gone before. You see, it was all just: now, now, now, now.'

Even in 1945, it was clear to the 18-year-old Martin Walser that he had to become a writer. As he later wrote: 'Everyone becomes a poet by virtue of the fact that he may not say what he wants to say.'[68]

CHAPTER EIGHT

The End of Their Story

You, who shall resurface following the flood

In which we have perished

Contemplate

When you speak of our weaknesses

Also the dark time

That you have escaped.

— Bertold Brecht, 'To Those Who Follow In Our Wake'

I cleaned my conscience for years, until it lay gleaming like a pebble in the stream of history. My generation knew from the outset what lessons we had to learn from that history.

In the face of the crimes that were committed between 1933 and 1945, not by us personally, but in the name of our nation and our forefathers, there could only be one conclusion: we had to ensure that nothing of the kind could happen again.

We grew up with our grandparents remembering, admonishing, and commemorating. What had happened didn't pertain to us, but we were inevitably affected by it. From the very beginning, we were informed about the abysmal depths of the Third Reich, the horrors of the Holocaust, and German war crimes.

And not only that. We were also informed that a cloak of silence and repression had settled over history back then, and that we were the first to be fully informed about those crimes, knowledge of which our teachers had needed to struggle to acquire.

When we went abroad and were greeted with malicious glee by people shouting 'Heil Hitler', we were hurt. It didn't happen often, but it did happen, and when it did we were justified in feeling vicarious embarrassment — because of our history, but also because non-Germans were so determined to assure us of our inherited guilt. As blameworthy as our recent history might have been, we were equally virtuous with our enlightened convictions.

While earlier generations of German schoolchildren were inoculated with the poison of nationalism, we were fed guilt, shame, and responsibility by the spoonful. It was liberating, but also unsettling, and like all medicines this one had its side effects. If dismay becomes a ritual, the danger arises of another kind of repression. Then a formulaic cult of memory and a habitual willingness to become enraged stifle any attempt to find one's own answer to the question: How could it happen?

Lawyer and well-known author Bernhard Schlink recently analysed the contemporary gesture of moral rage in an essay entitled 'Culture of Denunciation'.[1] In the essay, Schlink, who taught Public Law and Legal Philosophy at Humboldt University until 2009, reported on discussions he had had with his students about the moral obligations of lawyers. Schlink had tried to consider the work of lawyers under the Kaiser and in the Third Reich in the context of their times: What latitude did they allow themselves? How could their thoughts and actions be assessed in view of the existing conditions of the state and power politics? 'But the students were at the level of contemporary morality and weren't interested in yesterday's morals,' Schlink writes, summing up his observations before addressing the cause of the culture of denunciation among the students: 'At school, instead of understanding the behaviour in and out of the world of the "Third Reich", they are drilled in moral evaluation of it.'[2]

Schlink places responsibility for this on the shoulders of a historical scholarship that has paraded moral criticism rather than factual knowledge. He cited the authors of *Das Amt und die Vergangenheit* (*The Ministry and the Past*), a 2010 study of the Auswärtiges Amt, as a prime example of this kind of contemporary treatment of moral judgements in academia, when they described the Foreign Ministry in the Third Reich as a 'criminal organisation' and conjured a 'wave of rage'. If we judge history from a contemporary perspective, as if it were the present, the history ceases to be, and at best we replace a historical partiality with a contemporary one.

A good commentator on this topic is a former president of the Federal Republic, Richard von Weizsäcker. His speech on the 40th anniversary of the end of the war in 1985 went into the history books because he described 8 May 1945 not as a defeat, but as a 'day of liberation' from National Socialist tyranny. The reinterpretation of defeat as liberation marked the dawn of a new historical and political era, although Weizsäcker's attitude was a source of controversy at the time, even in his own party, the CDU. 'I made myself very unpopular in the parliamentary group with my attitude,' the former president said when I visited him in January 2012.'[3]

Weizsäcker wanted to put a positive spin on the future. As a former soldier who had lost a brother in the first weeks of the war, and who later, as a young lawyer, defended his father in the Nuremberg Wilhelmstrasse Trial, Weizsäcker was also an eyewitness who was very familiar with the moral hardships of dictatorship. Weizsäcker had never been a member of the NSDAP, but the question of the guilt and complicity of each individual German also preoccupied him in his 1985 speech: 'There is people's discovered guilt and the guilt that has remained hidden. There is guilt that people have admitted or denied. Everyone who experienced that time with full awareness is now asking himself quietly about his own involvement.'[4]

When I met him in 2012, Weizsäcker admitted that he had never talked to his father about his NSDAP membership. It hadn't interested him: 'In many cases there were certainly practical, personal reasons for joining the NSDAP, not political convictions. The overwhelming majority only found out what terrible cruelties were associated with the word Auschwitz shortly before the end of the war.'[5]

Weizsäcker was addressing the same generational conflict between eyewitnesses and the contemporary youth that Schlink describes. In his 1985 speech, the president had exhorted young and old to help each other understand 'why it is vitally important to keep memory alive. It is not a matter of overcoming the past. That can't be done. It cannot be changed retroactively, or made not to have happened'.

The further back in the past the events are, the greater our informational advantage over those who witnessed them. Today we have an overview of the horrors of National Socialism that even the main perpetrators couldn't have had at the time. In more than ten years of research, the academics at the Washington Holocaust Memorial Museum have drawn up a list of places of National Socialist persecution during the Holocaust. As *The New York Times* reported in March 2013, researchers counted some 42,500 camps and ghettoes that formed a Europe-wide Holocaust network.[6]

Even Adolf Eichmann could not have had such a detailed overview. But can those alive at the time therefore claim to have known nothing about Auschwitz? Did the guilt come only with shame, when the extent of the crimes committed by the Germans became clear after 1945? That was also something which Weizsäcker addressed in his 1985 speech: 'No one who kept his ears and eyes open, who wanted to keep himself informed, could miss seeing the fact that the deportation trains were rolling.'

During our conversation in 2012, I asked him if he included himself in that. 'Yes, of course,' Weizsäcker nodded. Everyone who had lived at the time was affected. I wanted to know if it was easier for us to talk about this responsibility today than it was 20 years ago. After all, the publication in 2010 of the Auswärtiges Amt study *The Ministry and the Past* had shown that, among the responsible historians and eyewitnesses such as Weizsäcker, there was deep dissent about the evaluation of the role of the Foreign Ministry in the Third Reich. Other studies of that same ministry make it equally clear how apt Bernhard Schlink's observation about the moral differences in perspective between eyewitnesses and contemporary commentators really is.

There is no denying that, over the last 20 years, much exemplary research has been done into the Third Reich. The awkwardness begins when its insights or conclusions influence the public and political treatment of memory, as in the case of *The Ministry and the Past*. The fact that a historian such as Norbert Frei, who co-authored the study, does not balk at speculating publicly, without adequate empirical evidence, about the collective enrolment of half-year groups of the Hitler Youth without those individuals' knowledge is another striking example of knee-jerk moral judgement — regardless of whether it serves the purposes of exoneration or denunciation.

It is a paradox: the more we learned about National Socialism, Schlink believes, the harder it became to imagine ourselves in the situation of people — whether victims or perpetrators — who were living at the time.

> For more than sixty years people have been researching, writing, reading about the twelve years of the 'Third Reich', new findings have been made and old ones rediscovered and reassessed, there has been analysis and reflection. It is not impossible that the results of this process of research and reflection have been projected into the minds of people acting at the time — as if they had known and considered at the time everything that has come to light over more than sixty years.[7]

This explains the bafflement and incomprehension with which evidence of the NSDAP membership of exemplary democrats was received. It forces us to imagine ourselves into the world of those affected at the time, a world very different from our own.

According to a cliché of politically engaged writing often evoked today, authors are 'writing against forgetting'. This always means the forgetting of others, of the masses who must be dragged from the sleep of innocence by wide-awake guardians of virtue such as Günter Grass, Martin Walser, and Dieter Wellershoff. But the truth is more complicated and subtler than we thought. Yes, they have written against forgetting — not only against ours, however, but also against their own. In Walser's work, that still happens between the lines, as we have seen, because the author denies ever knowingly becoming a member of the NSDAP. In Grass's case, it was a bombshell when, in his memoir *Peeling the Onion*, he shook off the burden of his never-forgotten membership of the SS by publicly remembering it. Grass was the only one to risk such a clean break. Walser, Wellershoff, Jens, Henze, Genscher, Luhmann, Loest, and all the rest wrote, composed, researched, and participated in politics against their own forgetting. One can, but need not, see the restless creativity of these *Flakhelfer* as an act of atonement for being led astray as youths. It is an achievement, at any rate.

In judging the *Flakhelfer* generation, we are judging ourselves, and finding ourselves satisfactory. Never led into temptation, we have done everything right. This attitude of moral superiority and rebellious 'memorialising' serves to anaesthetise our own conscience. 'Even more than that,' as Schlink puts it, 'they seem to eradicate the stain of the German past that members of the third and fourth generation still feel — if they are interested in history and define their identity not only on the basis of life in the present, but also on the basis of life with the past.'[8]

How different is the story that the *Flakhelfer* generation can tell us: a story of moral hardship, ethical conflicts, human weakness, and human greatness. It will draw towards a close when the last members of that generation die, but it will return in a new form, and then their story will remind us that we were not born better people, but owe it solely to the happy chance of our birth that we were not led into temptation.

In 1946, the American newspaper correspondent Judy Barden wrote of de-Nazification in Bavaria: 'It will take 72 years, until 2018, to complete the task.'[9] While de-Nazification was officially declared finished in 1948, the Nazi pasts of many of the *Flakhelfer* generation still surprise and preoccupy us even today. But it would be wrong to try to retroactively de-Nazify exemplary democrats such as Martin Walser, Walter Jens, or Hans-Dietrich Genscher by simply denying the existence of their NSDAP membership cards.

On the contrary: the life's work that these *Flakhelfer* created after 1945 as artists, academics, or politicians deserves to be acknowledged all the more for having been produced under the most unfavourable conditions imaginable. Seduced and betrayed, they were released by the Third Reich into an uncertain future — one which they mastered. So they didn't just contribute to the democratic success story of the Federal Republic. Their fate effectively embodies the transformation from bad to good.

Thomas Mann was one of the first to think, in 1945, about the causes of Germany's defeat at the hands of the Nazi barbarians. In his essay 'Germany and the Germans', the author, exiled from Germany by the Nazis, did not exempt himself from the guilt that weighed upon his compatriots, indeed upon the whole of German culture. After all, Mann had profound personal experience of the temptations of German introspection. So he declared:

> This story may bring one thing before our minds: that there are not two Germanys, an evil one and a good one, but only one, whose best was turned to evil by devilish cunning. Evil Germany is the good gone wrong, the good in misfortune, guilt and downfall. So it is just as impossible for a German-born spirit entirely to deny and to explain the evil, guilt-ridden Germany, and to declare: 'I am the good, the noble, the just Germany in the white robe, I leave the evil for you to eradicate.'[10]

Thomas Mann would not live to see the guilt-ridden, destroyed, morally corrupt post-war Germany become a genuine democracy. But he would have been able to confirm his view that there are not two Germanys, and that most Germans wore neither the white robe of innocence nor the black cloak of pure evil, but felt their way forward in the grey overalls of compromised reality. The *Flakhelfer* generation personally experienced that, and worked positively away at it.

So their story has a happy ending, because it proves that things can go the other way, and that the good can grow from the bad.

Notes

Prologue

1 'Im Westen viel Neues', *Hessische/Niedersächsische Allgemeine*, 21 June 2006.

2 Letter from the Kassel state Wilhelms Gymnasium to Frau Consul Walter Herwig, Kassel, Skagerrakplatz 30. Dated 3 March 1938.

Introduction: The Recruits

1 S. Fischer, *Reiselieder mit böhmischen Quinten: Autobiographische Mitteilungen 1926–1995*, Frankfurt 1996.

2 Max Nyffeler, 'Mit Schönheit den Schrecken gebannt', *Neue Zürcher Zeitung*, 29 October 2012.

3 Christian Wildhagen, 'War Hans Werner Henze Mitglied der NSDAP?', *Frankfurter Allgemeine Zeitung*, 13 February 2009.

4 'Mehr vom selben', *Süddeutsche Zeitung*, 17 May 2012.

5 Michael Buddrus, 'War es möglich, ohne eigenes Zutun Mitglied der NSDAP zu werden?' report of the Institute for Contemporary History Munich–Berlin for the *Internationale Germanistenlexikon 1800–1950*, in: *Zeitschrift für Geshchichte der Germanistik* 23/24 (2003), 21–26.

6 According to Nolzen, from the 18 million young men who were members of the Hitler Youth from 30 January 1933 until their 18th year, in total only around 7 to 8 per cent were accepted into the NSDAP, although the quotas for individual year groups were higher in some cases. Cf. Armin Nolzen, 'Vom "Jugengenossen" zum "Parteigenossen". The enrolment of members of the Hitler Youth in the NSDAP', in: Wolfgang Benz (ed.), *Wie wurde man Parteigenosse? Die NSDAP und ihre Mitglieder*, Frankfurt am Main 2009, 123–150; 149f.

7 Heinz Bude, *Deutsche Karrieren: Lebenskonstruktionen sozialer Aufsteiger aus der Flakhelfer-Generation*, Frankfurt am Main 1987, 182. Schelsky

quote ('without ties and entangled') *ibid.*, 179.

8 Bude 1987, 182.

9 Response from the German federal government of 14 December 2011 to the survey of the political party Die Linke. Printed matter 17/8134.

10 US State Dept. to National Archives/BDC, Request for records disposition authority, Washington, DC: Records of the Berlin Document Center, BDC Directorate Files, 4 December 1991. Cf. Glenn R. Cuomo, 'Opening the Director's Safe: an examination of the Berlin Document Center's restricted collection of NSDAP records'. Unpublished manuscript.

1. The Funeral Pyre

1 Katja Iken, 'Skizzen des Schreckens', http://einestages.spiegel.de/static/topicalbumbackground/24248/1/skizzen_des_ schreckens.html. Cf. also http://www.ghetto-theresienstadt. de/pages/g/gradowskibericht.htm (both accessed 28 January 2012).

2 Quoted in Erich Kuby, 'Die Russen in Berlin 1945', *Der Spiegel,* 5 May 1965.

3 Cf. Josef Henke, 'Das Schicksal deutscher zeitgeschichtlicher Quellen in Kriegs- und Nachkriegszeit', *Vierteljahrshefte für Zeitgeschichte* 4 (1982), 557–620; 564, and Hans-Stephan Brather, 'Aktenvernichtung durch deutsche Dienststellen beim Zusammenbruch des Faschismus', *Archivmitteilungen* (1958), 115–117.

4 Henke 1982, 564.

5 BStU MfS HA IX 21118. (Archive of the Federal Commissioner for the Stasi Records)

6 Stefan Heym, 'Eine wahre Geschichte', *Die Kannibalen und andere Erzählungen,* Leipzig 1953, 51–76; 51ff.

7 NSDAP-Mitgliedsliste aufgefunden', *Neue Zeitung,* 18 October 1945, and 'Gesamtliste der NSDAP gefunden', *Allgemeine Zeitung,* 19 October 1945. Gwyn Lewis, 'What the Complete Records of the Nazi Party Show — Amazing Story of How They Were Found: the man who held them hated the Nazis', *Sunday Express,* 21 October 1945.

8 Kathleen McLaughlin, 'Revenge Spurred Hunt for Nazi List', *New York Times,* 21 October 1945.

9 Sven-Felix Kellerhoff, 'Brisante Papiere aus dem Müllhaufen', *Die Welt,* 2 November 2005.

10 Christopher Robbins, *The Test of Courage: Michel Thomas: a biography of the Holocaust survivor and Nazi-hunter,* 2012.

11 *Ibid.*

12 Robert Wolfe, 'A Short History of the Berlin Document Center'. With thanks to Robert Wolfe for access to this and other documents from his decades-long service at the National Archives and for our personal

conversation in Alexandria, Virginia on 11 September 2011.

13 Robbins 2012.

14 'Revenge Spurred Hunt for Nazi List'.

15 Astrid M. Eckert, *Kampf um die Akten. Die Westalliierten und die Rückgabe von deutschem Archivgut nach dem Zweiten Weltkrieg*, Stuttgart 2004, 60.

16 Heym 1953, 71ff. In Heym's version, Huber the miller is called Bachleitner and is skilfully portrayed in a propagandistic manner by the GDR author, but played off somewhat unfairly against the ostensibly incompetent and eager-to-brag US officers. At the end of the story, Heym even indirectly compares the US soldiers with the SS men.

17 'Revenge Spurred Hunt for Nazi List'.

18 Eckert 2004, 60.

19 'Revenge Spurred Hunt for Nazi List'.

20 Wolfe, 'A Short History …'.

21 Eckert 2004, 59.

22 *Ibid.*, 72.

23 *Ibid.*, 59.

24 US Group CC Ministerial Collection Center Fürstenhagen, Instructional Memorandum 15 July 1945 (NARA).

25 *Ibid.*

26 Headquarters, European Theater of Operations United States Army, 29 June 1945 (NARA).

27 *Ibid.*

28 Ministerial Collecting Center, Control Commission for Germany (British Element), Kassel, 14 September 1945 (NARA).

29 Control Memorandum No. 13, 28 April 1945 (NARA).

30 NND953317, Anweisungen an den rangältesten deutschen Beamten (NARA).

31 *Ibid.*

32 2011.09.14-3, 390. USGCC, 12 June 1945 (NARA).

33 Vgl. Lester H. Born, 'The Ministerial Collecting Center near Kassel, Germany', *The American Archivist*, Jg. 13, Heft 3, July 1950, 237–258.

34 Eckert 2004, 68.

35 All details in Wolfe, 'A Short History …'.

36 Heinz Fehlauer, 'Deutsch-Amerikanische Archivgeschichte. Die Bestände des Berlin Document Centers: Kriegsbeute im Bundesarchiv', in: *Datenreich im Verborgenen. Das Berlin Document Center in Berlin-Zehlendorf*, ed. Sabine Weißler and Wolfgang Schäche, Marburg 2010, 27–40; 31.

37 Quote in Eckert 2004, 72.

38 Eckert 2004, 71.

39 Workers in the Munich warehouse of the Library of Congress, for example. Eckert 2004, 70.

40 'Volk ohne gestern. Das Schicksal der deutschen Akten - Sammeln, ehe es zu spät ist!', *Christ und Welt*, 23 March 1949.

41 Eckert 2004, 74.

42 *Ibid.*

43 Wolfe, 'A Short History ...'

44 BSTU MfS HA IX/11 PA 2193: Günther Nollau.

45 30.8.1945 to the Rechtsanwaltskammer Dresden, BSTU MfS HA IX/11 PA 2193: Günther Nollau.

46 BSTU MfS HA IX/11 PA 2193: Günther Nollau.

47 SMAD 201/47 Bundesarchiv.

48 *Ibid.*

49 Cf. Sandra Meenzen, *Konsequenter Antifaschismus? Thüringische SED-Sekretäre mit NSDAP-Vergangenheit*, Erfurt 2011, and 'Der Fall Hans Bentzien. Hitlerjunge, NSDAP-Mitglied und 1. Sekretär der SED-Kreisleitung Jena-Stadt', *Gerbergasse* 18, 57, II/2010, 9–13.

50 SMAD 201/47 Bundesarchiv. Richtlinien zur Anwendung der Direktiven Nr. 24 und Nr. 38 des Kontrollrats über die Entnazifizierung.

51 BSTU MfS HA IX/11 PA 2193: Günther Nollau.

52 30 August 1945 to the Rechtsanwaltskammer Dresden, BSTU MfS HA IX/11 PA 2193: Günther Nollau.

53 Klaus Marxen, Gerhard Werle, *Strafjustiz und DDR-Unrecht: Dokumentation,* Band 5, Teil 2, S. 1031.

54 *Die Welt,* 5 June 1975: 'Seine Weste war von Farbflecken übersät'. Quotation translated into English by the text's translators.

2. Members Only

1 Mario Wenzel, 'Die NSDAP, ihre Gliederungen und angeschlossenen Verbände. Ein Überblick', in: Benz 2009, 19–38.

2 Printed in: *Die tödliche Utopie. Bilder, Texte, Dokumente. Daten zum Dritten Reich,* ed. Volker Dahm *et. al.,* 5th edition, München 2008, 272.

3 Benz 2009, 16.

4 *Ibid.*, 10.

5 *Ibid.*, 148.

6 *Ibid.*

7 *Ibid.*, 142.

8 *Internationales Germanistenlexikon 1800–1950,* ed. Christoph König, 3 volumes, Berlin 2003.

9 'Von Goethe zu Hitler', *Der Spiegel,* 24 November 2003.

10 'Kommunikatives Beschweigen', *taz,* 16 August 2006.

11 *Ibid.*

12 'Von Goethe zu Hitler'.

13 *Ibid.*

14 *Ibid.*

15 *Ibid.*

16 Buddrus 2003.

17 *Ibid.*

18 *Ibid.*

19 Benz 2009, 148.

20 For example, the entry 'Walter Höllerer' in *Internationales Germanistenlexikon 1800–1950,* volume 2, 766.

21 Buddrus 2003.

22 The first part of this section, with minor changes, corresponds to my article 'Hoffnungslos dazwischen', *Der Spiegel,* 16 July 2007.

23 'Die unbekannte NSDAP-Mitgliedschaft: Martin Walser, Siegfried Lenz und Dieter Hildebrandt in der Kartei', *Neue Zürcher Zeitung,* 2 July 2007.

24 'Es ist ein Stück von ihnen: Die Dichter, die NSDAP und das Beschweigen danach', *Die Welt,* 7 June 2007.

25 Cf. 'Hoffnungslos dazwischen'.

26 'Neue Parteimitglieder', *Die Zeit,* 5 July 2007.

27 *Ibid.*

28 Norbert Frei, 'Hitler-Junge, Jahrgang 1926', *Die Zeit,* 11 September 2003.

29 *Ibid.*

30 The Rector of the Friedrich-Alexander-Universität of Erlangen, on behalf of: Prof. Grether, 21 November 1947. Typewritten letter with attachment.

31 *Ibid.*

32 Nolzen 2009.

33 Bude 1987, 68.

3. The Boys Left Standing

1 Conversation with Erich Loest, Leipzig, 8 March 2011.

2 Loest 1984, 22.

3 Conversation with Erich Loest, Leipzig, 8 March 2011.

4 Loest 1984, 22.

5 *Ibid.,* 27.

6 *Ibid.,* 26.

7 *Ibid.,* 29.

8 *Ibid.*

9 Loest, *Jungen die übrig blieben,* Frankfurt am Main 1985, 157.

10 Loest 1984, 43.

11 *Ibid.,* 54.

12 *Ibid.*

13 *Ibid.*, 71.

14 *Ibid.*, 105.

15 Loest, *Man ist ja keine Achtzig mehr. Tagebuch*, Göttingen 2011, 134f.

16 *Geschichte, die noch qualmt. Erich Loest und sein Werk*, Ed. Carsten Gansel und Joachim Jacob, Göttingen 2011, 285.

17 *Ibid.*

18 Loest 1984, 47.

19 *Ibid.*, 48.

20 *Ibid.*

21 'Die Schau wird für Rechte nicht ergiebig sein', *Aachener Zeitung*, 15 October 2010.

22 Loest 1984, 53.

23 Hans Werner Henze, *Reiselieder und böhmische Quinten. Autobiographische Mitteilungen 1926– 1995*, Frankfurt am Main 1996, 575f.

24 *Ibid.*, 45.

25 In: *Hans Werner Henze. Politisch-humanitäres Engagement als* künstlerische Perspektive, Ed. Sabine Giesbrecht and Stefan Hanheide, Osnabrück 1998, 16f.

26 Iring Fetscher, *Neugier und Furcht: Versuch, mein Leben zu verstehen*, Hamburg 1995, 9.

27 Interview with Iring Fetscher, 15 February 2011.

28 Fetscher 1995, 10.

29 *Ibid.*

30 *Ibid.*, 11.

31 *Ibid.*, 52.

32 *Ibid.*, 12.

33 *Ibid.*, 72.

34 *Ibid.*, 115.

35 *Ibid.*, 117.

36 *Ibid.*

37 *Ibid.*

38 Iring Fetscher, *Joseph Goebbels im Berliner Sportpalast 1943. 'Wollt ihr den totalen Krief?'*, Hamburg 1998, 8.

39 Fetscher 1995, 333.

40 *Ibid.*

41 'Ich war lange Jahre angepasst', *Süddeutsche Zeitung*, 8 December 2003.

42 *Ibid.*

43 *Ibid.*

44 *Ibid.*

45 Götz Aly, 'Was wusste Walter Jens? Wahrscheinlich geschah seine

Aufnahme in die NSDAP ohne eigene Kenntnis. Rekonstruktion einer akademischen Jugend', *Die Zeit,* 7 March 2008.

46 'Ich war lange Jahre angepasst'.

47 *Ibid.*

48 *Ibid.*

49 *Ibid.*

50 Tilman Jens, *Demenz. Abschied von meinem Vater,* Gütersloh 2009, 89.

51 Mathias Schreiber, 'Entschwinden des Partners', *Der Spiegl,* 13 July 2009.

52 *Ibid.*

53 *Ibid.*

54 Dieter Wellershoff, *Der lange Weg zum Anfang,* Cologne 2007.

4. The (Former) Lives of Others

1 BStU MfS HA IX/11 PA 40.

2 Roger Engelmann, Frank Joestel, *Die Zentrale Auswertungsund Informationsgruppe* (MfS-Handbuch). ed. BStU., Berlin 2009, 3.

3 Interview on 11 September 2011.

4 BStU MfS AS 2490/67.

5 BStU MfS ZAIG 10608.

6 Richard Evans, 'The German Foreign Office and the Nazi Past', *Neue Politische Literatur* 56 (2011), 179.

7 BStU MfS AS 2490/67.

8 BStU MfS HA 1 17658.

9 *Ibid.*

10 *Ibid.*

11 'Carstens: Ich habe so dunkle Erinnerungen,' *Der Spiegel,* 13 November 1978.

12 *Ibid.*

13 MfS HA VII 48.

14 *Ibid.*

15 *Ibid.*

16 *Ibid.*

17 Interview with Dieter Skiba, 17 April 2012.

18 Cf. Henry Leide, *NS-Verbrecher und Staatssicherheit: Die geheime Vergangenheitspolitik der DDR,* 2. ed., Göttingen 2006, 35ff.

19 For a detailed overview of the organisational development cf. *ibid.,* 96ff.

20 Claus Christian Malzahn, 'Politbüro-Geld bringt Beate Klarsfeld in Bedrängnis', *Welt Online,* 9 March 2012. http://www.welt.de/politik/deutschland/article13913556/ Politbuero-Geld-bringt-Beate-Klarsfeld-in-Bedraengnis.html (accessed 1 May 2012).

21 Nobert Frei, *Karrieren im Zwielicht,* Frankfurt 2001, 228f.

22 BStU MfS HA IX/11 PA 40 (Genscher); MfS HA IX/11 PA 41 (Achenbach).

23 BStU MfS HA IX 20452.

24 *Ibid.*

25 'Für ehrliche Zusammenarbeit', *Der Spiegel,* 19/1994.

26 BStU MfS HA XX/4 2621.

27 BStU MfS HA XX/4 2481: Kirchenmitglieder (Ost).

28 BStU MfS HA XX/4 2618. Analyse über die Konzentration ehemaliger faschistischer Offiziere in der Ev. Kirche in der DDR, 27 November1962.

29 BStU MfS HA XX/4 2619: Kirchenmitglieder.

30 BStU HA XX/42474.

31 BStU MFS HA XX/4 2617: Fall Willi R., der wegen Beihilfe zur Republikflucht seiner Kinder seit 1964 im Gefängnis saß: 'Eventuell kann seine vorherrschende Unsicherheit für eine Werbung genutzt werden'.

32 Numerous examples in Leide 2006, 195ff.

33 'Für ehrliche Zusammenarbeit'. Cf. Leide 2006, 61, 209.

34 BStU MfS Rechtsstelle 443.

35 BStU MfS HA IX 20452: Organisation der HA IX/11 und des Dokumentationszentrums Mitte der 1980er Jahre.

36 BStU MfS HA IX 20911.

37 *Ibid.*

38 BStU MfS HA IX 20604.

39 Meenzen 2011.

40 *Ibid.,* 13.

41 *Ibid.,* 12.

42 Olaf Kappelt, 'Mein "Weihnachtsgeschenk" an Erich Mielke. Über die Reaktionen des MfS auf ein Buch über Altnazis in der DDR', *horch und guck* 40 (2002), 6–9.

43 Meenzen 2011, 13.

44 *Neues Deutschland,* 11 February 1962.

45 'Bericht des Politbüros an die 2. Tagung des ZK der SED am 12 April 1963', *Neues Deutschland,* 13 April 1962.

46 MfS ZAIG 11176 Abt. Agitation, 11 February 1969.

47 BStU MfS ZAIG 27507.

48 *Ibid.,* annex 3.

49 *Ibid.*

50 *Ibid.*

51 *Ibid.*

52 BStU MfS HA IX 20911.

53 BStU MfS HA VII 2086.

54 *Ibid.*

55 Cf. Nolzen 2009, 149.

5. In Mr Simon's Safe

1 Cf. Glenn R. Cuomo, 'Opening the Director's Safe: an examination of the Berlin Document Center's restricted collection of NSDAP records'. Unpublished manuscript.

2 Daniel Simon to the US Minister, 17 September 1987, NARA NND953317.

3 Cf. Cuomo.

4 Details in Cuomo. Cf. also idem 'The NSDAP's Enduring Shadow: putting in perspective the recent outing of brown octogenarians', *German Studies Review* 35.2 (2012), 265–288.

5 Cf. Cuomo.

6 US State Dept. to National Archives/BDC, Request for records disposition authority, 4 December 1991, NARA [= NARA 2011.09.12-1, p5].

7 NARA RG 242, 190, 20, 05/ 06, 06/ 02 BDC directorate files 1945–1994, Stack 190 20/ 05/ 06 – 06/ 02 Box 20 'Personalities'.

8 Auswärtiges Amt (ed.), *100 Jahre Auswärtiges Amt. Begrüßungsworte des Bundesministers des Auswärtigen Walter Scheel und Festvortrag von Professor Golo Mann,* Bonn, 9 January 1970, 7–8.

9 Cf. 'Carstens: Ich habe so dunkle Erinnerungen'.

10 Kurt Becker, 'Die Schatten der Vergangenheit. Scheel, Carstens und das höchste Amt im Staate', *Die Zeit,* 17 November 1978.

11 'Scheel: Verständnis für Horst Köhler', *Neue Osnabrücker Zeitung,* 14 June 2010.

12 Cf. 'Die Schatten der Vergangenheit'.

13 *Ibid.*

14 Cf. Thomas M.T. Niles to Neal M. Sher, undated [1985] [NARA 2011.09.14-1, 946].

15 NARA FOIA NND953317 (along with Périot, Waldheim etc. released from the National Archive at my request).

16 In Department RG 242, Request files 1982–94 in the National Archives there are three thick folders of requests made by the Simon Wiesenthal Center between 1986 and 1994. On 20 May 1986, a member of the center's staff requested information about a German diplomat (and former secretary of state for the Foreign Office under Genscher). The request was turned down by the BDC with reference to the rules of procedure: 'We are aware that [W] is alive and we are unable to find evidence that he was ever tried or accused in court of law; therefore, in accordance with our access policy, we are precluded from checking our files.'

17 NARA, Memo JK to Koblitz, 9 September 1986.

18 *Ibid.*

19 Cf. Eckert 2004, 326f.

20 Dieter Krüger, 'Archiv im Spannungsfeld von Politik, Wissenschaft und

öffentlicher Meinung', *Vierteljahrshefte für Zeitgeschichte* 1 (1997), 49–74; 50.

21 Robert Wolfe, 'Transfer of the Berlin Document Center', German Studies Association, Dallas, 30 September 1994 (manuscript).

22 Report to the Conference Group on Central European History, American Historical Association, 28 December 1969, Washington D.C., National Archives Liaison Committee, Professor Gerhard L. Weinberg, Univ. of Michigan, Professor Willard A. Fletcher, University of Delaware, Professor William S. Allen, Wayne State University.

23 *Ibid.*

24 *Stuttgarter Nachrichten*, 4 January 1972 (there is an English translation of this article in the administrative files of the BDC in the National Archives, Washington).

25 'Dinarisch mit Einschlag', *Der Spiegel*, 19 April 1976.

26 Cf. Krüger 1997, 51 and Verhandlungen des Deutschen Bundestages, 7. Wahlperiode, 227. Sitzung, 11 March 1976, 1580f.; 233. Sitzung, 1 April 1976, Anl. 26, 16294.

27 Cf. *Frankfurter Rundschau*, 4 August 1979.

28 Cf. Krüger 1997, 51 and Verhandlungen des Deutschen Bundestages, 7. Wahlperiode, 247. Sitzung, 3 June 1976, S. 17549 . Cf. *Der Spiegel*, 19 April 1976, 41f.

29 'Dinarisch mit Einschlag'.

30 'Kragen geplatzt', *Der Spiegel*, 13 March 1978.

31 'SPD-Fraktion rügte Äußerungen des Abgeordneten Hansen', *Tagesspiegel*, 7 March 1978.

32 *Ibid.*

33 'Kragen geplatzt'.

34 Karl-Heinz Hansen, 'Die ungeliebten Akten des US-Document-Center', *Deutsche Volkszeitung*, 19 February 1988, in: Krüger 1997, 52.

35 'Schmidt ist beleidigt', *Der Abend*, 8 March 1978.

36 Federal Chancellor Helmut Schmidt to Foreign Minister Genscher, Minister of the Interior Maihofer, and Justice Minister Vogel, 17 March 1978 (PA AA, B86, AZ 553.00/ 06, Nr. 1589-1591).

37 File List–Security Container. Simon Era Files. Drawer 1. NARA.

38 NARA Declassified NND953317. Robert D. Johnson to Daniel Simon, 23 July 1979.

39 Conversation with Helmut Schmidt, Hamburg, 17 December 2012.

40 Hans-Peter Klausch, *Braunes Erbe – NS-Vergangenheit hessischer Landtagsabgeordneter der 1.– 11. Wahlperiode (1946–1987)*, Ed. Die Linke Fraktion im Hessischen Landtag, Wiesbaden 2011.

41 *Ibid.*

42 *Ibid.*

43 American professor of German Studies Glenn Cuomo has taken the trouble of comparing the later microfilms ('MFKL REFILM') with those in the main card files, to find out which file cards ended up in the safe and were replaced by placeholders ('plugs') in the main card file. Cuomo found the names of 74 prominent German post-war politicians on the Refilm roll. They largely coincide with the list I quote in the next paragraph. Cf. Glenn R. Cuomo, 'Opening the Director's Safe: an examination of the Berlin Document Center's restricted collection of NSDAP records'. Unpublished lecture manuscript.

44 'Index, Filing Cabinet, Drawer# 1', NARA. From number 110 onwards, names — presumably in the 1970s — have been added to the list by hand, including the aforementioned Genscher, Eppler, Dregger, Carstens, and Zimmermann, as well as Josef Ertl, Matheus Hagin, Otto Rahn, Alfons Bayerl, Paul Gerhard Flämig, Hermann Höcherl, Linus Memmel, Leo Wagner, Ernst Achenbach, Kurt Jung, Lothar Haase, Walter Becher, Siegfried Zoglmann, Fritz Kempfler, Alfred Biehle, Dionys Jobst, Oskar Schneider, Karl-Heinz Lemmrich, Karl Spilken, and Rolf Böger. These names were crossed out after the transfer of the file holdings in the Washington National Archive, with the note: 'Not in the files August 1997'. They were either recatalogued in the card file or destroyed.

45 Eckert 2004, 156, note 168.

46 Bonn 7 February 1986 (PA AA B 86, Bd. 1990).

47 'Ein ganz normales Archiv oder eine politische Zeitbombe?', *Volksblatt*, 3 July 1983.

48 'SPD bemängelt Zugangsregelung zu Beständen des Document Center', *Tagesspiegel*, 13 April 1984.

49 *Ibid.*

50 'Ein ganz normales Archiv oder eine politische Zeitbombe?'.

51 Mainhardt Graf Nayhauss, 'Bonn greift nach dem Berlin Document Center', *Welt am Sonntag*, 9 September 1984.

52 *Ibid.*

53 The scepticism of the Americans was reinforced by the fact that Périot clearly didn't speak German, even though he claimed he was trying to write an academic study of denazification in post-war Germany. In 1969 Périot had therefore asked to bring in Vincent von Wroblewsky, a Jewish Communist of French origins (and translator of Sartre) as interpreter. But Wroblewsky lived in East Berlin, and had completed his doctorate there at the Philosophical Institute at the Academy of Sciences, which already aroused the suspicion of the Americans. His brother, the musician and mime-artist Clément de Wroblewsky (b. 1943) travelled officially to West

Berlin in 1984. In March 2004 it was revealed that as 'J.M. Ernst' he had provided the Stasi with reports on the singer Udo Lindenberg.

54 NARA FOIA 20 March 1972, Richard Bauer to US Minister David Klein.

55 Late in 1971 the US Minister in Berlin approached his French counterpart and admitted that they had had some initial concerns about Périot's request, but would set these aside on the grounds of reassurances from the French delegation, and give Périot information (NARA FOIA 28. Dec. 1971: Min. Klein to Fr. Min. Jean-Louis Toffin). The magnitude of these concerns is apparent from confidential documents in which the Americans urged their French allies to withdraw their support for Périot's application. The American government supported the research of academics who belonged to recognised institutions and were able to demonstrate a convincing interest in research. In Périot's case, neither of these things was the case. In fact, in 1970, he had presented a list of names containing practically every leading judge and state prosecutor in the Federal Republic and asked for information about their political background. Périot could only be granted access on condition that the French government assume full responsibility should there be any diplomatic consequences in Germany (NARA FOIA, Draft letter Minister Klein to Gouv. Militaire Francais de Berlin, Division Politique. Ref. no 186/ POL in ref. to letter of 9 December 1971).

56 NARA FOIA 28 March 1972, Richard Bauer to US Minister via Mr V. Larson.

57 BDC-Auskunftsbogen zu Emil Kuhlmann und Marta [*sic*!] (NARA NND 953317, declassified on 3 July 2012).

58 On the BDC information file (Auskunftsbogen) for Helmut Schmidt a member of staff had written the note 'No!!' in March 1972 (NARA NND 953317, declassified on 3 July 2012).

59 NARA FOIA 14 February 1973 Dept. Director BDC Bauer to BDC Director Matild E. Holomany.

60 Subsequently Périot tried to get hold of all the information he wanted anyway. He even accused BDC Deputy Director Bauer of being a German. The Americans coolly replied that he had German-Jewish roots, and that he emigrated at the age of 16 while his family were killed in the Third Reich. So he had no reason to protect former Nazis (NARA FOIA Memo Gespräch Periot & Bauer, 30 March 1972).

61 NARA Memo Don Koblitz, 28.3.72.

62 The receipt for NSDAP membership contributions from a certain Bernhard zur Lippe-Biesterfeld, for example, was handled discreetly, because the gentleman in question was really the German father of the Dutch Queen Beatrix, Prinz Bernhard zur Lippe-Biesterfeld. The Americans kept to

themselves the discovery of a number of letters from Theodor Heuss, signed 'Heil Hitler', and a Gestapo memo according to which Heuss 'had lately been well behaved'. The documents were very innocuous, argued a political adviser to the US delegation in Berlin, 'but some of them could be used to slander the first President of the Federal Republic' (NARA FOIA [201] 10 July 1975, Memo from Pol. Adviser Peter Semler to USBER Minister George).

63 *Ibid.*

64 'Die Schatten der Vergangenheit'.

65 Cf. Heiner Meyer, *Berlin Document Center. Das Geschäft mit der Vergangenheit*, Frankfurt am Main 1988.

66 RG 242 Marwell Era Box 14.

67 Bundesdrucksache, 11/ 1926 (cf. Krüger 1997, 54).

68 Verhandlungen des Deutschen Bundestages, 11. Wahlperiode, 137. Sitzung, 20 April 1989, 10136–10141, bes. 10136, 10140f. Cf. Krüger 1997, 56.

69 Bundesdrucksache 11/ 2024, 16.3.1988, and *ibid.*, 11/ 2061, 25.3.1988, Pkt. 1– 4; *ibid.*, 11/ 2609, 1.7.1988. Verhandlungen des Deutschen Bundestages, 11. Wahlperiode, 68. Sitzung, 10.3.1988, 4646–4653, esp. 4646 f., 4651. In: Krüger 1997, 54.

70 Daniel Simon to Don Koblitz, 12 August 1987.

71 US-Botschaft Bonn an RUEFC/ Secstate WashDC 8829, 10 October 1989. NARA NND953317.

72 Harry Gilmore an RUEHC/ SECSTATE WASHDC, 21 February 1990. NARA NND453317. 292

73 Statement of Mary Ann Peters, Deputy Assistant Secretary of State for European and Canadian Affairs, Before the Subcommittee on International Security, International Organizations, and Human Rights, Committee on Foreign Affairs, House of Representatives, April 28 1994. BDC Electronic Mail, 23 April 1994.

74 *Tagesspiegel,* 15 March 1990.

75 Bekanntmachung des deutsch-amerikanischen Abkommens über die Übertragung der Berliner Dokumentenzentrale, 26 October 1993, BGBl. 1993 II, S. 2033–2035. Cf. Krüger 1997, 57.

76 Gerald Posner, 'Letter from Berlin: secrets of the files', *The New Yorker*, 14 March 1994.

77 Federal Archive Act § 5, Para 5.

78 Statement of Mary Ann Peters, Deputy Assistant Secretary of State for European and Canadian Affairs, Before the Subcommittee on International Security, International Organizations, and Human Rights, Committee on Foreign Affairs, House of Representatives, April 28 1994.

79 BDC Electronic Mail, 23.4.1994 [NARA 2011.09.14-1, 259].

80 *Ibid.*

81 Statement of Chairman Tom Lantos, Hearing on 'The U.S.-German Agreement on the Transfer to German Control of Nazi Party Records in the Berlin Document Center', 28 April 1994.

82 Krüger 1997, 53.

83 Cf. Wolfe 1994.

84 David Marwell to Malte Herwig, 31 January 2013.

85 Antwort der Bundesregierung auf die Große Anfrage der Abgeordneten Jan Korte, Sevim Dagdelen, Ulla Jelpke, weiterer Abgeordneter und der Fraktion DIE LINKE. Drucksache 17/8134. 14.12.2011.

86 Drucksache 17/8134, 9.

87 Drucksache 17/8134, 4. The report refers to two works in particular: Sabine Mecking, *'Immer treu'. Kommunalbeamte zwischen Kaiserreich und Bundesrepublik*, Essen 2003; and Bernhard Gotto, *Nationalsozialistische Kommunalpolitik. Administrative Normalität und System-stabilisierung durch die Augsburger Stadtverwaltung 1933–1945*, Munich 2006.

88 Drucksache, 17/8134, 4.

89 Akten Bundeskanzleramt, Referat 5, Vermerk vom 21 August 1963 (released in response to application MH 2012).

6. Last Ink: Günter Grass

1 *Eintagsfliegen*, Göttingen 2012, 89.

2 Letter, Lübeck, 2 May 2012.

3 Heinrich Detering, 'Mal sehen. Rede zum 85. Geburtstag von Günter Grass', 14 October 2012. Unpublished speech manuscript.

4 http://www.kiwi-verlag.de/news/23102012-eva-menasse-ueber-gunter-grass (accessed 25 November 2012).

5 *Aus dem Tagebuch einer Schnecke*, GGW 5 [=Günter Grass, *Werke*, Göttingen 2007], 315.

6 *Ibid.*, 446f.

7 *Ibid.*, 448f.

8 'Fehlbar und verstrickt', *Der Spiegel*, 21 August 2006, 63.

9 Ute Scheub, *Das falsche Leben. Eine Vatersuche*, Munich 2006.

10 *Ibid.*, 188.

11 'Wie sagen wir es den Kindern?' GGW 11, 1062.

12 *Ibid.*

13 Cf. Frank Schirrmacher, 'Das Geständnis', *Frankfurter Allgemeine Zeitung*, 12 August 2012.

14 'Wie sagen wir es den Kindern?', 1063.

15 *Im Krebsgang (Crabwalk)*, GGW 10, 109.

16 'Warum ich nach sechzig Jahren mein Schweigen breche', *Frankfurter*

Allgemeine Zeitung, 12 August 2012.

17 Quoted in Bude 1987, 69.

18 'Warum ich nach sechzig Jahren mein Schweigen breche'.

19 Hilmar Hoffmann, *Ihr naht Euch wieder, schwankende Gestalten: Erinnerungen*, Hamburg 1999, 18.

20 'Warum ich nach sechzig Jahren mein Schweigen breche'.

21 *Ibid.*

22 *Ibid.*

23 Hermann Kurzke: 'Der Mythos als Ruine. Die "Blechtrommel", nach dem vierfachen Schriftsinn gedeutet', in: *Ein Buch schreibt Geschichte. 50 Jahre "Die Blechtrommel"*, ed. Jörg-Philipp Thomsa, Lübeck 2009, 83–91; 90.

24 *Die Blechtrommel* (*The Tin Drum*), GGW 3, 736.

25 Kurzke 2009, 89.

26 *Beim Häuten der Zwiebel* (*Peeling the Onion*), Göttingen 2006, 127.

27 *Ibid.*, 221.

28 *Ibid.*

29 Günter Grass to Malte Herwig, 16 February 2011.

30 *Im Krebsgang*, 190.

31 Quoted in Michael Jürgs, *Günter Grass. Eine deutsche Biografie*, München 2007, 434. Günter Grass, 'Ich erinnere mich', in: *Die Zukunft der Erinnerung*, ed. Martin Wälde, Göttingen 2001, 27–34; 27.

32 *Im Krebsgang*, 199.

33 *Eintagsfliegen*, 42.

34 *Im Krebsgang*, 205.

35 *Schreiben nach Auschwitz*. (*Writing after Auschwitz*) *Frankfurter Poetik-Vorlesung*, Frankfurt 1990, 8.

36 *Hundejahre* (*Dog Years*), GGW 4, 849.

37 *Ibid.*, 173.

38 *Schreiben nach Auschwitz*, 18.

39 *Hundejahre*, 886.

40 *Schreiben nach Auschwitz*, 7.

41 *Hundejahre*, 887.

42 *Schreiben nach Auschwitz*, 32.

43 *Ibid.*

44 *Ibid.*, 42.

45 'Günter Grass schreibt an Karl Schiller. Beichten Sie, es wäre eine Erleichterung!', *Frankfurter Allgemeine Zeitung*, 29 September 2006.

46 *Ibid.*

47 *Ibid.*

48 'Das Geständnis'.

49 *Schreiben nach Auschwitz*, 13.

50 *Ibid.*, 18.

51 Dieter Schlesak, 'Oskar Pastiors Spitzelberichte: Die Schule der Schizophrenie', *Frankfurter Allgemeine Zeitung*, 16 November 2012.

52 'Verspäteter Schutzbrief für Oskar Pastior', *Eintagsfliegen*, 50.

7. 'The need to spell out our lives': Martin Walser

1 Martin Walser, 'Erfahrungen bein Verfassen einer Sonntagsree' in: *Die Walser-Bubis-Debatte. Eine Dokumentation*, E. Frank Schirrmacher, Frankfurt am Main 1999, 7–17.

2 *Ibid.*, 13.

3 *Ibid.*, 15.

4 *Ibid.*, 11.

5 *Ibid.*, 9, 14.

6 *Ibid.*, 16.

7 *Ibid.*, 17.

8 *Ibid.*

9 'All diese Karteikarten der NSDAP', *Frankfurter Allgemeine Zeitung*, 2 July 2007.

10 'Erinnerung kann man nicht befehlen', *Der Spiegel*, 45/1998.

11 *Ibid.*

12 *Ibid.*

13 'Warum sind sie in einer oder keiner Partei', *Der Abend*, 9 July 1964.

14 Ruth Klüger, *weiter leben. Eine Jugend*, Göttingen 1992, 213.

15 *Ibid.*, 212.

16 *Ibid.*, 217.

17 *Ibid.*, 213.

18 Hans Dieter Schäfer, *Das gespaltene Bewusstsein. Vom Dritten Reich bix zu den langen Fünfziger Jahren*, Göttingen 2009, 324.

19 'Die menschliche Wärmelehre', in: *Die Verwaltung des Nichts. Reden und Aufsätze*, Reinbek 2004, 165.

20 Jörg Magenau, *Martin Walser. Eine Biographie*, new edition, Reinbek 2008, 15.

21 *Ibid.*, 493.

22 *Märkische Allgemeine*, 6 July 2002.

23 *Leben und Schreiben. Tagebücher 1963–1973*, Reinbek 2009, 28 (9 April 1963).

24 *Ibid.*, 34.

25 *Ibid.*, 36.

26 *Ibid.*, 30.

27 Cf. the interesting contribution to the debate by Tilmann Moser in 'Erinnerungen an eine Kindheit in der NS-Zeit oder Wieviel musste Martin

Walser wissen vom damaligen Schrecken?', *Deutschlandfunk*, 11 December 1998.

28 Walser 1999, 12.

29 'Erinnerung kann man nicht befehlen'.

30 *Ibid.*

31 Interview, 29 August 2012.

32 *Ein springender Brunnen* (*A Leaping Fountain*), Frankfurt am Main 1998, 90.

33 'Protokoll der Fuldaer Bischofskonferenz betr. Stellungnahme zur NSDAP' (17 August 1932), in: *Akten deutscher Bischöfe über die Lage der Kirche 1933–1945*, vol. 1: 1933–1934, Ed. Bernhard Stasiewski, Mainz 1968, 843f. This also includes other documents on the question of the administering of the sacraments and related issues.

34 'Erinnerung kann man nicht befehlen'.

35 *Ein springender Brunnen*, 9.

36 *Ibid.*

37 *Ibid.*, 367.

38 *Ibid.*, 370.

39 *Ibid.*, 282.

40 *Ibid.*, 282f.

41 *Ein springender Brunnen*, 344.

42 'Unser Auschwitz', *Werke in Zwölf Bänden* 11, 159.

43 *Ibid.*, 167.

44 *Ibid.*, 169.

45 'Erinnerung kann man nicht befehlen'.

46 *Der schwarze Schwan*, Frankfurt 1965, 81.

47 *Ibid.*, 85.

48 *Ibid.*, 94.

49 Magenau 2008, 216f.

50 'Wärmelhere', 165.

51 Magenau 2008, 216.

52 'Erinnerung kann man nicht befehlen'.

53 'Auschwitz und kein Ende', *Werke in Zwölf Bänden* 11, 636.

54 'Unser Auschwitz', 166.

55 *Ibid.*, 168.

56 *Ibid.*, 170.

57 *Der schwarze Schwan*, 81.

58 *Ein springender Brunnen*, 352.

59 This is apparent from the website of the Bundesarchiv: http://www.bundesarchiv.de/oeffentlichkeitsarbeit/bilder_ dokumente/00757/ind ex-6.html.de (accessed 14 January 2013).

60 Groth/Jentzsch, AZ 145/11G09 Gr/EnD865, 29.5.2012. Land-gericht Hamburg.

61 Anordnung 1/44 des Reichsschatzmeisters, http://www.bundesarchiv.

62 http://www.bundesarchiv.de/oeffentlichkeitsarbeit/bilder_
dokumente/00757/index-16.html.de (accessed 1 November 2012).

63 'Die Partei ist die Heimat der Jugend. Reichsjugendführer Axmann eröffnet
die weltanschaulichen Monatsappelle der Hitler-Jugend', *Südschwäbisches
Tagblatt*, Lindau, 28 February 1944.

64 'Das vergangene Wochenende', *Südschwäbisches Tagblat*, Lindau, 28
February 1944.

65 http://www.bundesarchiv.de/oeffentlichkeitsarbeit/bilder_
dokumente/00757/index-16.html.de (accessed 1 November 2012).

66 *Ibid.*

67 *Ein springender Brunnen*, 374.

68 'Wärmelehre', 164. Cit. in Magenau 2008, 17.

8. The End of Their Story

1 Bernhard Schlink, 'Die Kultur des Denunziatorischen', *Merkur* 745 (June
2011), 473–486.

2 *Ibid.*, 476.

3 Conversation with Richard von Weizsäcker, Berlin, 26 January 2012.

4 *On the 40th Anniversary of the End of the War in Europe, and of the
National Socialist tyranny*. Address by President Richard von Weizsäcker
on 8 May 1984, commemoration in the Plenary Hall of the German
Bundestag.

5 Conversation with Richard von Weizsäcker, Berlin, 26 January 2012.

6 'The Holocaust Just Got More Shocking', *The New York Times*, 1 March
2013.

7 Schlink 2011, 479.

8 *Ibid.*, 484.

9 Cit. in Cuomo 2012, 283.

10 Thomas Mann, 'Deutschland und die Deutschen', in: *Gesammelte Werke in
dreizehn Bänden*, XI, 1146.